Trembling in the Ivory Tower

Excesses in the Pursuit of Truth and Tenure

By Kenneth Lasson

bancroft
press

Baltimore, MD

Other Books by Kenneth Lasson

Representing Yourself: What You Can Do Without a Lawyer

Mousetraps and Muffling Cups:
One Hundred Brilliant and Bizarre United States Patents

Private Lives of Public Servants

Proudly We Hail: Profiles of Public Citizens in Action

The Workers: Portraits of Nine American Job Holders

Learning Law: The Mastery of Legal Logic
(with co-author Sheldon Margulies)

Getting the Most Out of Washington:
Using Congress to Move the Federal Bureaucracy
(with co-author William S. Cohen)

Your Rights As a Vet

Your Rights and the Draft

Published by Bancroft Press
P.O. Box 65360, Baltimore, MD 21209
800.637.7377
www.bancroftpress.com

Library of Congress Control Number: 2001096588

ISBN 1-890862-08-8 cl
Printed in the United States of America
First Edition

Dedicated to open-minded scholars everywhere,

some of whom know who they are.

Table of Contents

A Note about the Notes

Scholarly publications are almost always heavily anno-tated. This weighty exercise has two purposes: to lend an air of authenticity to the work, and to allow the author long-winded tangential digressions (some of which may actually be relevant to the main themes).

The traditional justification for footnotes is that they enable skeptical readers to verify for themselves that the writer's sources are legitimate. That in itself can be an exceed-ingly tedious exercise even for editorial cite-checkers—and one that is rarely undertaken by other people who have some-thing (anything?) better to do with their time.

Curious readers are sometimes drawn to glance at the notes, a practice they inevitably abandon as soon as their eyes begin to glaze over. Thus the annotations presented herein are designed to be reader-friendly, to lend texture to the text. They have been festooned with academic seals (⚘) and set off in shaded boxes. Even so, they can be passed over without ill effect by impatient readers, or by those who must limit their intake of salt. More traditional notes—supplied solely to sat-isfy finicky source-seekers—are adorned with the standard tiny-type superscript numbers and appear at the back of the book. (I proposed skipping the latter altogether—or offering to supply them gratis to anyone who'd send me a self-addressed stamped envelope—but the publisher insisted on them, probably at the suggestion of his lawyers.)

Introduction

What are the chances of anyone actually reading this little flagon of well-aged whine?[1]

Veritas vos liberabit, chanted the scholastics of yesteryear.

The truth will set you free, echo their latter-day counterparts in the academy—intoning the mantra reverentially, but with increasingly more hope than confidence, more faith than conviction. By and large, universities would like themselves to be perceived as places of culture in a chaotic world, protectors of reasoned discourse, peaceful havens where learned professors roam orderly quadrangles and ponder higher thoughts. Slick brochures and elegant catalogues depict a community of scholars serious- and fair-minded at both work and play, all thirsting for knowledge in sylvan tranquility, all feasting on the fruits of unfettered intellectual curiosity, all nurtured in an atmosphere of invigorating academic freedom—an altogether overflowing cornucopia in the ever-bustling marketplace of ideas.

The real world of the academy, of course, is not quite that wonderful—nor nearly as bad as many would suggest.

The ironies become palpable, however, when those same institutions, which almost universally view themselves as bastions of free speech, are seen instead to stifle debate that is politically incorrect or otherwise embarrassing. Academic administrators naturally shy away from conflict and contention. They shun controversy. In fact they abhor negative publicity of any kind, quelling it as heavy-handedly as conservative corporations whose primary concern is to ensure a profitable bottom line.✿

> ✿The general counsels at a number of universities now caution against catalogue language representing their clients' devotion to free speech and the rights of students to procedural fairness—lest they might be required by courts to honor such promises.[2]

Because life in the Ivory Tower is largely insular, however, its residents' perception of the world outside is likely to be somewhat different than that of non-academics.

We live in interesting times—a fascinating and frustrating age of harmony and contradiction: at once blessed with widespread wealth and plagued by endemic poverty; graced with virtually unfettered liberty and subjected to pernicious deprivations of rights; overwhelmed by an abundance of technological marvels that increasingly seem to invade our privacy while they whir away in an intellectual wasteland. We participate daily in an abandonment of common sense, even as we yearn almost universally for its application. We shun traditional morality as we search for traditional values. We seek simplicity as we indulge in excess.

Often (if not always) on the cutting edge of such conflicting forces is the academic enterprise. Universities are both the birthplaces of monumental achievements and the breeding-grounds for unnecessary if not outrageous indulgences. "He who enters a university walks on hallowed ground," said one president of Harvard; its task, said another, is "to keep alive in young people the courage to dare to speak the truth, to be free, to establish in them a compelling desire to live greatly and magnanimously." Intoned Robert Maynard

Hutchins, former president at the University of Chicago: "Freedom of inquiry, freedom of discussion, and freedom of teaching—the university exists only to find and to communicate the truth."[3]✸

> ✸Hutchins also said that a truly world-class university must provide three things: "sex for the students, parking for the faculty, and football for the alumni."

But the pitched battles currently taking place in the Ivory Tower—whether in the pursuit of truth and tenure, rights and trifles, or minds and manners—are not always noticed by the people upon whom they have the most impact. The loonier elements of the academy, epitomized over the years by the eccentric professor or the abstruse course title, have long been easy targets for satirists. As the acquisition of a college degree becomes ever more central to the American dream, however, closer attention needs to be paid to what is being taught on the campuses. For what is learned there is certain to reverberate ever more loudly in the broader world in which we live.[4]

At stake as well is the relationship between the university and society at large. The traditional role of the university has long been that of a place for reflection upon culture and society, inherently objective and self-critical in its search for truth. But that view has been largely replaced by one that insists upon a variety of coexisting cultures, and implies a university that is political at its core and to its peak—one that discredits what it perceives to be an oppressive "dominant" culture and empowers whose who are perceived to be "marginalized" and "disadvantaged." The modern university forbids critical scrutiny of the latter; to this end, according to one dismayed observer, "it casts the giants of Western thought and art as running dogs of some prohibited -ism." The result is a society that has been indoctrinated not in the values of healthy diversity, but in a narrow critique of an establishment viewed as inherently bad. As such, multiculturalism has become not ecumenical, but adversarial.[5]

A number of contemporary studies point to an alarming deficit in undergraduate learning—a decline in what colleges expect students actually to *know*. Fully one-quarter of seniors surveyed a decade ago could not say within fifty years when Columbus discovered America, and almost half were unable to date the American Civil War. Things have not improved over the last ten years. A 1996 study found a progressive disintegration of the liberal-arts curriculum. Students now spend significantly less time than their predecessors satisfying general education requirements. There are fewer mandatory subjects and recommended courses than ever before.[6]

Thoughtful critics like John Ellis, whose 1998 book *Literature Lost* noted "a startling decline in the intellectual quality of work in the humanities and a descent to intellectual triviality and irrelevance that amounts to a betrayal of the university," have concluded that the current, dramatic deterioration in the study of the humanities in America is a national tragedy.[7]

Things are not all that bad, of course. The Republic's soul and psyche, after all, depend more on religious values and a healthy economy than on the consistency of iambic pentameter in a Shakespearian sonnet. But there are serious problems in the Academy, and they deserve our honest attention.

For one, the current curricula are weighted heavily against traditional Western culture. For another, there is a growing perception (and reality) that students (and the parents who support them) are not getting their money's worth—increasingly encountering pop courses in place of the classics, abbreviated or canceled class schedules, and watered down instruction in the lecture halls. Thirty years ago, broad-based courses (both introductory and mandatory) were taught by experienced, dedicated, and often underpaid professors who sought to inspire their students' enthusiasm for the subject matter. Today, substantive survey courses have all but disappeared, and those that remain are frequently ministered by novice graduate assistants, many of whom are tinged with biases borne of political correctness.

Although good liberal-arts educations have amply proven their value, and strong native language skills have become necessary for individual success in free and prosperous societies, it is an unfortunate fact of modern higher education that more and more students leave college with inferior backgrounds in the humanities, weak language and writing skills,[8] and little respect for their professors.

The genesis of this book was a minor but personal academic odyssey: a trilogy of articles I wrote and saw published over the past few years, each of which sought in its own way to apply the sometimes harsh and shocking perspectives of common sense to everyday life in the academy.✸

> ✸*Scholarship Amok: Excesses in the Pursuit of Truth and Tenure,*[9] *Feminism Awry: Excesses in the Pursuit of Rights and Trifles,*[10] and *Political Correctness Askew: Excesses in the Pursuit of Minds and Manners*[11] The author quickly concedes he is not immune from excesses of his own, particularly a penchant for cutesy titles.[12] The standard of common sense applied here is my own, which I—like most people, but especially professors—feel is infallible.

In them I described trends and realities that may have begun as well-meaning reforms, but have long since calcified into narrow political agendas, revealing more their protagonists' egos and inflexibility than their nobility or high-mindedness.

From that perspective, this work could (and has been) regarded (or dismissed) as an angry screed indeed. Even so, I hasten to insist, these reflections were borne more out of bemusement than bitterness. They were less an expression of outrage than an occasionally fascinated or appalled observation—perhaps because I have not been personally victimized to any great extent by the excesses of coerced scholarship, radical feminism, or political correctness. To the contrary: the trilogy referred to above has brought me a measure of perverse notoriety and gratification.

Other academics, however, have suffered substantial injury, and by reasonable extension so have we all.

Scholarship Amok generated mixed but strong reactions among the few who read it: some were dismayed, some dismissive, some delighted. That piece took law professors sternly to task for their hard-nosed rules on tenure. Perhaps even more painful to some of my colleagues, it had been published in that holiest of holies, the august and revered *Harvard Law Review.* One must understand that an appearance in *Harvard* assures a modicum of both stature and credibility. So *how could it publish something like this?* I was asked on more than one occasion (and not only by my self-effacing alter-ego). Must be an aberration, some of my fellow professors assured themselves—and (in less cautious moments over cocktails at faculty receptions) me as well. All the more pleasing, then, to receive letters of congratulations from around the country and beyond.

Such as these (which I'm not at all too modest to reprint here)—

To the Editors:

It is somewhat unheard of to find an interesting and readable piece in a law review, let alone one of the big three or four. I found Professor Lasson's *Scholarship Amok: Excesses in the Pursuit of Truth and Tenure* very enjoyable and perceptive.

Congratulations also to your issue's deviant, oops devious, editor who gets my award for ironic juxtaposition. From the positionality of standpoint epistemology, one can only hope, generatively speaking, that Professor B——- soon will assume some knowability of Professor Lasson's work. Even I, in the hinterlands, would not wish fifty-nine pages of "counter-hegemonic perceptions" otherwise to go to waste. But seriously, I thought Lasson's piece worth the subscription price.

J. Nicholas McGrath
Aspen, Colorado

And—

To the Editors:

Before reading Mr. Lasson's article in the current issue of the *Review*, I had drafted a letter to you with a few questions about your publication. There is scarcely any reason now to send the letter. Mr. Lasson seems to have answered my questions. ...

What price scholarship? In attempting to answer this question I tried to estimate the price of the lead article in the second issue of Volume 103. The author of the article gives thanks to thirty-three named individuals, all the participants in workshops at seven universities, three research assistants, and the University of Chicago for its generous support. Using modest billable rates and estimates of time for the cost of the people involved in this marathon (excluding the time of the author himself) and estimating the generosity of the University of Chicago, I came up with a very big number.

The number is so whopping by my standards that I won't disclose it here. My methodology must be wrong. And maybe scholarship is beyond measure—priceless.

Beset by these questions, I turn for help to your readers, if you have any.

I think I have my answers now. Bravo to Mr. Lasson.

David Kilgour
Clinton, Ontario[13]

Bravo!?!

These letters of course went right to my head, and tipped my typical-scholar's intuitive insecurity well in the direction of Cheshire-cat cockiness. Moreover, I told myself, the sour grapes tasted by some of my colleagues may have been all the harder to swallow because there was so little they could do to me—fully tenured and promoted (I thanked my lucky stars) as I was—save for some genteel frontal back-stabbing and behind-the-back nitpicking and naysaying.[14] I suppose it didn't hurt that I'd already been widely published (even if barely read), and therefore somewhat protected from the standard criticism that those who denigrate scholarship don't engage in it.

The principal path to tenure, after all, is through publishing—especially articles in academic journals. The storied "publish or perish" pressure generates an incredible number of journals—in the 1970's some four hundred new ones were *founded* in modern languages and literature alone—which carry articles almost none of which will ever be widely read or subsequently cited.

One of the weaknesses I bemoaned in *Scholarship Amok* was the generally poor quality of writing published in the professional journals, much of which is virtually incomprehensible to a reasonably intelligent but non-academic reader. At the top (or bottom) of this *genre*, I noted, is a good deal of what is written by radical feminists.

Thus was born *Feminism Awry*, which drew blood even

before it was published. This piece was originally penned and submitted to law reviews under a pseudonym: although on sundry past occasions I had been called a gentleman or scholar, I divined that (Hell having no fury like a radical feminist scorned) upon publication I'd be re-cast as curmudgeon or cur. Nevertheless, encouraged by a number of women who had read the manuscript favorably, I came cowering out of the closet. Alas, my initial instincts were proven correct.

Shortly after the draft manuscript had been completed, a colleague noticed a copy of it on my secretary's desk, was shocked by its subtitle *(Excesses in the Pursuit of Rights and Trifles)*—and quickly convened a meeting of her feminist friends to determine how to handle this treachery in her midst. What later came to be known as the "Lynch Lasson Luncheon" produced a variety of responses, from a suggestion that I be asked to withdraw the piece altogether, to a campus-wide symposium on radical feminism in which I was roundly excoriated. All I can remember of the event was that, each time I tried to defend my thoughts, there was a general rolling of the eyes and widespread hissing.

After the article finally did appear, one of its featured characters—Catherine MacKinnon, perhaps the radical feminists' most arched-back cat—threatened me in print. It was exquisite *machismo* by a woman scorned:

> *To the Editors:*
>
> It is difficult—ultimately perhaps impossible—to separate the factually false from the unspeakably distorted, the superficially ignorant from the profoundly misogynist, in Kenneth Lasson's "Feminism Awry." Contemplating a response, one begins with using it to wrap fish and ends with the "cognitive therapy" of a fist in the face. . . .

Sincerely,
Catharine A. MacKinnon
Professor of Law, University of Michigan[15]

I haven't seen Ms. MacKinnon since, but her letter remains one of the minor highlights of my academic career to date. Although this was the first time I'd ever been called a misogynist (much less a profound one), I was inclined not to pursue any remedies for the damage that such a term (which means one who hates or distrusts women)—and its source— could have caused my reputation. And had my reaction to Ms. MacKinnon's letter been more that of a detached scholar than of an amused male, I suppose I would have written a learned law-review article in response (no doubt citing along the way pieces like Richard Slee, *Maxillofacial Surgery and the Practising Solicitor—An Overview*).[16] Instead, I penned a letter of my own to the *Journal of Legal Education,* in which I opined that Ms. MacKinnon's bluster spoke eloquently for itself.❀

> ❀Actually we did meet once, at a symposium on hate speech and the First Amendment. We were subsequently quoted in *Newsweek* as standing for the same proposition—that the First Amendment isn't absolute. But I was talking about Nazis preaching genocide, and she about men oppressing women. I never considered suing *Newsweek.*[17]

Not that there's likely to be much more of one. I've been told to forget any thoughts I may have once entertained of a "lateral move," much less an upward one. A strange article in an obscure feminist journal took me to task for *Feminist Awry's* "defensive belligerence": I had failed "to substantiate a number of crucial and controversial claims about feminism," and neglected "to consider whether feminists' negative statements about men are justified."❀

> ✺I noticed this article by sheer happenstance—having one day plugged my name into the Lexis-Nexis database (a standard form of ego-massage for professors who feel they are under-appreciated). I found it remarkable, though not surprising, that no one had sent me a copy. I had neither been asked to respond nor sent a reprint by the authors or editors. Nor to my knowledge has there been any comment pro or con from anyone else who may have happened to see it. I suppose this supports my contention that few people ever actually read law reviews.

And here I thought I had been fair, substantive, and considerate, especially in arguing that the standard radfem credo—"Men Oppress Women"—is simply untrue. "The whole purpose of much feminist analysis," my critics informed me, "is to change the culture so as to produce good men."[18] What, pray tell (I asked myself in the quiet of my study, fully insulated from the isolated but still-shrill catcalls for my misogynistic scalp), are "good men"? And in whom should be vested an exclusive right to define that term?

I soon came to understand that radical feminist scholarship is only one of the politically-correct fault-lines along which the modern university sits. But it often triggers major tremors, both curricular and extra-curricular, that are pervasive and continuing, and I went on to describe some of those quakes in *Political Correctness Askew.* That piece elicited a goodly number of phone calls in agreement but relatively little written comment.✺

> ✺One critic, a dean no less, dismissed my polemical efforts as little more than shooting fish in a barrel. That image has always struck me as curious: the few fish I've been able to hook are swamped by the multitudes swimming in PC schools all over the country; if they are in a figurative barrel, their victims are often over one. True enough, though, something here is fishy.

Again I was not surprised. Why should anyone rock a boat already controlled firmly by the mutineers?

At first the academic PC movement infected only language. "Oppressive language does more than represent violence," writes novelist and race critic Toni Morrison. "It must be rejected, altered and exposed."[19] This kind of lingual nihilism has been embraced by a great many American universities largely by way of stringent speech and conduct codes. Over 225 of such codes forbid "verbal abuse and harassment," and over 100 prohibit "advocacy of offensive or outrageous viewpoints.[20]

The most visible neo-linguists are the radical feminists, who have turned chairmen into *chairs,* manholes into *personholes,* and history into *herstory.*[21] Thus students in an American Literature class can object, with the approval of their faculty mentors, to use of the word *mankind* in the Declaration of Independence (in the process ignoring Jefferson's opening reference to "the course of *human* events).[22] On the other hand, practically all "girls" and "ladies" have become self-made *women.*❀

❀ Or *wimmin, wimyn, womyn*—all now accepted usages, according to the Oxford English Dictionary, together with their singular counterparts wofem, womban, womon, womyn, woperson, and person of gender. But wimmin academics appreciate what the system has done for them, as witness this passage from a feminist journal: "Wimmin are treated the best and have the most equality when we're in university systems. A sense of comfort develops for most wimmin while we're attending universities. Then, upon graduation, we are ripped apart, degraded, mis-treated, undervalued, de-valued, judged by our sexuality, and much more. This is as equal as it is ever going to be."[23]

While the exhortation to reject "oppressive language" may appeal to a common sense of decency and civility, it too easily runs afoul of the First Amendment's guarantee of free speech. That principle—whatever people might say is less important than their right to say it—is fundamental to the American ideal of individual liberty.

But preoccupation with politically-correct speech has ultimately given way to other concerns, as the universities' self-appointed PC proponents began to identify and proscribe politically-incorrect conduct and curricula. These perceived evils have in turn been combated by way of a new pedagogy: "deconstruction," "critical legal studies," and "sensitivity training," while "Eurocentrism," "traditionalism," and even modern science are increasingly scorned and denounced. Diversity is promoted as a noble goal unto itself. Students are subjected to mandatory intensive "prejudice reduction workshops." Professors are hounded by "sexual harassment task forces," and their teaching is evaluated on political grounds.[24]

In many quarters, the pervasive PC atmosphere can be seen as both the primary cause and clear reflection of a widely-perceived deterioration in the quality of higher education—an environment that stifles free inquiry and expression, reinforces racial and political preferences, and dilutes standards. Thus the traditional search for truth is subordinated to the accommodation of "historically under-represented groups." The biases are brought to bear most visibly in faculty hiring, where in many places no white heterosexual males should waste their time applying; in teaching, where traditional courses thought to be "Eurocentric" are cast aside in favor of deconstructionist or multi-cultural offerings; and in evaluation of students, where rampant grade-inflation in the cause of compensation for ethnic differences serves to camouflage ineptitude. In theory, there may have been some justification for affirmative-action programs; in practice, they have proven unfairly inflexible and counter-productive.

My own first-hand experience with academic excesses has come mostly from the stomping-grounds of legal education, but it has not been difficult to gather evidence from elsewhere in the humanities or the physical and social sciences.

The current and most serious abuses in political correctness began with wholesale changes to the established liberal-arts curricula beginning in the late 1970's. What arguably was meant to be an effort toward open-mindedness and "inclusiveness" eventually hardened into a narrow political agenda—specifically the ostracization of "Eurocentric" culture as personified by "dead white males." The result has been a "dumbing down" of the standard curriculum. This has occurred most noticeably in the humanities, where the animus against Western civilization is manifested in the promulgation of so-called "Oppression Studies."

In literature, the classics have been relegated to the archives. Thus, in many modern English departments, Shakespeare is not only regarded as just another man of letters, but he is tossed to the ash-heaps—no longer required reading at some large universities, even for those who major in English Literature! Such a seemingly moronic educational philosophy is a direct reflection of the multi-culturalists' widespread world-view, in which society is an arena of power and conflict between those who oppress and those who are oppressed.

In philosophy, multi-culturalism is often synonymous with radical feminism. The goal of radfem philosophers is not truth, but political change. That purpose is not bad in and of itself, except where it serves to *suppress* truth—as when arguments are advanced in the absence of empirical evidence, or where hostility to the scientific method excludes its consideration. The inevitable result is shabby scholarship, which can readily be seen in most of the self-righteous and self-perpetuating feminist journals.[25]

In the field of history, the excesses are even more obvious. Here radical feminists have joined forces with various ethnic lobbies in a union whose sheer numbers make them a power to be reckoned with. In their zeal they view scholarship as a means to overthrow the established culture. Their rhetoric takes on the shrill sound of Communist or Nazi: education, religion, art, even science are merely tools of indoctrination and control wielded by the ruling race, class, or gender. The importance of academia becomes primarily its utility in the struggle for liberation. Thus the new *National Standards of History* emphasize the role of women and minorities in World War II to the virtual exclusion of the millions of white males who gave their lives for their country. The first textbook written to conform with the *Standards* devotes more space to the internment of Japanese-Americans than to all the battles in Europe and the Pacific combined. The Renaissance gets seven lines of text, the Reformation none. Nothing is said about the great universities of Europe. Religion is virtually ignored as well, except as it can be seen to have exploited women. The effect, as an aggrieved traditionalist put it, has been to "reduce historical work to polemics tricked out with footnotes."[26]

The sciences have been somewhat less infected, perhaps because there can be no "people's science" apart from existing science, no exclusive feminist sociology that makes sense, no deconstructionist mathematical theory, no such thing as

"African protein chemistry." Academic scientists must nevertheless keep a wary eye on the politically correct extremes of affirmative-action policies.[27]

Such is the hostility towards traditional culture and values that in 1995 Yale University returned an alumnus' gift of 20 million dollars rather than honor the donor's request that it be used for a course of studies in Western Civilization. On the other hand, Yale requires freshmen and sophomores to live in coed dormitories. Dartmouth offers a class called "Introduction to Gay and Lesbian Studies" (and plans to hire a dean for gay students).[28] Stanford is proud to present "Black Hair as Culture and History."[29]

The ostensibly commendable goals of political correctness —civility, sensitivity, and equality—have been substantially perverted by what has come to be called "multi-culturalism." When that concept is truly pluralistic—that is, when it becomes a quest to enrich our common culture by making it more inclusive of positive elements from other cultures—it is entirely defensible. But too often what evolves is a pervasively *illiberal* agenda, which sees scholarship and curricula almost solely as conduits for political change. Nowadays we are frequently subjected to an academic bait-and-switch: the arguments for multi-culturalism are usually couched in pluralistic terms, but more often than not the goal proves to be furtherance of a particular and one-sided strategic objective.[30]

A truly pluralistic multi-culturalist would recognize that trying to deny the contributions of European culture to mankind is ultimately futile and self-defeating. All literature would be measured against uniform aesthetic standards, and not praised simply because it is non- or anti-traditional.[31] Thus scholars interested in communicating a perfectly reasonable point of view—such as, "we should listen to the views of people outside of Western society in order to learn about the cultural biases that affect us"—should avoid the pseudo-intellectual jargon that remains very much the norm—such as, "we should absorb the intertextual multivocalities of postcolonial others in order to countenance the phallogocentric biases that mediate our identities."[32]

On some of these issues the interest is understandably selective, if sexist. For example, radical feminist scholars tend to take up the cudgels primarily in tenure battles that involve women, or in zoning legislation which might define the typical family as heterosexual. But the illiberal multi-culturalist and radical feminist agendas cast their effects well beyond scholarship and the curricula. They are quick to come to the defense of any woman alleging rape or sexual harassment—often before hearing all the evidence, and sometimes even after a defendant has been acquitted.

As multi-culturalists have assumed greater degrees of power, the Academy has become a decidedly unwelcome nesting place for those with different points of view. Academic freedom is increasingly threatened by the vague standards currently describing sexual harassment. The conflict between perceived offensive conduct and free speech is often much sharper on campus than in the ordinary employment context. The rules regarding harassment deter not only genuine misconduct but also harmless (and even desirable) speech—which in higher education should be central both to the purpose of the institution and to the employee's profession and performance. Faced with legal uncertainty, many professors will avoid *any* speech that might be even remotely interpreted as creating a hostile environment. (Even *staring at a stranger* has been cited by some radical feminists as "a well-established cultural taboo.")[33] They know first- hand that the PC police can cause great harm to character and career, just as traditionalists who deign to challenge the wholesale removal of "Eurocentric" courses realize that they have become voices in the academic wilderness.✿

> ✿A friend who teaches at a small women's college in New England was put through several years' worth of harrowing litigation because he had suggested at a search-committee meeting that a lesbian candidate "might not be a good role model."

The acquisition of tenure remains the holy grail of most academics—and the standards for attaining it the altars before which faculty quake and genuflect. But trembling in the Ivory Tower may still best be characterized by the inhibition of free speech and thought. It remains the crux of the conflict between Political Correctness and the Constitution. For traditional scholars and libertarians, regardless of their political persuasion, the abiding concern about PC is the stifling effect that radical agendas can have on shared values, that coerced speech and conduct codes can have on both liberty of expression and academic freedom. (They might agree with the 73 percent of Americans in a recent poll who think our manners are worse today than they were several decades ago, but they are duly alarmed that 43 percent say it's worth placing limits on freedom of speech in order to enforce civility.) A college campus today may be the least safe place in America to speak dangerously: less safe than a radio or tv talk show, a newspaper, a street corner.[34]

How can the tensions be reconciled?

Only by redress within the bounds of the law—fully in

keeping with the Constitutional principles of civil liberties (freedom of speech, press, religion, and assembly), civil rights (due process, equal protection), and academic freedom (sustained by genuine scholarship and nurtured by unfettered inquiry)—and by refusal to exclude arbitrarily any common heritage of learning.

That's the purpose of this book, which seeks little more, but no less, than to encourage a return of common sense to the Academy. It is not about why Johnny (or Jane) can't read, but about why both are discouraged from reading Shakespeare or the history of Western civilization. It is about why they are both taught that, because Johnny has oppressed Jane throughout the ages, he must firmly and finally be put in his place—as must the patriarchal system that has so wrongfully perpetuated male biases. It is about why both have less regard for their traditional-minded professors, who in turn have come to quiver before their increasingly strident colleagues pressing political causes and promulgating exclusionary curricula.[35]

The following pages seek to explore the manifold excesses in the modern Ivory Tower, moving from one that is particularly representative (legal scholarship, specifically the relationship between tenure and coerced and ever-proliferating law-review articles) to another that is more generally pervasive (radical feminism, and its impact on modern faculties). They culminate in an examination of the most cosmic of contemporary intemperances—political correctness, and its corrosive effects on the entire academic enterprise.

Besides running the risk of offending colleagues, writing a critique of the modern academy is, of course, like trying to freeze an ever-evolving institution.[36] By the time this book is published, some of the more outrageous excesses described herein may well have been replaced by other (perhaps even more bizarre and egregious) curricular or extra-curricular reforms. Moreover, one who undertakes in a single book to reach the simple but elusive goal of a return to common sense faces some long odds. Scholarly writing itself is a lonely pursuit; writing about scholarship might be even lonelier; whining about either is almost inevitably unproductive.

Nevertheless, is it too much to expect that these pages will not only be read, but in some measure heeded—to hope that exposing the excesses will somehow suggest reasonable remedies?

Even skeptical scholars can be optimistic.

I

Scholarship Amok
Excesses in the Pursuit of Truth and Tenure

Not everything that man thinks must he say; not everything he says must he write, but most important not everything that he has written must he publish. —KING SOLOMON (1033-975 B.C.)[1]

Professors, the prized and often permanent residents of the Ivory Tower, are generally valued more for their writing than their teaching—which itself is often left largely to graduate assistants.[2] Administrators, meanwhile, are bent on measuring scholarship more by quantity than quality. For many if not most members of the faculty, "publish or perish" is both a simple reality of academic life and a ghoulish academic aphorism that will just not go away.[3]

No better proof of this proposition can be found than in law schools, where the great majority of junior professors must publish a certain number of articles within a certain number of years in order to win tenure or promotion.[4] But legal scholarship is unique. Unlike other disciplines (which may have their own problems with objectivity and scientific method), practically all of it is a form of advocacy. Moreover, as a Yale law professor named Fred Rodell said famously way back in 1937, there are two things wrong with almost all legal writing:

"One is its style. The other is its content."[5]

Here we are, three millennia after Solomon and over a half-century since Rodell, and what have we?

Fifty years ago there were about 150 law journals[6] (not to mention thousands of local newspapers and countless full-color comic books). Now, there are over *eight hundred* legal periodicals[7] (not to mention a drastically dwindled number of daily papers, and precious few comics). Both the wisdom of Solomon and the pithy sayings of Rodell have been all but forgotten. What, indeed, have we wrought? Although Rodell predicted his original critique would have no effect, could he have anticipated the sheer dimensions of this worst-case scenario—that his "professional purveyors of pretentious poppycock"[8] would have spawned so furiously, that the contemporary law reviews he collectively called "spinach"[9] would have mushroomed into such a gargantuan souffle of airy irrelevance?

Lo, the voices are heard once again in the wilderness, from the bewildered among us innocent (or ignorant) enough to try righting the wrongs perpetrated in the name of Scholarship.

Few professors today delude themselves about (or are able to luxuriate in) the long-romanticized lifestyle of Academia: walking the quiet quadrangles of neatly manicured college gardens, discoursing timelessly with colleagues, thinking higher thoughts. Fewer still aspire to scholarship purely in search of Truth. Nowadays the goal of publication is much less to find answers than to avoid perishing in pursuit of promotion and tenure.

The promise of lifetime job security—tenure—is usually defended as essential for the preservation of academic freedom: the right to think, speak, and write without fear of recrimination. From that perspective the concept of tenure has great merit.

But the system can be counter-productive. Tenure serves not to protect valuable diversity and dissent, argue its secret critics, but to perpetuate "an intellectually homogeneous," anti-conservative class. In fact it may chill the academic freedom of younger faculty who fear offending senior professors. The pressure that is placed on young teachers to write for their peers—who in turn determine whether to recommend tenure—can force authors to publish themselves into a narrow academic corner. The result may be scholarship that is written for the dean or the tenure committee, and no one else. Meanwhile, the faculty becomes entrenched, ultimately consisting of middle-aged professors whose political views reflect the liberal/radical temperament of the 'Sixties. At least that is the view of many non-academics, who see re-examination of tenure as part of a "largely wholesome turbulence" resulting from public dismay over the cost and quality of college education.[10]

Although various attempts have been made to change the tenure system,[11] for better or worse the principal path to the prize of total job security is still through publishing. In the 1970's alone some four hundred new journals were founded in modern languages and literature, carrying articles almost none of which were likely to be subsequently cited elsewhere. The term in the bookstore industry for faculty publications is "wallpaper." At many schools, the hardbound titles are nothing more than pretty shelf-fillers. "No one reads them," says the general manager of the Yale University bookstore. "Many of these books are so esoteric that they only sell two or three copies a year."

More than a few observers have complained that something should be done to reduce the amount of money libraries spend on scholarly journals. One new plan to cut down on the number of journals and junk scholarship would be to require certification of scholarship, as opposed to actual publication. (The new standard would thus be "certify or perish" rather than "publish or perish.")[12]

The threshold question, of course, is why Scholarship? *He who increases knowledge,* said Solomon, *increases grief.*[13]

Certainly there exist among us the genuine scholastics of yesteryear, dutifully reporting their original ideas and producing from time to time provocative prose and innovative agendas. (Rodell himself could have been considered among this small group, if for no other reason than having been the first to say publicly what so many of us—weaker-kneed, wimpier-eyed, and more thoroughly word-processed—privately bemoan within the *sanctum sanctorum* of the faculty lounge.)

But for every pure scholar we have a dozen-and-a-half of the innocent ersatz, for every diamond a heap of rhinestones. Some of them are decent enough thinkers stickied-up by pedestrian prose, industrious worker-bees who—simply by virtue of the thousands of articles with which they must periodically compete—must of necessity be deemed mediocre. In greater part, however, they are competent-enough teachers without anything original to write, doomed to scholarly mediocrity by academic imperative—coerced clones who are whipped into a hack's frenzy, urged to jump through hoops held up by the local promotion-and-tenure committee, forced to shimmy down the chutes of the publication process or (perish the thought) perish.

To some degree, all of them—whether genuine scholars, would-be wisemen, or coerced clones—are motivated by the gratification of ego, the satisfaction of habit, and the expectations of university image-makers. In turn these traits are fueled by faculty self-studies, administrative mission statements, and fiats laid down by the Association of American Law Schools,[14] most of which themselves become etched in ivory long before their floppy disks ever begin to fossilize.

Forget the traditional rights to freedom of thought or expression. Now, everything a professor says, writes, or publishes must be politically correct. Solomon would be dismayed.

These observations are intended as much to define scholarship as to debunk it, to separate the wind-blown chaff from the few kernels that might nourish the mind. Legal scholarship is largely illustrated by the (totally unillustrated) law reviews which, conversely, both contribute to and reflect the value system by which the academy is governed. Even a cursory perusal of the literature leads to an inescapable conclusion: the number of mind-enriching scholars is much smaller than that suggested by the burgeoning reviews, the number of whole-grain journals but a fraction of the fruited plains currently being harvested in law libraries across the land. Analysis, research, and writing are overblown, while classroom competence, community service, and non-law review scholarship are under-credited. The law schools have a problem. The system has run amok.

Multitudes and Minutiae

In an ideal world, people govern themselves and governments pass laws only when necessary, and then only those that are easy to understand and follow. Likewise, lawyers in Utopia are uniformly bright, energetic advocates—fair, ethical, and sensitive—having emerged from law schools that offer logical, interesting curricula taught by fair, ethical, and sensitive professors, whose courses are complemented by the fruits of their research, which itself is distilled into useful, interesting articles and published in well-edited reviews.

In the real world, all of the above may exist, but in greatly diminishing degree. Scholarship could be valuable, but most of it isn't. Whatever rich stew there once may have been quickly thins into bland gruel through the sheer multitude of journals seeking fodder for their troughs. Slops fill the law reviews. Simply put, there are too many of them.

Consider the numbers involved. Of the 800-plus journals cited by the relatively exclusive *Current Law Index,* most appear at least three times throughout the year, each with several lead articles apiece. By conservative estimate, that's *five thousand* new pieces annually. Could even a small percentage of this massive productivity (which law librarians privately label the Junk Stream) be worth readers' whiles?

And, one must hasten to ask, *what* readers? Most reviews have very limited circulations, consisting primarily of libraries and alumni. Few in the latter group pay any attention to the esoteric titles appearing on the cover, much less to the contents inside. For all the work professors put into law-review articles, one would think they'd be able to attract a larger audience than the sprinkling of colleagues who skim through off-prints out of courtesy or the handful of students who wade through them because they've been assigned. Even fewer practicing attorneys read such secondary sources out of non-billable interest.

Helping to perpetuate this endless multitude of articles are exhaustive "research tools," supplying comprehensive cross-references and mind-boggling databases. *The Index to Legal Periodicals* and the *Current Law Index* both reflect and contribute to the epidemic proportions of publication.

Beyond sheer numbers, consider the journals themselves. The *Harvard Law Review* is arguably the oldest, still among the toughest to break into, and certainly the one most emulated both in form and content.[15]✿

> ✿If so, certain enraged readers may ask, how could it have accepted a piece like this? The writer himself, though, rejected Groucho Marx's famous analysis—"I'd never join a club that would have somebody like me as a member"—and congratulated the editors on their good judgment. Truth to tell, given the central thesis presented herein, there was little doubt it would be published somewhere among the 800-plus journals currently clogging legal libraries everywhere; might as well start at the top. I offered any curious reader a confidential list of journals that rejected this article—the offer to expire when I ran out of self-satisfaction. No one asked.

Yet even *Harvard's* goals were exceedingly modest at the beginning. From Volume I, Number 1, which appeared in 1887:

> Our object, primarily, is to set forth the work done in the school with which we are connected, to furnish news of interest to those who have studied law in Cambridge, and to give, if possible, to all who are interested in the subject of legal education, some idea of what is done under the Harvard system of instruction. Yet we are not without hopes that the *Review* may be serviceable to the profession at large.[16]

How serviceable the *Harvard Law Review* has been in all the years since remains open to question, but it has supplied the overwhelming majority of the most-cited articles in the past half-century.[17]

Nevertheless, every law school now has at least one review to call its own, each looking and reading depressingly like the rest. Despite scattered attempts by editors to distinguish their journals by theme and discipline, redundancy abounds. Besides the fundamentally fungible general-interest reviews, we have the *Journal of Law and Religion* and the *Journal of Church and State;* the *International Lawyer,* the *Journal of International Law,* the *Connecticut Journal of International Law,* the *Yale Journal of International Law,* and the *Wisconsin Journal of International Law;* the *American Criminal Law Review,* the *Criminal Law Journal,* the *Criminal Law Bulletin,* the *Criminal Law Quarterly,* and the *Criminal Law Review.* The list goes on and on. Law reviews are published from Adelaide to Zambia. There's the *Pacific Basin Law Review,* the *San Fernando Valley Law Review,* and the *Samoan Pacific Law Review.* Don't know which one is best for your little gem-of-an-opus? *Try the Directory for Successful Publishing in Legal Periodicals,* which lists only the 495 choicest outlets.

The lead articles themselves are often overwhelming collections of minutiae, perhaps substantively relevant at some point in time to an individual practitioner or two way out in the hinterlands, and that almost entirely by chance. Otherwise, they are quickly relegated to oblivion, or if lucky to a passing *but see* in someone else's obscure piece.

True (and perhaps good), law today pervades all aspects of life—but must all aspects of life be treated in law reviews? Here's a sampling of recent articles:

"*The Unrecognized Uses of Legal Education in Papua New Guinea*"[18]

"*The Legal Status of Fish Farming*"[19]

"*Law and Landscape: The Legal Construction and Protection of Hedgerows*[20]

*"In Praise of the Efficiency of Decentralized Traditions and
    Their Preconditions"* [21]

*"Mongolian Bankruptcy Law: A Comparative Analysis with
    the American Bankruptcy System"* [22]

*"Epistemological Foundations and Meta-Hermeneutic
    Methods: The Search for a Theoretical Justification of
    the Coercive Force of Legal Interpretation"* [23]

*"If Spot Bites the Neighbor, Should Dick and Jane Go
    to Jail?"* [24]

"Judicial Review: From the Frog to Mickey Mouse" [25]

*"What's Love Got To Do With It? Critical Legal Studies,
    Feminist Discourse, and the Ethic of Solidarity"* [26]

"Official: During Pregnancy, Females Are Pregnant" [27]

"Morality or Sittlichkeit: Toward a Post-Hegelian Solution" [28]

"Toward a Legal Theory of Popular Culture" [29]

*"Toward an Economic Theory of Voluntary Resignation by
    Dictators"* [30]

*"The Differentiation of Francophone Rapists and Nonrapists
    Using Penile Circumferential Measures"* [31]

"Why Study Pacific Salmon Law?" [32]

Why, indeed?

One may not be able to tell an article by its title, but
originality is evidently in short supply among authors and editors wondering what to call their mind-numbing research.
According to LEXIS, the words "toward," "model," or "theory"
have appeared in no fewer than 19,558 titles during the past
twenty-four years[33]—making them the most popular titular
buzzwords since "integrated" and "functional" came down the
pike.

> ⚜The figures, tabulated as of March 2001, are absurdly easy to gather and verify by using a modern database like Lexis-Nexis. Readers of this tidbit will be rewarded with a further break-down (of the titles) if they take the pain to peruse the end-notes.

"Confusion" reigns at the top of 1,113 recent articles.⚜ In fact you can find almost any word you can think of—even "penile" has shown up fifteen times in recent years.⚜⚜

> ⚜Look it up yourself.
> ⚜⚜Could we be moving Towards a Model Penile Code?

Legislative analysis frequently turns into law-review manure. Do we really need 571 separate articles on waste-disposal laws? If only the promulgators of scholarship patterns recognize the dimensions of their own garbage-removal problem. Garbage in scholarship, of course, is not the exclusive province of the law reviews. A panel proposed for an academic conference in 1999 was entitled *"The Economy of Excrement in English Renaissance Studies."*[34] Literary scholars were invited to reflect upon the "tropes and representations of excrement and/or excretion in literature" and "waste management and the social order."

In fact a good deal of non-legal academia is similarly tinged with political or strategic agendas. A professor and graduate student at the University of Michigan co-authored a paper with this weighty title: *"When Ideology Hurts: Effects of Belief in the Protestant Ethic and Feeling Overweight on the Psychological Well-Being of Women."* The article's conclusions—that "overweight women perceive that the reason they experienced social rejection from an attractive male was due to their weight," that the Protestant work ethic forces them to ignore the fact that they are "victims of a discriminatory system," and that they instead blame "their lesser outcomes" on a "lack of self-discipline, hard work, and strong moral character"—were somewhat less than startling.

Moreover, scholarship can be and often is blatantly self-serving. The University of Michigan commissioned a study—to help defend itself against several lawsuits charging it with discriminating by race in its affirmative-action admissions process—which set out to prove that students attending racially "diverse" colleges go on to lead more racially diverse lives.[35]

Too often, the Junk Stream journals are more concerned with churning it out, and thus heavily pre-occupied with meeting publishing schedules. They certainly do not consider how much they pollute the intellectual environment—how much they miss the forests they destroy for the knotted trees in whose dark shade they obscurely bask.

But the journals continue to take themselves ever so seriously. That's another reason why the literature of the law is perhaps the most massive of any profession.❀

> ❀ One of my colleagues reports that the editors of a Midwestern law review were not amused when he asked them the status of their potato-law symposium issue.[36] Chances are they weren't having trouble digging up lead articles, but that they had too many sacksful to choose from.

The law reviews' pretentiousness and singular lack of humor is legendary. Rodell himself suggested a means by which that weakness could be overcome: "The best way to get a laugh out of a law review is to take a couple of drinks and then read an article, any article, aloud. That can be really funny."[37]

Value Among the Volume(s)

It's been said before that law reviews were made to be written and not read.❀ Regardless of their questionable benefit to bar and bench, however, they do have some value for the few students who "make law review" and no doubt receive exceptionally good training in logical thought and formal exposition, not to mention source-checking. Indeed, the reviews can correct deficiencies in, or at least complement, the traditional law school curriculum, which frequently provides precious little in the way of research and writing. They also offer an outlet for student initiative in the face of curricular boredom. However, the hard fact that the majority of law reviews are exclusive clubs, closed to all but those with the highest grades or demonstrated writing ability, calls into question the scope of their educational value.[38]

> ❀I haven't really tried to verify who said this, or if in fact it was said, but I know I've seen it somewhere, and even if I haven't, what difference does it make?

A good many professors can likewise benefit from researching and writing within their chosen fields of interest and discipline, in the process stimulating their involvement and dissipating that particular inertia which often permeates the Ivory Tower.

But the limited value of legal scholarship as it appears in law reviews is largely outweighed by its costs. The proliferation of research and writing tends more to increase quantity than quality. One article is no longer good enough for promotion. An aspirant must establish a "pattern" of publication.[39]

Professorial purposes can be accomplished better than through *omphaloskepsis* (a law-review-quality Greek term for "contemplation of the navel"). Others have called it "sesquipedalian tergiversation" (multi-syllabled evasiveness). But belly-button gazing should be a luxury allowed only those few whose writing is deemed both incisive and succinct. The rest should be encouraged to more logical productivity as teachers and community leaders.

Considering the scholarly stuff many obscure writers have to offer, they richly deserve the anonymity promised by the multitude of lesser journals. Some might even prefer it.

Meanwhile, the impact of law reviews on the judiciary is diminishing.[40] Would their absence cause the courts to cease viewing issues analytically? Probably no more than closing down the Office of Information and Public Affairs in the Rural Electrification Administration of the Department of Agriculture would have any effect whatever on television watching in Appaloosa. In fact, as a casual glance through *Shepard's Law Review Citations* will reveal, the overwhelming majority of articles are noted not by courts or legislatures, but by *one another!*[41] Remarkably few are ever cited in the primary sources—case reports or annotated codes.

There are so many publications clamoring to fill their pages with Law Most Learned, however, that few contributors need worry about dwindling forums for their prose. Moreover, all of the participants in the process—pupils, professors, practitioners, printers, and publishers—are quite content to go on greasing one another's palms and egos.[42]

Much of this enormous hodge-podge has a built-in obsolescence as well, largely by virtue of the law reviews' extended editing process. Most often the lag is so long between the first dull gleam in an author's eye and the finished product that whatever may be timely and relevant is largely lost on whatever few readers might be out there. The stuff is simply stale, stupid, or stultifying. (Scholarship in the scientific community, by way of comparison, is of considerably greater utility and immediacy. That may explain why articles in medical journals, for example, are generally much shorter, contain fewer footnotes, and are often grist for the popular media.)[43]

Here and there amidst the morass of law reviews are occasional stabs at candid self-criticism. For example, various observers have noted that supposedly analytical commentaries are predominantly descriptive and mildly plagiaristic;[44] that those published during pending litigation interfere with the judicial process;[45] that the scholarly voice lacks factual discipline;[46] and that objectivity is impossible because of lawyers' inalienable commitment to advocacy.[47]❀ Supreme Court Justice William O. Douglas said that law-review articles are written by paid hacks espousing the views of their clients.[49] Others see the extraordinary proliferation of published articles as "harmful for the nature, evaluation, and accessibility of legal scholarship."[50] They "lack originality, are boring, too long, too numerous, and have too many footnotes, which also are boring and too long."[51] It was Rodell, again, who summed it up best—over fifty years ago: "This centripetal absorption in the home-made mysteries and sleight-of-hand of the law would be a perfectly harmless occupation if it did not consume so much time and energy that might better be spent otherwise."[52]

> ❀ One critic wrote that "scholarship qua scholarship on law may not even exist," but I don't know what that means.[48]

But these criticisms are few and far between and—perhaps also because they are published in law reviews themselves—widely ignored.

Instead, as another lonely voice put it, we go on "blithely continuing to make mountain after mountain out of tiresome technical molehills,"[53] not to mention the sacrifices made in personal income. Law professors, it would seem, must be either independently wealthy or married to rich spouses. "Else why—once they have won their full professorships, at any rate—do they keep submitting that turgid, legaldegooky garbage to law reviews—for free?"[54]

Here's a modest (and unoriginal) proposal for reform: let the local reviews enhance the educational value needed to justify their existence by making themselves accessible to all the local law students and professors, and reduce their publication costs by putting all articles onto a computerized database instead of into print. Students and professors alike would thereby be able to polish their research and writing skills—without wasting the time of printers and publishers, postal workers, law librarians, and compulsive readers of junk mail.[55]

Scholarship: We Know It When We See It

It is quite possible that reducing the number of law reviews might only address the symptoms of a deeper malaise—in particular the value system reflected by promotion-and-tenure policies as they are worshipfully applied through the criteria of "research, analysis, and writing."

Webster's defines scholarship simply as "a fund of knowledge and learning."[56] Faculties of law have much more difficulty with the concept. They grapple with the meaning of scholarship in much the same way that Justice Potter Stewart was unable to define pornography. "But," he said, "I know it when I see it."[57]

For purposes of promotion and tenure, "scholarship"

means written and published materials which meet all of the following criteria: they are "analytical," "significant," "learned," "well-written," and "disinterested."[58] Each of these terms is likewise chewed over like cud, all the while defying objective definition.

To be *analytical,* according to the bylaws of the typical faculty, "the materials must provide a detailed, well-supported and sophisticated analysis that increases our understanding of the topic, and must do more than describe a body of law or a legal problem."[59] A colleague of mine speaks of "massaging ideas" (whatever *that* is). As we shall see shortly, no amount of analysis seems to increase our understanding of the term itself.

To be *significant,* "the materials must make a significant contribution to the legal literature. They must do more than reiterate or rephrase previous analyses of the topic and they must not represent the work of others."[60] But the words "significant" and "more than" are inescapably subjective. If they were applied strictly, a significant portion of all law review material would be thrown out as representing in some way the work of others.

To be *learned,* "the materials must demonstrate deep familiarity with and understanding of the body of knowledge associated with the topic."[61]

To be *well-written,* they "must be written in a manner appropriate to the subject matter, and must demonstrate the candidate's ability to convey his or her ideas effectively."[62] Again, these are patently subjective criteria that in most cases give no more guidance in promotion and tenure decisions than does the gut feeling of how well a candidate gets along with his colleagues.

Indeed, the only objective standard is the last. To be *disinterested,* "the materials must not be published to serve the interests of any client, either paid or pro bono."[63] But the over-inclusiveness of this standard belies a failure of common sense. Suppose a pro bono article goes *against* a client's interests? Suppose a professor is *commissioned* to do an exhaustive study? In neither case should his scholarship be discredited out-of-hand—but it is.

Besides their inherent subjectivity, the promotion-and-tenure standards of most faculties focus unduly on articles published in law reviews. Often neither briefs nor practice manuals—no matter how learned or useful—are considered "scholarship." Nor would a casebook or treatise be deemed as satisfactory as a law review article. One wonders how the promotion and tenure committee would handle Socrates, who never published a word (but on whose Socratic method law professors widely rely).✿

> ✿ I didn't think of this myself, but neither, I'm sure, did the journalist (whose name I forget) from whom I stole it.

One senior professor summed up the importance of scholarship to promotion and tenure from a much more practical and concrete point of view, giving this advice to a junior colleague: the way to get ahead, he advised, is to "take an obscure little problem that no one has thought much about, blow it out of all proportion, and solve it, preferably several times, in prestigious law reviews."[64]

Law schools generally consider scholarship to be an amalgam of research, analysis, and writing. Each is taught as part of a required course in the first year, and genuflected upon in all years afterward (even through practice and retirement). Scholarship can be largely demystified, however, by examining those traditional components.

Research: Bushwhacking Through the Thickets

Legal research is at once objective—that is, there are a finite number of sources to be gathered and culled—and an open-ended art form.

With the advent of computerized data banks such as *Lexis* and *Westlaw*, gleaning all the cases on point is as easy as playing Trivial Pursuit and maybe even more fun. Finding everything that's ever been written on the subject requires little more than leafing through the *Current Law Index* or its older but equally adequate counterpart, the *Index to Legal Periodicals*. And the whole mass can be saturation-bombed with cross-references by resorting to an endless array of *Shephard's Citations*. (There, I've given away the secrets of legal research in a mere three sentences!) As for gleaning the most relevant and salient authorities, the possibilities are infinite—and are what separate the grown-up academics from the *wannabe* boys and girls.

Nowadays, unfortunately, research skills often amount to little more than mastery of the citation forms. The genuine scholars, besides being creative writers, are highly selective in their choice of relevant data. But many modern professors tend to toss their excess research into the annotation hopper and leave it to their readers (or editors) to separate the salient stuff from the midly tangential. That's why it's harder to write without footnotes than with them: it takes a good writer to decide what's on point and what's not. It's far easier to keep baby and bathwater in the same textual tub. And it's safer, both intellectually (allowing the writer to straddle any issue by taking a strong position in the text while waffling below) and morally (permitting him to stave off plagiarism with grudging acknowledgments in four-point type), as well as more ego-gratifying (enabling intricate citation of arcane sources at stupefying length).

Yet the number of notes in an article is still deemed a measure of its erudition. Although there are occasions of reverse snobbery—where it is implied (as in this polemic)[65] that notes are beneath an author's time, dignity, or expertise—the more common scholarship seeks to impress by both magnitude and multitude of bottom-matter. The longer the note, the greater the breadth of its author's knowledge. The more numerous the references, the more comprehensive his treatment of the subject matter. The current individual record-holder is Arnold S. Jacobs, Esq., who drew his readers away from the text no fewer than 4,824 times—easily eclipsing the former mark held by Dean Jesse Choper (1,611) as well as the group title (3,917) held by the *Georgetown Law Journal* staff.[66] Too bad no promotion-and-tenure credit is given for the transcendent task of bushwhacking through such unintelligible thickets.

> Even the shortest article in law-review history, Erik M. Jensen's provocative three- worder, *The Shortest Article in Law Review History*, contained two footnotes totaling 109 words. Equally useful information: Disney animators drew 6,469,952 black spots for the film *101 Dalmations;* there were 17,500,000,000 charcoal briquettes sold in 1988; and 24% of all Iowans display lawn ornaments.

Some writers limit their notes strictly to citations of authority, disdaining what they consider flights of creative irrelevance and esoteric nit-picking. But such purists are passé.

The new chic in noting is to write rambling distinctions laced with "fugitive" sources—exotic references, rare books, or "letters or documents on file with the author." Incomprehensible law-and-economics graphs and diagrams are also In.[67]

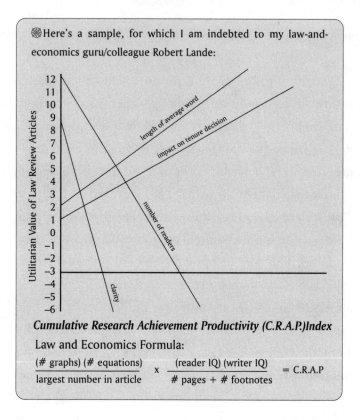

Here's a sample, for which I am indebted to my law-and-economics guru/colleague Robert Lande:

Cumulative Research Achievement Productivity (C.R.A.P.)Index

Law and Economics Formula:

$$\frac{(\#\ graphs)\ (\#\ equations)}{largest\ number\ in\ article} \times \frac{(reader\ IQ)\ (writer\ IQ)}{\#\ pages + \#\ footnotes} = C.R.A.P$$

Two primary strains of footnote virus were identified early on in the law review epidemic: (1) the explanatory type (or *if-you-didn't-understand-what-I-wrote-in-the-text-here's-another- stab-at-it)* type, and (2) the vainglorious variety (or *if-you're-from-Kalamazoo-just-take-a- gander-at-this).* [68]

Most scholars, however, refuse to recognize footnoting as a disease at all, arguing the benefits that inure to both writer and reader of teensy typography. Indeed, they spare readers a barrage of unneeded technical trivia, enable them to uncover shortcomings in authority, and allow for a smoother-running text. At the same time, they let a writer more easily separate basic concepts from nuances, and sometimes force him to justify his positions. [69]

On occasion, notes become more important than text. Witness the famous footnote #4 in *United States v. Carolene Products Co.*,[70] in which Justice Harlan Stone announced the landmark principle of constitutional jurisprudence that statutes affecting "discrete and insular minorities" must be given strict scrutiny. There's also note #59 in *United States v. Socony-Vacuum Oil Co.*[71] and note #16 in *Terry v. Ohio*[72] (which has been cited well over a hundred times).

The most lucid analysis of the subject is an article by Arthur Austin,[73] whose tongue-in-cheek tone is somewhat overwhelmed both by serious assertions in defense of footnotes and by 107 of his own.❀ "In today's publish or perish environment," Austin writes, "footnote trashing is the slothful tenured establishment's last refuge of snobbery."[74] *Au contraire,* he suggests that footnoting permits one author to differentiate his work from another's—an "artistic and abstruse discipline that functions as a subtle, but critical, influence in the determination of promotion, tenure, and professional status."[75] Moreover, footnotes "serve as embryos for new ideas and an underground source for humor"[76] (no doubt referring to classics such as *The Common Law Origins of the Infield Fly Rule*[77] and my own *Mockingbirds Among the Brethren*[78]). He also points out that footnoting helps create the aura of elevated status that ultimately furnishes academics with hefty consulting fees.[79]

❀My congratulations to the reader discerning enough to question how I have the gall to chide Austin for his apparent hypocrisy, when I offer several hundred notes of my own. My somewhat lame excuse ("the editors made me do it!"—see "A Note about the Notes," *supra)* is hereby accompanied by both abject apologies and an offer to supply another version of this same piece—unannotated—to anyone who asks. I don't expect any takers.

But as with the reviews themselves, the negatives far out-weigh the positives. Even traditionalists recognize the criticism that footnotes have become "a serious embarrassment to legal scholarship."[80] Others have called them "phony excrescences,"[81] "a means of concealment,"[82] "hedges against forthright statements in the text,"[83] and a "foible [that] breeds nothing but sloppy thinking, clumsy writing, and bad eyes."[84] Various judges have complained that footnotes "cause more problems than they solve," represent "dubious erudition," and are an "abomination."[85]

> ✸The late Supreme Court Justice Arthur Goldberg may have resigned in part because of footnotes. Complaining about an appellate opinion with over 500 notes, he observed: "Had I remained on the Supreme Court, I would have reversed him on this ground because of the sheer impossibility of reviewing an opinion of this type."

It's hard enough to keep track of a modern scholar's train of thought without having to jump back and forth from text to note. "If footnotes were a rational form of communication," said one judge, "Darwinian selection would have resulted in the eyes being set vertically rather than on an inefficient horizontal plane."[86] Or, as Noel Coward put it, encountering a footnote "is like going downstairs to answer the doorbell while making love."[87]

But it's virtually impossible to comprehend footnotes that slavishly follow the signals required by *A Uniform System of Citation* (the "Bluebook"). Show me someone who can explain the difference between *"but see"* and *"but cf."* and I'll show you a world-class master of utterly useless distinctions.[88]

The core of the problem is the lack of moderation. The notes often take on a life of their own, snuffing out whatever line of logic the writer seeks to impart. If originality is the goal, why such excessive attribution? (Compare the typically bloated American law-review article with its British counterpart: the latter is generally leaner and cleaner, with far fewer footnotes—and hence eminently more readable.)

Scholarship is no different from any other writing in its basic function: communication. But the geometric growth of footnote density is fundamentally at odds with that purpose.[89] Recognition of such counter-productivity has been slow in coming, but bubbles up here and there in new journals that publish shorter, more provocative articles, and in a few established law reviews, hoping to counter similar criticism of their own deadweight pieces, which include relatively note-free "Essay and Dialogue" sections.[90]

Analysis: Separating the Taut from the Tautological

Webster's defines "analysis" simply as (1) "separation of a whole into its component parts" and/or (2) "an examination of a complex, its elements, and their relations."[91]

For purposes of promotion and tenure, however, the term appears to defy definition—even though virtually every Promotion and Tenure Committee requires that, for scholarship to pass muster, it must be "analytical." Consider again the attempt made by the typical faculty manual noted earlier: to be analytical, "[t]he materials must provide a detailed, well-supported and sophisticated analysis that increases our understanding of the topic, and must do more than describe a body of law or a legal problem."[92] Talk about tautology: to be *analytical,* the materials must provide an *analysis!*

In virtually every case, determination of whether an article increases our understanding of the topic or does anything more than describe a body of law or a legal problem depends almost entirely on subjective factors. The more familiar the reader with the subject matter, the less analytical the article; the more the reader favors a candidate, the better the analysis; and if the reader dislikes the candidate for any of many reasons, he can discreetly dismiss the analysis as wanting. This can be done in all manner of obfuscatory language. For example, a tenured associate generally regarded as an effective teacher was recently denied a promotion, largely based on a committee report stating that his work "did not disprove an accepted understanding of what the law is or how it works"; it did not provide "a fresh conceptual framework"; it did not "break new ground."[93]

We'd be more intellectually honest (and fair) if we were to apply a more liberal meaning to the word "analytical." A workable definition, it seems to me, is "that which describes a body of knowledge, and offers an opinion about it." The true measure of an article's quality should be how well it describes the subject, how tautly it is written, and how cogent we think the opinion—even if we disagree. A more honest approach (with ourselves and our colleagues) would begin by conceding the semantic truism that practically everything is analytical to a degree, and by making our sincere and subjective judgment based on how well we like it (or its author).

Changing our definition of analysis to give it practical meaning would also help us escape the law review mind-set, and thereby allow us to reward the writer of useful, enlightening, and provocative essays—as well as restatements, treatises, practice manuals, model legislation, op-eds, and all manner of interdisciplinary texts.

Writing: Bugaboo of the Poobahs

It may be hard to say whether good writers are born or made, but it's painfully obvious that few of them are legal scholars. Law-review prose is predominantly bleak and turgid. Moreover, it seems to be self-perpetuating. The brightest students, should they become teachers, are still browbeaten into writing what has been called a "wonderful profusion of humbug."[94] Many observers have noted the apprehension with which the law school elite regard a student or professor who resists legalese and insists on simple prose in writing and speech. The scholarship of such rare beasts is often regarded as suspect.[95]

Similarly, length remains a hallmark of erudition. *Let your words be few,*[96] said King Solomon himself, but the legal scholars continue to exalt quantity. Thus if a good writing professor suggests to the poobahs on the curriculum committee that they reduce the number of required pages in students' first-year memoranda or their third-year independent research papers, he will likely be voted down. Few faculty members understand that the shorter a memo, the more clear and effective it usually is. Nor do they fathom that it's often more difficult to be concise. (Mark Twain once apologized for a lengthy letter by saying that he didn't have enough time to write a brief one.) These are the same folks who make promotion-and-tenure decisions based on the length of law-review articles. ✾ Next we'll be measuring page size as we tally up the footnotes.

> ✾ One faculty I know passed a by-law that a law-review article of twenty pages or longer would presumptively satisfy its promotion-and-tenure standards but, for anything shorter, the burden of proof would shift to the candidate.

The way law-review articles are written may be the primary reason they are so widely unread. The legal scholar's standard prose has been criticized as everything from "patronizing"[97] and "pompous patois"[98] to unintelligible "gibberish."[99] Its long sentences, awkward syntax, and overweening commitment to noncommittal buzzwords are at once impressive-sounding and useless.

Obscurity persists in both style and substance, as witness this little sample from a feminist law professor:

> [T]he possible undervaluation of motherhood entailed by the mother/soldier parallel is similar to the possible under-valuation of women's work implied by the elementary school teacher/garbage collector. ... Undervaluing the traditionally female half of the parallel is only additional evidence of the culture's phallocentrism; it does not justify refusing to revalue nurses, teachers, and mothers at least to the extent that real estate appraisers, garbage collectors, and soldiers are valued.[100]

This article runs fifty-eight pages and 34,072 words; forty-two of which are either "phallocentrism" or "phallocentric" (meaning male dominance).

The reasons behind such poor writing may have as much to do with the perceived purpose of legal scholarship—indeed the scholar's understanding of the purpose of law itself—as with an inability to follow basic rules of grammar, syntax, and style.

Let us suppose that the purpose of law is the betterment of society. Although it is hard to see how the esoterica so often offered up by law reviews has any measurable application to real-life problem-solving,[101] let us assume these writers do have something serious to say that may be of value to society's decisionmakers, whether it is about law and literature, critical legal studies, feminist law—or dog bites in South Carolina.[102] Is there any justification for not saying it with greater clarity?

All too frequently the language of scholars is "far removed from the emotions, language, and understandings of the great majority of human beings,"[103] and the law they seek to analyze, criticize, explain, or change is lost in a sea of verbal molasses. Those who want to influence social policy in a more liberal direction have even greater reason to write understandable English. The intellectual movers and shakers need the support of workers, activists, and politicans alike; new social orders are impossible when such diverse groups cannot comprehend one another's language—or feel alienated by it. Programs championed in the Ivory Tower, but unheard or unfathomed in town or in board- or caucus-rooms, are unlikely to see life beyond the scarcely-read pages upon which they are printed—a brief flicker between the time they come off the presses and when they begin to yellow, tightly bound, in dusty library stacks.[104]

But let us suppose further that there is value in scholars discoursing among themselves, that it is easier and more efficacious for them to use the specialized terminology familiar to those in the discipline. A central problem here is that such highly technical or narrowly targeted articles frequently appear in the general-interest law reviews. The tension between necessary jargon and editorial clarity, between influencing a small audience and accommodating a broader one, is overwhelming if not impossible. The lay lawyer reading a scholarly legal essay is hard put to understand it, much less see its search for Truth. Its length, style, and substance all too often combine to yield a soporific result: the eyes glazeth over.

One might argue that medical journals are every bit as

impenetrable to the average doctor as law reviews are to the lawyer, yet no one criticizes them for being too technical. But the analogy is weak: the "truths" sought are essentially different (a medical researcher examines the safety or effectiveness of a particular drug or procedure or therapy or policy, and bases his conclusions on specific empirical data), and most medical reviews are explicitly aimed at specialists in the field who understand the terms of art. (There are relatively few general-interest scientific journals.) Law professors, on the other hand, often engage in philosophical discourse that has little practical application, and their colloquies are seldom confined to special-interest reviews.

Communicating clearly, however—even about complex legal ideas—should not be an impossible task.

Charles Alan Wright recalls a legal writing seminar he took while a law student at Yale, in which his professor—none other than the aforementioned Fred Rodell—asked a guest scholar to pick one of his own articles, open it at random, and read a paragraph. The scholar obliged, says Wright, and read a paragraph "filled with the jargon and convolutions that mark most legal writing." When he finished, Rodell asked him what the paragraph meant. "[He] sputtered for a moment and then gave a brief and clear explanation of the proposition he had stated at much greater length in the article. 'Why didn't you write it that way?', [Rodell] asked. The point was made." To which Professor Wright adds: "I am sure that thirty years of very orthodox academic writing have corrupted my style, but I like to think that even today my books and articles and briefs are better because of what Fred taught me in that seminar."[105]

Students who may be naturally predisposed to avoiding difficult legal concepts will surely avoid coming to grips with the nebulous ideas presented in a great many law-review articles. The scholarly voice invites analysis by generalities and lacks the discipline demanded by empirical research. It requires students to learn a new, complex language that will probably be irrelevant to their future careers.[106]

The best way truly to appreciale the difficulties of understanding academic writing is to get down and dirty with some of it. Consider the following examples, selected more or less at random from recent reviews.

On law and literature:

> It is one thing ... to blur the divide between the creation and criticism of literature, and quite another to blur the distinction between the creation and criticism of law. Historically, the consequence of the blending of the law and the moral basis from which we criticize law has almost always been a politically regressive insistence upon the morality of existing power; and the present decade's fashionable denial of the difference between fact and value (whether indulged by the political left or by the political center) has proven to be no exception. The most obvious and compelling implication of the claim that there is no real difference between the law that is and the law that ought to be is that the law which is, is perfect: the law that is, is as it ought to be. The anti-positivist blurring of that which is from that which ought to be entails a non-critical, accepting complacency with the status quo.[107]

> ❋ The names of the perpetrators of this and the next several passages have been withheld, in the hopes of preventing hard feelings and libel suits. Genuinely curious or skeptical readers should jump to the end-notes.

Granted, this passage is taken out of context, but take it for granted that the context is every bit as abstruse. If you would rather flagellate yourself by attempting to understand such "scholarship," try answering these questions: how can the "creation" and "criticism" of either law or literature be regarded as parallels capable of distinction? How can the difference be blurred between the *creation* of a book (or film or work of art) and its *criticism?* How can the law and "the moral basis from which we criticize law" be blended? What is the difference between 'fact" and "value," or between "the law that is" and "the law that ought to be"? What is the writer trying to tell us? That his sense of syntax is out to lunch? Most readers of general-interest journals, unfamiliar with the specific scholarly voice, would not easily be able to discern a clear meaning.

Such illustrations appear all through law reviews aimed at broad readerships. On Critical Legal Studies (this from *Harvard):*

> The two internal critical themes stand by synecdoche for the two major traditions of criticism of modern society that antedate the rise of modernist literature and philosophy. One of these traditions objects to the denial of solidarity and to the absence of the varieties of communal life that could mediate between the isolated individual and the large-scale organizations of the social world. The other tradition emphasizes the continuity of group domination under forms of practice and thought that both conceal and reproduce it. The deviationist doctrinal argument shows how the two traditions can merge into a more comprehensive and satisfactory line of criticism once analysis descends to institutional detail. The practical and theoretical solutions to the problem of overcorrecting and undercorrecting contract converge with the implications of the attempt to soften the antagonism between contract and community.[108]

> ❀Despite entreaties from editors at the *Harvard Law Review*, I found it hard to shorten this excerpt. Its length not only underscores its long-windedness, but accurately suggests that this passage is one of many in the article equally difficult to decipher.

How many readers will be able to define or divine what "synecdoche" means? How many intellectual gear-shifts can they be expected to make in order to plow through the hazy double-negatives in *"objects* to the *denial* . . . and to the *absence* of . . . that could *mediate between"*? In the third sentence, does the closing "it" refer to "tradition," or to "continuity," or to "domination"? Where has the "analysis" in the next sentence been, before it "descends to institutional detail"? What is the intended connotation of "contract" in the last sentence? Responsible scholarship (or editing) would supply clarifications where needed, either in text or footnote.[109] All too often, though, the words stare back.

And finally, these words-to-live-by from another feminist "scholar":

> The first purpose of this essay is to put forward the global and critical claim that by virtue of their share embrace of the separation thesis, all of our modern legal theory—by which I mean "liberal legalism" and "critical legal theory" collectively—is essentially and irretrievably masculine. My use of "I" above was inauthentic, just as the modern, increasing use of the female pronoun in liberal and critical legal theory, although well-intended, is empirically and experientially false. For the cluster of claims that jointly constitute the "separation thesis"—the claim that human beings are, definitionally, distinct from one another, the claim that the referent of "I" is singular and unambiguous, the claim that the word "individual" has an uncontested biological meaning, namely that we are each physically individuated from every other, the claim that we are individuals "first," and the claim that what separates us is epistemologically and morally prior to what connects us —while "trivially true" of men, are patently untrue of women. Women are not essentially, necessarily, inevitably, invariably, always, and forever separate from other human beings: women, distinctively, are quite clearly "connected" to another human life when pregnant. In fact, women are

in some sense "connected" to life and to other human beings during at least four recurrent and critical material experiences: the experience of pregnancy itself; the invasive and "connecting" experience of heterosexual penetration, which may lead to pregnancy; the monthly experience of menstruation, which represents the potential for pregnancy; and the post-pregnancy experience of breast-feeding. Indeed, perhaps the central insight of feminist theory of the last decade has been that women are "essentially connected," not "essentially separate," from the rest of human life, both materially, through pregnancy, intercourse, and breast-feeding and existentially, through the moral and practical life. If by "human beings" legal theorists mean women as well as men, then the "separation thesis" is clearly false. If, alternatively, by "human beings" they mean those for whom the separation thesis is true, then women are not human beings. It's not hard to guess which is meant.[110]

Let's try to take this passage weakness by weakness. In the first sentence the plural possessive "their" does not agree with the singular noun it modifies, "theory." Or should "claim" be plural? By "inauthentic," does the writer mean "not genuine"? The standard student Webster's informs us that "experiential" means "empirical"; why use both? The singular collective noun "cluster" at the beginning of the third sentence disagrees with the plural verb "are" near the end—a nitpick, perhaps, in view of the seventy-eight words piled on in between. What is meant by "epistemologically" as it is juxtaposed here with "morally"? Or by "'trivially true'" as it is placed within quotation marks? Is there any meaningful difference among the words "essentially," "necessarily," "inevitably," "invariably," "always," and "forever"? Why use them all, except to betray the writer's anger? (And if that's the case, why not add "fundamentally," "basically," and "elementary"?) Slogging through the rest of the paragraph, we are staggered by the syllogism at the end; it's doubtful that open-minded readers (particularly nonfeminists) will have an easy time guessing which conclusion is intended. What's it all mean? Those who have been especially dogged in trudging through this polysyllabic sludge may be left with little more than the flimsy notion that it is, after all, a man's world.

Is this brilliant insight, or intellectual quicksand? You decide.❀

> ❀In the interest of fairness I conducted a mini-survey regarding this last excerpt. Of the ten readers asked if they understood it, two (a professor familiar with feminist literature, and the editor-in-chief of a leading law review) offered a"yes-I-think-I-do-but-it's-not-very-clear." The eight who said "no-I-can't-figure-it-out" included a practitioner who graduated magna cum laude from Harvard, a feminist librarian, a law-review faculty advisor, a law-and-economics professor, a housewife with a master's degree in education, an author of nine published books, a law school dean, and a former Rhodes Scholar.

Meaning aside, elementary matters of grammar, style, and syntax—what Swift referred to as "proper words in proper places"[111]—are often beyond the ken of authors and editors.❀

> ❀Examples of weak syntax are easy to find, and likewise not limited to radical legal scholarship. Here are several from articles I've cited earlier: "Their environmental sensitivity, immense migrations, and economic value, combined with a long history of bitter allocation struggles, make anadromous fish a fruitful area for legal study." And, "Finally, it must be noted that there may well be situations where an animal attacks without provocation and has failed to behave in a manner reasonably calculated to provide the owner with prior notice or warning regarding its tendency or inclination to attack."[112]

If good writing is a reflection of clear thinking, the poobahs of scholarship must be a bunch of bumbleheads, because they produce bad writers by the barrelful. My criticism of the above excerpts is less about their substance than about their form; whatever messages they seek to deliver are lost in a jumble of jargon and gibberish. The point is this: if our purpose as scholars is to explain and persuade, we are most likely to succeed if we write simply and clearly.[113]

Narcissism and Other Perceptions

Why such passionate preoccupation with the irrelevant, such obeisance to the obscure? A final word about motivation is in order.

Vanity of vanities, saith the Preacher, . . . all is vanity![114]

Besides the life-force craving for promotion and tenure, image is easily as important as substance for many a professor. To treat the arcane in traditional academic prose is to impress one's colleagues. To be published, even cited, in an Ivy League journal is considered to be a feather in one's professional cap. To be spurned by the *East Parsipanny Journal of Nursery School Law and Literature,* on the other hand, is ignominy most bitter (and usually suffered alone, without informing even one's spouse).

Habitual publication is especially useful to those professors who view themselves as Traveling Scholars, available on short notice to grace the halls of fellow universities for a semester or two with their particular brand of out-of-town expertise. But even here the shinola quickly rubs off. And to be roundly ignored while visiting may be the worst blow of all to self-esteem, a measure of inferiority that is often visited in turn upon one's colleagues at home.

Scholarship thus becomes inalterably bound up in politics. It was a wise professor who said the reason academic politics are so sordid is that the stakes are so low.

Olive Branches and Apologia
(Conclusion and Self-Praise)

Biting the hand that feeds can be very satisfying for one who is protected by tenure and academic freedom. But the purpose of this piece is to urge that we move away from rewarding "scholarship" alone. Let's let the writers be writers, the scholars scholars, the teachers teachers, and the leaders leaders—and give them credit accordingly.[115] Let's recognize good writing as valuable, even if it's not in an academic journal, and promote service to the community at least every bit as much as journal scholarship of questionable worth. Let's mold faculty as position players, not as clones of one another. Let's require all to be at least minimally competent in the classroom and the library, but not require proof of professionalism by way of intellectual coercion or passage through the publication chute. Surely there are better ways to measure quality.

An olive branch to the Good Reader and Scholar alike: we should all be forgiven for giving in to the system, for nurturing it out of a strong sense of self-preservation—seeking if nothing else to put bread on our tables in the way we know best. We mean no harm, even if we offer little of lasting value.

I utter this Apologia with full recognition of my own knowing participation in the process, completely aware that whatever few readers are out there may indeed view Lasson's Scholarly Production as utterly useless—itself little more than the pretentious pap he so roundly excoriates. True, I like to *think* I have had something original to say (and have guiltlessly accepted remuneration via research grants or summer stipends). Yet all of my "scholarship"—like that of most others—must be viewed as exceedingly modest when compared to that of a true scholar.[116]

❀ Those interested in bashing my own scholarship are enthusiastically invited to do so, especially if the citations are plentiful and reasonably accurate. Among my more recent pieces are Holocaust Denial and the First Amendment: The Quest for Truth in a Free Society;[117] The Tintinnabulation of Bell's Letters;[118] Mad Dogs and Englishmen: A Ditty Dedicated to First-Year Law Students, Confused on the Merits;[119] Religious Liberty in the Military: The First Amendment under Friendly Fire;[120] On Letters and Law Reviews: A Jaded Rejoinder;[121] To Stimulate, Provoke, or Incite?:First Amendment Purposes and Group Defamation;[122] and Racism in Higher Education: Brown's Effect on Campus Bigotry.[123] Note, however, that I regard myself as in a no-lose situation. If I attract a lot of flack for my failure to understand or appreciate somebody else's scholarly prose, at least I will have finally provoked a thoughtful (or outraged) response to my work. And the article upon which this chapter is based, first published in the Harvard Law Review, will have been cited once again. On the other hand, if I get no response, well, that proves my point, doesn't it?)

Moreover, I am cognizant of the possibility that—though Solomon may have had a point—I myself may be unable to avoid cooking up yet another black pot of scholarly porridge, and thereby run the risk of various other professorial kettles recalling my past aspersions cast asunder.

II

❧

Feminism Awry
Excesses in the Pursuit of Rights and Trifles

> *When I see the elaborate study and ingenuity displayed by women in the pursuit of trifles, I feel no doubt of their capacity for the most Herculean tasks.*—JULIA WARD HOWE

> *Being a woman is a terribly difficult task, since it consists principally in dealing with men.*—JOSEPH CONRAD

A goodly portion of what passes for academic scholarship these days is sparked if not dominated by social theorists who seek wholesale changes in the way faculties are appointed, curricula are developed, and students are taught. They do not consider themselves simply as anti-conservative progressives, but as revolutionaries with a clear vision of the evils of an oppressive traditional social order and the educational philosophies that inform it.

Much of the trembling in today's Ivory Tower is triggered by radical feminists, who also churn out a fair share of the new abstruse literature. Just as their voices and visions are far from clear, neither are they easy to define—or, unfortunately, to defuse.

Lessons from Olympia: Some Foregone Conclusions

By providence or happenstance, modern feminism has achieved mythic proportions. The classic case of *Hercules v. Juno,* in which the heroic son of Zeus was sentenced to seemingly impossible labors by the vengeful goddess of women, is as relevant today as it was in ancient Greece. *In heavenly minds can such resentments dwell?* asked Virgil. Well, yes. The Battle of the Sexes is, after all, the true Mother of All Conflicts—a war that has been waged ever since Lysistrata exercised her wiles and maybe even back to Eve.✾

> ✾Though created as Adam's "helpmate," Eve proved herself to be a notably independent thinker (see Genesis, Chapter III:1-6). Lysistrata was Aristophanes' Athenian femme fatale, who sought to end the Second Peloponnesian War by persuading all Greek wives to deny their husbands sexual relations so long as the fighting lasted. Assuming that the men would be unable to endure prolonged celibacy and in order to hasten the war's end, Lysistrata exposed a nude girl before the two armies—whereupon the Athenians and Spartans, both presumably panting with frustration, declared peace quickly and departed for home and (presumably) connubial contentment. Though modern critics would likely reject any "big bang" theory as to the origins of feminist jurisprudence, mythological references are gaining currency. A Jungian psychiatrist, for example, advises women to meditate on the Greek goddesses and to imagine themselves as heroines in the myths of their own lives.[1]

Perhaps it's best to begin with the positive. From virtually any perspective, feminists in the Twentieth Century have improved the quality of life for many women in a number of noteworthy ways. They have helped win the right to vote, to own property, to make contracts, to serve on juries, to use contraceptives. They have succeeded in asserting the need for enhanced economic opportunities: equal pay for equal work, maternity leave, flex-time for mothers. They have made significant advancements against both domestic battery and workplace sexual harassment. As a consequence of all these efforts, more women than ever before are in professional schools, city halls, state houses, and courts.✿

> ✿On this point, I am challenged by one of my research assistants, who observes that the rights to vote, own property, make contracts, and serve on juries were all won in the late nineteenth and early twentieth centuries. "Have feminists been spinning their wheels for the last 70 or 80 years," she asks, "or what? One Supreme Court justice, a few heads of state, and lots of female law students don't seem like much of an accomplishment compared with what was done [earlier]."

Such well-deserved victories, however, have been achieved at the cost of a good number of Pyrrhic ones, not the least of which have been wholesale changes in language, literature, and even law—most of it force-fed to the silent majority of women who are relatively satisfied with the conditions of their gender. Good people of both sexes have been stampeded into corners of stilted parlance and tortured logic by self-appointed thought police. Big Sister has imposed herself upon us all. Nowadays she throws no pots and burns no bras, but brandishes instead a sacred and unabridgeable Lexicon of Political Correctness.[2]

It is not just labeling lawyers who apply the "reasonable man" standard as profoundly sexist,[3] nor forcing substantial expenditures to render the text of codes and constitutions "gender-neutral"[4]—nor even likening the first movement of Beethoven's Ninth to the murderous rage of a rapist.[5]✿ The vernacular required by Feminist Newspeak is thus as inconsequential as it may be silly or supercilious.

> ❀One lover of language I know (a male, who wishes to remain anonymous) has suggested a universal pronoun—the shortest possible contraction of "she," "he," and "it"—which he claims is especially appropriate because it is not only gender-neutral but expresses our common humanity as well.

Nor does it cause anything more than a mild ripple among the *cognoscenti* when feminist professors demand removal of a Goya nude from a university lecture hall,[6] or loftily lump male professors in with all the other licensed lechers seen to saturate the establishment.[7]❀

> ❀This particular kind of stereotyping appears to be endemic among the growing number of radical feminist law students. A professor at the University of Baltimore School of Law was chastised by one of his feminist students for asking his law-and-economics class whether a particular (male) expert witness might be considered a "whore"—a term the student felt was "misogynistic." (The student happened to be president of the school's increasingly vocal Lesbian Student Association. Were we living in the Gay Nineties then, or what?)

These are but the piddling quibbles.

More serious and wasteful—and ultimately more dangerous —is the attention paid to shrill rantings by self-appointed feminist spokespeople with inordinate access to the media and political arenas,[8] and the even more obsequious homage accorded the obscure ravings of their academic counterparts, the radical feminist scholars.[9]❀

> ❀The Good Reader who has gotten this far is kindly requested to pardon the polemics: it's merely meeting ire with ire.

As noted in Part I, whether on the hustle or the hustings their words are often virtually incomprehensible, their writings filled with shrill jargon and polysyllabic gibberish—their voices as outraged as their messages outrageous. Whatever they lack in clarity is made up for in volume: they dominate the discussion of the agenda they so stridently dictate, lashing out against all those who do not accept their world view with the same unadorned scorn they heap upon tellers of off-color jokes. In so doing, they serve to obfuscate the legitimate gains of the women's movement by shrouding it in the clothes of shrill revolutionary discourse. Many women have thus come to see the feminist movement as anti-male, anti-child, anti-family, and anti-feminine.[10]

What we consider to be feminist jurisprudence has been with us for at least a quarter-century.[11] It is part of the curricula of many law schools, and the focal point of an increasing number of law-review articles.[12]

> ❀At least a hundred professors (presumably all female) teach or have taught courses on women in the law. Examples of the courses offered: Feminist Jurisprudence (Cornell), Feminist Theory (University of California, Hastings College of Law), Colloquium on Women and Rights (Columbia), Seminar on Feminist Theory (University of Chicago), and Sexual Harassment (Boalt Hall). Interestingly, the Ivy League tends to have more such courses than do other law schools. Predictably, perhaps, there are no courses on feminist law or related topics at more traditionally conservative places, such as William and Mary, Washington and Lee, or Catholic University. Faculty-selection committees, especially at law schools with more liberal pretensions, are also influenced by feminist-oriented affirmative action pressures. Some schools (e.g., the University of Maryland School of Law) even have students evaluate their professors according to how "gender-neutral" they have been in class.[13]

If this is "scholarship," what is it all about? Does the virtual absence of any meaningful challenge mean that the majority of male scholars tacitly agree with their feminist colleagues? Or are they too intimidated, bored, amused, or confused to respond?[14]✾

> ✾The intimidation factor is real. More than one fully tenured and promoted law professor has said that, although he may have more strongly negative views than I do about radical feminism, he would not assert them publicly for fear of being ostracized by the Academy, and thus rendered unable to obtain a teaching position elsewhere.

Perhaps that is the primary reason criticism of modern-day feminists is often more harsh from women than from men. Camille Paglia has observed that women's studies "is a jumble of vulgarians, bunglers, whiners, French faddists, apparatchiks, doughface party-liners, pie-in-the-sky utopianists, and bullying, sanctimonious sermonizers." Brigitte Berger, a professor of sociology at Wellesley College, notes that professional feminists are "unfettered by any serious intellectual resistance" and are "driven by their presuppositions toward ever more radical conceptualizations."

Perhaps the most outspoken male critic of radical feminism is Michael Levin, a professor of philosophy at the City College of New York. He challenges feminists who deny that innate sex differences have anything to do with the basic structure of society and who therefore interpret observable differences between male and female roles to be the result of discrimination and restrictive social conditioning rather than to flow from the free expression of basic preferences. Levin concludes that feminist proposals for remedying this imaginary oppression serve systematically to thwart individual liberty. Elsewhere he describes "a grand gesture of intellectual affirmative action" in which "the predominantly male academic establishment continues to allow feminists to get away with anything." In his view such deference to feminist excess "may be partly due to misplaced chivalry and an understandable reluctance to provoke further feminist anger, but it derives primarily from guilt about the massive oppression supposedly suffered by women."

How much does the current literature continue to reflect a plaintive cry for equality by a sex unjustly scorned—and how much of it is strewn with the petty mewlings of pouty prima donnas who are intellectually dishonest to boot? Which are the rights, and which the trifles?

Such quaeres themselves, of course, can be criticized as gender-biased, and it is a virtual certainty that the answers suggested by this book—that the best-known feminist legal scholars have unfairly arrogated to themselves the right to speak for all women, that their advocacy is confounded by their language, and that what they can or should get is more often limited by logic and the natural human condition than by an oppressive masculine society—will be dismissed as the misguided misogyny of a society dominated by male chauvinists.

So be it. The time is past due for an intellectually responsible challenge to the radical feminists who have assumed command of the Ivory Tower and the world beyond to which it beckons. Abdication of that responsibility—whether because it is felt the feminists themselves are unfathomable, or their agenda illogical, or that fighting them could be career-threatening —amounts to endorsement of an authoritarian ideology that runs roughshod over the few scholars who dare to question its merits. The recent history of academic feminism shows what can happen to an enterprise when its guardians do not "root out the first cropping of intellectual mischief," either because it appears too silly or in the misguided hope that it will eventually die out on its own.[15] Just ask the handful of outspoken women who have had the temerity to call feminist scholarship "a travesty of the intellect,"[16] "bald ignorance,"[17] and "pop fascism."[18]

In truth, the thesis is a simple one: the legitimate gains achieved on behalf of all women—largely by the Herculean efforts of both latter-day Lysistratas and their high-minded male colleagues—are seriously diminished by the self-anointed high priestesses of women's rights who minister their metaphysics from behind the protective wall of an unquestioning Academy.[19]

Venus Redux: Feminism Identified
First feminism, then law. —CATHARINE MACKINNON

As any psychologist will tell you, the worst thing you can possibly do to a woman is to deprive her of a grievance. —BEVERLY NICHOLS

Feminist scholars come in as many incarnations as did Venus, who was goddess of everything from fertility to love and marriage to venal lust.✸

> ✸The many faces of Venus include those as *Aphrodite Urania*, goddess of noble love; as *Aphrodite Genetrix*, who favored and protected marriage and to whom unmarried girls prayed in order to obtain husbands; and as *Aphrodite Pandemos* or *Porne* (!), the goddess of lust and patroness of prostitutes. Venus was also the wife of Hephaestus, the ugliest and most graceless of gods, and took wicked delight in rousing the passionate desires of the Immortals and launching them on amorous adventures.[20]

It is unclear how many of them would agree with Mackinnon, their current guru, or would instead treat feminist legal scholarship as an integral part of a broader contextual framework, arguing simply that new social orders require new legal structures.

But neither feminism nor feminist law is easy to define. A recent article in the *Harvard Law Review* talked about a "self-consciously critical stance toward the existing order with respect to the various ways it affects women 'as women.' "[21] What does *that* mean? The author goes on to make three points: (a) gender must be the central category for analysis; (b) specific needs of women are either actively frustrated by men or go otherwise unsatisfied; and (c) society must do everything necessary to meet such needs. Feminism has also been called "an exploration of the implications of gender (how it affects expectations, desires self-perceptions, and choices) — in other words, the effects of treating men and women differently or similarly.[22]

MacKinnon defines feminism, with great clarity even if only for its shock value, as that which "stresses the indistinguishability of prostitution, marriage, and sexual harassment."✿

> ✿ Such "indistinguishability" may be one reason why MacKinnon's efforts on behalf of various American anti-pornography statutes have been found unconstitutionally vague.[23]

Conceptual definitions, however, do not really describe the phenomena currently in vogue. Because radical feminist scholarship is predominantly *ad hominem*, such attempts to categorize are regarded with suspicion in that they reflect what is considered a typically male thought-process. Similarly, even subjective definitions, in the style of Justice Potter Stewart's characterization of pornography ("I can't define it but I know it when I see it") can be called chauvinistic.[24]

Perhaps the most acceptable way to define feminist law is by reference to the victories that have been won through trenchant challenges to entrenched rules. Both politicians and employers have become increasingly sensitive and responsive to gender bias. One result has been progressive legislation relating to marital property, spousal abuse, and the workplace environment.[25]

But radical feminist scholars often reject such a litany of victories when it is recited by a male. Definitions of feminism are likewise tainted and thus disclaimed. What suggests the question, is it it is necessary to be a woman in order to be a feminist? Even on this fine point, there is a certain amount of disagreement among the professional feminists, centering around whether women "present a valid category for analysis."[26] Not all women are the same, after all; they may in fact be more dissimilar from each other than from men.✿

> ✿Source-checkers: You need to verify *this?*[27]

In the final analysis, however, what makes defining feminist scholarship a most idle and frustrating pursuit is the difficulty readers have in understanding it. Trying to grasp either its logical gist or substantive grist can addle even the most analytical of well-meaning minds. Like octopi, many feminist scholars hide themselves in their own inklings.✿

> ✿Modern scholars have been called "Ph. D. Squid," a spineless species whose primary impulse is to squirt ink in response to any stimulus.[28]

Feminist Scholarship: Across the Divide

Getting a grip on the broad range of feminist literature is a daunting task. Scholars in the field appear to be interested in a wide gamut of issues, including abortion, alimony, career restrictions, child care and custody, comparable worth, divorce, domestic violence, interracial marriage, language bias, lesbian rights, pornography, pregnancy, prostitution, rape, sexual freedom, sexual harassment, sexual innuendo, surrogate motherhood, tenure, toilets, and zoning ordinances.[29] Gender-bias legislation also covers the judicial process: selection of judges, jurors, and court personnel; attitudes by and toward lawyers; and treatment of women as litigants and witnesses.

On some of these issues the interest is selective, even sexist. For example, feminist scholars tend to take up the cudgels primarily in tenure battles that involve women, or in zoning legislation that might define the typical family as heterosexual. They are quick to come to the defense of any woman alleging rape or sexual harassment—often before hearing all the evidence, and occasionally even after a defendant has been acquitted.

On other issues, most notably abortion, there are substantial disagreements as to why there should be disagreement. Besides the inherent tension between pro-choice and pro-life (control over reproduction vs. protection of unborn fetuses), some feminists argue that abortion increases the availability of women for the sexual satisfaction of men because it removes the excuse that the woman might get pregnant. Similarly, feminist scholars who favor women having as much sexual freedom as men are opposed by those who say that free sex, by increasing the availability of women, contributes to their subordination. Likewise, there are sharply differing views on pornography—which some feminist scholars feel obliged to defend on First Amendment grounds, and which others attack as a mechanism for oppression.[30]

The appropriate remedies for these perceived wrongs are debated just as vigorously. Some women scholars argue that *all* feminist points of view should be considered in public law-making, while others believe that issues such as abortion should be removed from the legal arena entirely, and decided exclusively as private matters.[31]

Although having some notion of common feminist goals should help define the purposes of feminist scholarship, the current literature is so filled with radically sex-centered intro-spection that the picture presented is thoroughly confused, with strident but unfocused arguments scattered about as if by blunderbuss.[32]

But if radical feminist scholarship is to be challenged it must be fathomed and put in perspective. For that purpose it is helpful to analyze the different approaches so passionately taken toward the issues addressed.

Descriptive Scholarship

The primary level of feminist legal scholarship is inves-tigative and descriptive, with a proliferation of titles like "Women in the Law,"[33] "The Comparative Sociology of Women Lawyers,"[34] and "Reflections on Women in the Legal Profession: A Sociological Perspective."[35] In this group are case studies of women at work, the specific demands they place on the law and their representation in fiction.[36] As with much legal scholarship, a few of these articles are reasonably under-standable and well-argued, and others are somewhat petty—examining, for example, the extent to which female scholars are not cited in the mainstream law reviews and calling for the inclusion of more women writers in law-school reading lists.[37] On occasion there is an interesting intramural skirmish, such as that on the mediation of wife-abuse cases: some feminists welcome extra-judicial remedies, while others claim that the new alternative methodologies for dispute resolution mask and perpetuate inequalities of power.[38]

"The Women's Questions"

There are also numerous studies in contemporary feminist literature asking "The Women's Questions." The game here is to identify rules that are masked as neutral but in truth are "masculine"; the goal is to expose how such rules operate, and suggest how to correct them. Good examples of this approach can be found in diverse places, from law reviews of all kinds to autobiographies of Jewish feminists. Here are the "women's questions" presented in a *Berkeley Women's Law Journal* article, appropriately entitled "To Question Everything: The Inquiries of Feminist Jurisprudence":

1. What have been and what are now all women's experiences of the "Life Situation" addressed by the doctrine, process or area of law under examination?

2. What assumptions, descriptions, assertions and/or definitions of experience—male, female or ostensibly gender neutral—does the law make in this area?

3. What is the area of mismatch, distortion, or denial created by the differences of women's life experiences and the law's assumptions or imposed structures?

4. What patriarchal interests are served by the mismatch?

5. What reforms have been proposed in this area of law or women's life situation? How will these reform proposals, if adopted, affect women both practically and ideologically?

6. In an ideal world, what would this women's life situation look like and what relationship, if any, would the law have to this future life situation? (and)

7. How do we get there from here?[39]

Such broad inquiries lend themselves to specific and personal adaptations, such as the efforts by feminist Bible students who seek to place women at the center of a reconstructed past, and by revisionist historians who say things like: "The study of the woman question in Judaism is as important as the study of the Jewish question in general history."[40]

The "women's questions" have thus become sacred cows for radical feminist scholars, providing a virtually endless amount of cud upon which they can chew and achieve tenure.

Old and New Strands of Feminist Law

Regardless of the approach taken, heated arguments occur as well between advocates of the old and newer strands in feminist thought. Different observers apply different labels, but most categorize feminists as either liberal, cultural, or radical.[41]

Liberal Feminism: Vesta and the Virgins ✿

> ✿Vesta was the goddess of fire; her name means hearth or home. In Rome the task of always keeping a fire lit and dedicated to her was entrusted to a group of maidens, called vestal virgins; woe (i.e., live burning) to any of them who let the fire go out or who lost her virginity.

Sometimes called liberal feminists or rational empiricists, those who reason on the basis of equality seek to minimize the differences between men and women and to focus on issues of equality. Proponents of this point of view argue that it is arbitrary and irrational to make any distinction between the sexes;

their primary goal is passage of an Equal Rights Amendment; their principal voice is the National Organization of Women (NOW).

The equality approach has been responsible for most of the practical victories that have been won by women in the workplace. Using traditional analytical methodology, liberal feminists reason on behalf of free choice and equal opportunity, even if that means accommodating women who find satisfaction in their roles as wives and mothers. They call for equality in areas where they can demonstrate irrational differences in the treatment of men and women. They want to avoid being perceived as overturning the world order.

But liberal feminists are sometimes faced with the practical problem that equality can work *against* women. Consider various areas of the law in which women once had a certain favored status. For example, NOW has helped quash legislation that would allow adoption of out-of-wedlock children only by the mother's consent, void statutes requiring that only a husband need pay alimony, and oppose the male-only draft. In so doing, NOW clearly does not speak for all women.

When she was president of NOW, Patricia Ireland undoubtedly caused a backlash from people of both sexes when she announced that in addition to her husband she has had a concurrent "love relationship with a woman." Nor does NOW speak for all women when it denounces signs in bars that warn against drinking during pregnancy.

Feminists get suspicious when men argue along these lines—that is, that organizations such as NOW may work against women—and suggest that it is analogous to the bad joke that rape victims should keep quiet and enjoy the experience. It is just as likely, however, that men are simply bemoaning the decline of chivalry at the expense of feminism. How must men react, however, when a woman judge overturns the conviction of ten females found guilty of exposing their breasts in public, ruling that as a matter of equal protection of the law women's breasts should not be legally distinguished from men's?

Other anomalies abound. Sentences vary widely for battered wives convicted of clobbering their husbands. Fewer men are charged with first- or second-degree murder for killing a woman they have known than are women charged with first- or second-degree murder for the homicide of men they have known. Note further that a male spouse can now generally get as much of a dependency allowance on income-tax returns as his female counterpart.[42]

Liberal feminists seem to agree that it does not matter whether the real differences between men and women are natural or constructed. The role of feminists, they say, should be to reduce inequality by revaluing occupations, pursuits, and lifestyles. Women want to be taken seriously at work, but many of them have come to place a newfound priority on family matters.[43] This justifiable ambivalence is perhaps the most significant and accepted aspect of what used to be called the women's liberation movement, particularly since women have begun to exercise more power in the workplace. Thus the recent burgeoning of a pro-family feminist camp, which promulgates policies recognizing the importance of comparable worth, day care, paid maternity leaves, and the creation of opportunities for fathers to share household responsibilities.[44]

Other liberal feminist scholars criticize the concept of a "Mommy Track"—arguing that women in the workplace should be treated without deference to their sex, that working women should realize they cannot have it both ways.[45]

Working women with children, however, do not need scholars to tell them what it means to be caught between conflicting hopes for themselves and the expectations of family. For many of them the dilemma is too profound to be resolved simply be equalizing the roles of men and women.[46]

Cultural Feminism: Minerva and the Muses ✹

> ✹Minerva (Athena to the Greeks) was the goddess of wisdom, science and art, and is said to have sprung (fully dressed in armor) from the forehead of her father Zeus. She never married and is variously depicted as wearing a helmet and carrying a spear, or holding a distaff (a tool for spinning thread) or a twig of an olive tree. The Muses, nine sisters each the symbol of one of the arts, were originally represented as virgins of strictest chastity; they later became less shy and had numerous love affairs.

Cultural feminists take a more chauvinistic tack. Differences between the sexes, they say, are both profound and immutable. Further, the "different voice" of women—a truer, more caring nature—is one on which a superior feminist jurisprudence can be based.[47]

The academic description of cultural feminism is predictably difficult to understand. According to Robin West:

> Women's potential for a material connection to life entails (either directly as I have argued or indirectly, through the reproduction of mothering) an experiential and psychological sense of connection with other human life, which in turn entails both women's concept of value, and women's concept of harm. Women's concept of value revolves not around the axis of autonomy, individuality, justice and rights, as does men's, but instead around the axis of intimacy, nurturance, community, responsibility and care. For women the creation of value and the living of a good life, therefore depend upon relational, contextual, nurturant and affective responses to the needs of those who are

dependent and weak, while for men the creation of value, and living the good life, depend upon the ability to respect the rights of independent co-equals and the deductive, cognitive ability to infer from those rights rules for safe living. Women's concept of harm revolves not around the fear of annihilation by the other but around a fear of separation and isolation from the human community on which she depends, and which is dependent upon her.[48]

Cultural feminists maintain that all legal theory is male-oriented because all legal theory is based upon the notion that each individual is separate. Women, on the other hand, are not separated but connected. They reason differently from men; they are more sensitive to situations in context; they emphasize practical results over abstract justice; they resist universal principles and generalizations. The attack on the male-oriented theory emphasizes the distinctive way in which women approach problems—advocating negotiation rather than conflict, making the most of the feminine mystique, and rising above principle.[49]

In other words, women are nurturing and altruistic, men individualistic and (it is to be inferred) insensitive.

Radical Feminism: Discordia and the Amazons🏵

> 🏵 Discordia (Eris), the sister of the war god Ares, was considered a dangerous deity; she spread discord in Olympus as well as on earth and was feared by everyone until Zeus finally drove her out of heaven. The Amazons were perhaps the earliest radical feminists; from infancy, they were trained for the chase and for war and were often characterized by their horror of men.

Radical feminists (the focus of this section) go even further than their cultural counterparts, beginning with the explicit assumption that men by their very nature consciously and systematically oppress women—who in turn are the primary victims of the male-hierarchic society.

The differences between men and women are not just biological, say the radical feminists, but diabolical as well.✿ Because the shrill voice is often the one most heard, the readicals dominate both the popular media and the academic literature, and they do not hide how they feel. They are angry. That their ire triggers such trembling in the Ivory Tower is as much a commentary on their colleagues as it is on themselves.

> ✿Compare this point of view with that of the critical race theorists. The radfems rarely note facts that might contravene their theory, e.g., that in the United States women live longer than men, or that they still legally possess most of the wealth.[50]

Fates and Furies:
The Agenda Unmodified✿

> ✿The Fates, three sisters who held the mysterious thread of man's life, were governed by Fortuna, a blind Roman goddess said to preside over the lives of all humans. Nothing could prevent them from cutting the thread of life once the hour of fate had struck. Fortuna is represented in three distinct modes: with a horn of plenty as sovereign of riches; with a scepter as an emblem of her power; or holding a wheel, which acts as a symbol of her fickleness and instability. The Furies were ministers of vengeance. Hell hath no Fury like a You Know What.

I went out at night; to smash a man's face in. I declared war. My nom de guerre *is Andrea One. I am reliably told there are many more; girls named courage who are ready to kill.* —ANDREA DWORKIN

Leaving sex to the feminists is like letting your dog vacation at the taxidermist's.—CAMILLE PAGLIA✿

> ❀ Prof. Paglia might have added the motto of a veterinarian who doubled as a taxidermist: "Either way, you get your pet back."

Rights and Trifles

Cast in the light of Dworkin's belligerency, Phyllis Schlafly's take on the radical feminists—"they hate men and they're out to destroy any man who stands in their way"[51]— appears sufficiently succinct. But an even more lucid statement of the radical philosophy comes from a feminist herself, as it appeared in a recent issue of the *University of Chicago Law Review:* "The important difference between men and women is that women *get f-----* and men *f---*."[52] ❀

> ❀ The Uniform System of Citation says nothing about vulgarisms. Those who are unable to divine the expurgated words by counting the hyphens may consult the original text in the Chicago Law Review itself, which apparently has no compunctions about corrupting its younger readers. Although the quoted declaration would undoubtedly offend feminists if it were made by a male, it is unlikely that the scholar who wrote it has ever been inside a men's locker room or college fraternity-house—where a traditional rallying cry is, "Let's go out and get l---!"

One difficulty with this theory is that it disregards the power women have over men concerning sex;[53] another is that women may actually enjoy making love. ❀ MacKinnon's logic is as follows: The only reason women may enjoy sex with men is that women have learned to enjoy degradation. Compare this view with the findings of Nancy Friday in her 1991 book *Women on Top,* which reported that women like sex as much as (if not more than) men.

> ❀ This has been fertile ground for dispute ever since the ancients. The Greeks told of how Zeus and Hera called upon Tiresius to settle their dispute over whether men or women derive more pleasure from making love. When Tiresius answered that women have ten times more fun (and consequently changed his gender from male to female), an enraged Hera caused him to become blind, whereupon Zeus gave Tiresius the gift of prophetic sight as a consolation. (Tiresius is said to have discovered which sex had more pleasure by killing a female serpent in the act of mating. Still another version is that Tiresius was blinded by Minerva for having watched her as she undressed and bathed.)

Ms. Friday also provides details of women's sexual fantasies, including those that have themselves as perpetrators of rape and willing participants in bondage and bestiality.

Happily for men and women who take pleasure in heterosexual liaisons, cultural feminists are quick to rebut: the argument that the sex act is a form of submission "fails to capture the phenomenological experience of intercourse as one of positive intimacy ... not invasive bondage."[54]

But from their narrow perspective the radicals appear to be fundamentally opposed even to that kind of heterosexual activity, which to them entails two forms of oppression and subordination—intercourse and pregnancy. The leading exponents of this point of view are Dworkin and her academic Echo, MacKinnon. ❀

> ❀ Echo was a nymph who served Zeus by distracting Juno's attention with chattering and singing every time his master paid court to another female. For this Juno punished Echo by depriving her of speech, and condemning her to repeat only the last syllable of words spoken in her presence. Echo was thus unable to declare her love for the young Thespian named Narcissus, and she died of a broken heart. Her bones turned to stone; all that remained was her voice. The gods in turn punished Narcissus for spurning Echo's love by making him fall in love with his own image. (There is a moral in here somewhere.)

It is difficult to quote either of them, however, without offending the casual reader's sensibilities or violating contemporary standards of decency.✥

> ✥At least not in the text. For x-rated but typical passages from Dworkin and MacKinnon, see excerpts in the end-notes to this section.[55]

In their obsessive determination to root out their male oppressors, radical feminists press the assertion that practically all heterosexual relationships amount to rape, assault, or at the very least harassment. For MacKinnon, no less than 92 percent of all women are sexually assaulted or harassed; anywhere from 25 to 75 percent of women experience serious violence in the home; 44 percent of all women are victims of rape or attempted rape; and 14 percent of married women have been raped by their husbands.[56] "Recent experimental research," she declares, "makes normal men more closely resemble convicted rapists attitudinally, although as a group they don't look all that different from them to start with."[57] She goes on to claim that "the family legitimizes violence to women and calls that civilization."[58]

Radical feminists also vociferously oppose cultural feminists, asserting that all women will be sold short by anything less than a cosmically changed social order. Neutral criteria, say the radicals, deprive women of the few protections they once had; they now lose more child-custody battles than before; they don't get as much alimony as they used to. Women do not need a declaration of equality, which would inhibit the law from recognizing that men *start* with an unfair advantage. What women need, say the radicals, is an aggressive affirmative-action program—an Anti-Subordination Amendment rather than an Equal Rights Amendment.

Cultural feminists are likewise attacked by the radicals on the ground that those qualities traditionally ascribed to females—for example, compassion and empathy—are in truth neither natural nor inherent, but simply an adjustment to the social subordination of all women by all men. The differences that exist between the sexes are not to be celebrated, but deplored. Radical academic feminists thus align themselves with lesbian-rights groups, which likewise attack the notion of a male's right of access to women (and ultimately a rite of passage and conquest). The radicals see sexual coercion as the root of the whole "women problem." It is that mindset which empowers their forays into the legislative and jurisprudential arenas, especially in the areas of sexual harassment and pornography. As to the former, the radical feminists take an unwarranted amount of credit. For example, the concept of sexual harassment as discrimination evolved as a common creation of both men and women practicing equal-rights advocacy; MacKinnon was still a law student when the pioneering cases came to trial in the mid-1970's, and to some critics her book *Sexual Harassment of Working Women* was largely derivative.[59]

MacKinnon is more properly given credit for co-authorship (with Dworkin) of anti-pornography legislation for the City of Minneapolis. That ordinance, however, was uniformly rejected by various lower federal courts and the Supreme Court itself, on the ground that it was unconstitutionally vague. The Feminist Anti-Censorship Task Force called it "squarely within the tradition of the sexual double-standard." The American Civil Liberties Union found the proposed law "extraordinarily ill-drafted," "fatally overbroad" (it would have prohibited even clinical illustrations in medical texts), filled with "multiple uncertainties," and "riddled with discriminatory distinctions."[60]

⚛A similar ordinance in Indianapolis was likewise found unconstitutional. Nevertheless, MacKinnon celebrated a recent holding
by Canada's Supreme Court—that violent or degrading pornography can be constitutionally outlawed—as vindicating her position that all pornography degrades women and should therefore
be prohibited. On the one hand, she probably misread the Court's
narrowly focused and carefully worded decision; on the other, her
radical feminist interpretation of what is pornographic—that
which is violent or degrading—should likewise cause the censorship of such pop fiction as Ice and Fire by her co-religionist
Andrea Dworkin, and maybe even such classic works as The
Taming of the Shrew by Shakespeare.[60]

These are rather harsh critiques of a woman appointed at
various times to the law faculties of Stanford, Minnesota,
Chicago, Yale, and Michigan, and who has also been selected
as a distinguished guest lecturer on civil liberty at Harvard.

Here is a bit of MacKinnon the Libertarian:

[T]he First Amendment has become a sexual fetish through
years of absolutist writing in the melodrama mode in
Playboy in particular. You know those superheated articles
where freedom of speech is extolled and its imminent
repression is invoked. Behaviorally, Playboy's consumers are
reading about the First Amendment, masturbating to the
women, reading about the First Amendment, masturbating
to the women, reading about the First Amendment, masturbating to the women.[61]

For feminist scholars, the belly-button gazing engaged in
by Playboy readers is evil incarnate, and cannot be compared
with the *omphaloskepsis* (contemplation of the navel) undertaken by academic tenure-seekers.

To discern the difficulty people like MacKinnon and
Dworkin have with the First Amendment, all one need do is
compare their position on pornography (which they would

ban) with their own vulgar views on the oppressive male culture (such as in Dworkin's *Intercourse)*. Or contrast their condemnation of Brett Easton Ellis' morbidly grotesque *American Psycho* with their support of Helen Zahavi's equally obscene *Dirty Weekend.* Both involve serial torture-killers; both were universally panned by book reviewers as uniformly disgusting. The only ostensible difference between the two is that Ellis's protagonist is a male and Zahavi's (like Dworkin's in *Mercy)* a female. Zahavi herself calls *Dirty Weekend* a "deeply moral" book. Dworkin rallied to her defense by castigating the reviewers as "literary police [who] punish any fool who gets out of line; that is their job." Dworkin was quoted with favor by her comrade-in-arms Naomi Wolf (author of *The Beauty Myth),* who argued that women writers such as Zahari and Dworkin are "ritually punished" because they "are genuinely subversive."[62]

The radicals have similar problems with due process and other rules relating to the fair administration of justice. Compare, for example, their routine condemnation of all sexual-assault defendants (both before and after hearing all the evidence) with what the law schools teach their students about rules of hearsay and other constitutional safeguards.

But in a broader sense the arguments of radicals like MacKinnon defy attempts at analysis or rebuttal. Those who challenge MacKinnon's manifesto are dismissed as having been *programmed* to do so by a male-dominated culture, or they are said to be simply seeking reaffirmation of the status quo, or to be rejecting revolution out of hand because fundamental change is always unpleasantly traumatic. Thus, her views become unassailable.

To equate marriage with sexual harassment and prostitution, however, is to debase language and to dilute the plain meaning of words merely in order to serve an argument. At what point can the case against MacKinnon's rhetorical declarations-of-fact be rested? How does one go about proving the negative—that most men do not *oppress* most women? How does one illustrate the likelihood that most men fully understand the horror of rape and, for that matter, abhor *any* aggressively violent behavior against another human being, whether within marriage or not? How does one refute the equation of marriage and prostitution, other than to assert that the experience of all those couples whose marriages are reasonably happy proves the absurdity of that idea?

The radical feminists would have us believe that there are few if any reasonably happy marriages. MacKinnon's claim that men systematically enforce their sexual domination of women in multi-nefarious ways is supported by little more than the passionate and unbending expression of her convictions.[63] To be sure, she offers an abundance of statistical data, but they are selective and uncontroverted. When challenged even cursorily, they become highly suspect.[64]

As one reviewer of *Feminism Unmodified* points out, MacKinnon's logic "depends on slogans, false premises, half-information, sinister innuendo and ad hoc reasoning," and her arguments "sink into sweeping, indiscriminate accusations that are never substantiated."[65] For example, she seeks to prove that the legal changes fought for and won by liberals who call themselves feminists have, for the most part, failed.

Why? Because (she argues) there has been a concurrent increase in reported rapes and a decrease in convictions. Does that necessarily mean that rape is outpacing other violent crimes? To what extent could the alleged increase in rapes simply reflect greater documentation of assaults encouraged by a climate more supportive of the victim? Must it be assumed that more reported assaults will automatically engender more convictions?[66]

Similarly, despite considerable evidence that coercion is rare in the porn industry, MacKinnon cites as the norm the "slave training" of certain actresses. Her proof is the experience of one woman; completely ignored is the ample testimony of many other porn queens who insist that coercion is rare (and unnecessary), as well as evidence that women may enjoy pornography themselves.[67] Such selective perception permits MacKinnon to ignore or discredit anyone with a contradictory opinion.[68] For MacKinnon, the only true feminists are the radicals.[69]

Satyrs and Sirens✸

✸Satyrs (or Fauns) were scattered about in the country, chiefly serving Bacchus, the god of wine. Poets made them the terror of shepherds and nymphs. They should not be confused with satyrists (such as writers of books like this one), or pundits (such as the eighteenth-century Englishman who wrote that "Women have more strength in their looks than we have in our laws; and more power in their tears, than we have by our arguments."). The Sirens were three sea nymphs who lived on an island and sang so sweetly that passing sailors were drawn to them, spellbound, and promptly shipwrecked on the isle. Odysseus stuffed the ears of his crew with wax and ordered them to tie him to the mast until they were safely through.[70]

The more recent literature leads us farther and farther down the barbed primrose path, with an almost fatal attraction to the world of absurdity. Naomi Wolf's best-selling book, *The Beauty Myth: How Images of Beauty Are Used Against*

Women, describes a society dominated by males who use pulchritude as a political weapon to hold women back. The author lashes out against what she calls the Professional Beauty Qualification (PBQ)—a man-made measurement she believes is "extremely widely institutionalized" as a condition under which women are hired, fired, and promoted. She rails about a male conspiracy that has created a "cult of thinness," which in turn causes women to hate their bodies, to starve themselves, and to "mutilate" their flesh under the knives of (mostly male) plastic surgeons.✿

✿Could the author be a sheep in Wolf's clothing? Her thesis may be complicated by her own publicity tours, where she appears to be an attractive woman who does not disdain fashionable clothes, jewelry, or makeup. Has she been so victimized by the culture that she has no choice but to succumb? Not likely. Nor would Ms. Wolf be likely to countenance the suggestion (made to the writer by both male and female readers of this manuscript) that women dress more for other women than for men. Even hard-core feminists find such theories a bit hard to take. Betty Friedan, whose 1963 book The Feminine Mystique made her a mother of the women's liberation movement, says she finds Wolf's message "a bit distorted" and that "I don't think the great enemies of women today are beauty pornography or beauty preoccupation. . . . I think the real danger lies in the new feminine mystique that tells women to go back home again, and that preoccupation with sidebars on beauty is a digression from the real need to address the terrible social problems women need to face." It would be interesting to know how Wolf reacted to the recent book by Gloria Steinem, another mother of the movement, who now admits that she has long had serious problems with the way she looks and suggests that she has always wanted to feel attractive.[71]

Another common characteristic of radical feminist legal theory is that it is anti-mainstream and ever-more-often revisionist and revolutionary. By definition it regards the existing order as oppressive to women. Its primary attack is against contemporary law itself, whose rules and methodology conceal and perpetuate oppression. The radicals take aim at the basic verities of all institutions and traditions—starting with religion and ending with the family. God the Father is anathema. The family is the principal focal point of oppression—perpetuating as it does a sexual hierarchy and promoting heterosexuality as the norm. Because they regard marriage as a form of prostitution, radical feminists have a detailed program for ridding the world of the nuclear family. They would like to see the term "family law" changed to "household law," so that, whether married or not, they could enjoy individual benefits and tax allowances. They would abolish all sorts of immunities from suit in litigation of one spouse against another.

For them, solving "the women's problem" is usually not enough: the "women's problem" must be seen as part of a larger injustice. Their articles therefore attack all the ills of the world: poverty, discrimination, and social as well as economic exploitation—or as one feminist scholar puts it, the whole range of "racist, misogynist, homophobic, patriarchic and economic hierarchies."[72] In seeking a holistic theory of justice, feminist scholars conclude that *all* of our values have to be transformed. The code word is "empowerment." Political power is what radical feminists seek above all else—their agenda unmodified. Though feminist theorizing is never far removed from "political struggle,"[73] the radicals have little patience for conjecture about the nature of law, for precedent or jurisprudence. For them, power is at the core of legal decision-making. Their view of the world is that of a male-dominated engine of oppression, which they would like to shift into reverse. Women would give the orders. It is They Who Must Be Obeyed.✿

> ✿The phrase is from John Mortimer's *Rumpole of the Bailey:* "I, Horace Rumpole, barrister at law, 68 next birthday, Old Bailey Hack, husband to Mrs. Hilda Rumpole (known to me only as She Who Must Be Obeyed) and father to Nicholas Rumpole (lecturer in social studies at the University of Baltimore. I have always been extremely proud of Nick) ..." [Author's note: No, I did not make up this quote, although there is no "social studies department at my own University of Baltimore.] An equally acerbic male observation about obedience, this one from an Irishman: "Women never truly command, till they have given their promise to obey; and they are never in more danger of being made slaves, than when the men are at their feet."[74]

But shifting gears runs the risk of stripping them. Consider, for example, the feminist-legal scholars' current criticism of typical marital-property laws. When such laws were first being passed in the 1970's, feminists strongly supported them as necessary to deal with a "women's problem"—men who did not pay court-ordered alimony. Under the marital-property acts, spousal assets would be divided at the time of divorce, with the woman getting a lump sum. Usually, there is no alimony, so no need to enforce monthly payments. Lobbyists supporting the acts persuaded legislators that the new laws would also solve a "men's problem"—that is, divorced women refusing to get a job or to remarry because they could live better off of their ex-spouses' alimony payments. These days, though, radical feminists *attack* marital property acts as unjust, because older untrained women, wealthy when married, are now being denied alimony and forced to take minimum-wage jobs. Judges are likewise being criticized for abusing their discretion, particularly where financial awards appear to favor the male party. The radicals' remedy is to increase the number of female judges. Left unaddressed is the possibility that increasing the number of female judges might only throw the bias toward women or bring about inconsistency in how the law is applied.[75]

Radical feminists often cite favorably a 1992 report by the American Association of University Women entitled *How Schools Shortchange Girls.* They are likely to ignore a contrary study (published by a contrary woman professor in 1998) which provided empirical data that women more than hold their own in the academic arena: they receive higher grades than men in every subject in high schools, attend college and graduate schools in greater numbers, and cope better with the challenges presented by university educations.[76]

In trying to resolve such tricky strategic dilemmas, radical feminist scholars derive solace from the critical-legal-studies people. Together, they argue that the law is indeterminate, that courts can do anything they please, and that all decisions are political. Law professors in particular are seen as overwhelmingly male, white, middle class and obsessed with status and superiority over students and other staff; that is why (it is argued) women students participate less in class, receive less professional attention, and find law school dispassionate and dehumanizing. The enterprise is to prove that all legal doctrine is a "patriarchal construct" that should be "deconstructed"—its facade torn away so that the underlying infrastructure of oppression can be revealed. Once that is done, the remedy is not accommodation, but revolution.[77]

With strident revolutionary declarations, however, radical feminists frequently skewer themselves, ignoring what could be much more persuasive arguments. A great deal of feminist philosophy is flawed precisely because it puts politics first, thus making the goal political change, not truth. Feminist scholarship is often marked by hostility to scientific method and characterized by a lack of empirical evidence and argument.[78] For example, radical feminists could (but do not) assert that the changes they advocate would benefit men as well as women, in that working wives and mothers take some of the strain off men to provide for families. They should (but do not) emphasize the universal merits of a system where *everyone* places a greater value on raising children, friendly relationships in the workplace, or care for the elderly. They would do well to recognize (but do not) that men have human frailties as well.[79]

In short, instead of directly addressing the contentions that their arguments exhibit logical failings and historical inaccuracies, they condemn all such challenges as predictably and hopelessly sexist.[80]

Dominoes and Dominees

Feminist scholarship has by now been institutionalized into full-scale academic departments, foundations, and political interest groups, all of which have come to pervade the media, professional associations, and the government itself. It is lavishly funded, both privately and publicly.[81] Its spokeswomen are courted as avidly by universities as free agents are in professional sports—though their playing quality may be just as suspect. Catharine MacKinnon has adorned the cover of the *New York Times Magazine.*[82]

Many colleges have yielded to feminist demands for special departments, courses, and requirements in such traditional disciplines as history and science. In so doing, they ignore studies that find both empty and pernicious the claim that men and women are different in the way they conduct scientific investigations.[83] They also help educate a generation of students who know more about Harriet Tubman than about George Washington or Abraham Lincoln or Winston Churchill.[84] If they had their way, the radicals would continue to increase the number of "subjective" courses, as well as adopt guidelines for non-masculinist writing and grading of female students that is sensitive to their presumed non-dominant attitudes.[85]

Stanford University's "Innovative Academic Courses" and "Student Workshops on Political and Social Issues" promulgated, among a number of other courses, a three-credit offering called "Issues in Self-Defense for Women." But instead of teaching women the physical skills needed to protect themselves from aggressors—to overcome their natural disadvantages in strength, size, and quickness—the course seeks to give women a sense of "empowerment" through a feminist ideology. "It is less important that we teach individuals in our classes how to defend themselves," said the instructor, "than it is to change society." She described the course as an important step toward a "feminist utopia," which would end sexism, starvation, classism, and hierarchy.

In 1993, because of the need to comply with federal regulations that prohibit gender discrimination at universities receiving federal funds, Stanford's feminist studies department was forced to add a new men's section. A faculty member of the "Women Defending Ourselves Collective," the group charged with teaching such a class, complained that its purpose is "empowerment," and that "it wouldn't make much sense to teach that to men who already control all of the power." 🌼

> 🌼 Stanford Law School sponsored a conference entitled "Women of Color and the Law." The keynote speaker was Angela Davis, a professor of "the history of consciousness" at the University of California (Santa Cruz) and the quadrennial vice-presidential candidate of the American Communist Party. "I have always found the law to be one of the most terrifying dimensions of the social order," said Professor Davis. Another speaker was Haunani-Kay Trask, who strongly advocates that Hawaii declare its independence from the United States. Native Hawaiians "must beware of white liberals," said Ms. Trask, "particularly lawyers, anthropologists and archaeologists, and other scientists and technicians" who are motivated by "some personal/psychological problem, such as guilt about being part of an oppressive white ruling class in a stolen Native country." At various points in the conference all those who were not"women of color" were asked to leave the auditorium, because only "women of color" could possibly "understand" whatever would be said next.[8]

Thus is diversity excluded even within the Academy. For example, radical feminists have supported the exclusion of a male student from a class in feminist methodology because he proposed a project that included women and men as subjects of research.[87] Mary Daly, a radical feminist professor of theology at Boston College, was dismissed for refusing to allow male students access to her course on "Introduction to Feminist Ethics." Among Daly's teachings: Men are "lethal organs" of a "rapist society," misogynists who feed parasitically on female energy, and who invent evil technologies to compensate for their inability to bear children; the birth-control pill and estrogen therapy entail "the poisoning of women"; or the only contraception women need is a "mister-ectomy." Women who don't accept Daly's views are mocked as "honorary white males."[88]

Besides men, people who are not "of color" are also frequent targets of the radicals. Even more deleterious is the ghetto-ization of certain women professors, a number of whom complain that they are discriminated against in appointment, promotion, and tenure decisions because they do not teach "feminist" courses or adhere to the radical philosophy.[89] This intolerance also takes the form of blunderbuss charges in the name of political correctness, which in turn causes the idea of sexual harassment to be trivialized and diluted.[90]

The schism at Harvard, an active participant in the rad-fem follies, is particularly severe. A random look at Women's Studies offerings there: English 193, "Issues and Approaches in Twentieth-Century Literary Theory") in which *Macho Sluts* is required reading; Women's Studies 132, "Shop 'Til You Drop: Gender and Class in Consumer Society"; Women's Studies 154, "I Like Ike, But I Love Lucy: Women, Popular Culture, and the 1950's."[91]

Harvey Mansfield, a notoriously outspoken professor of philosophy at Harvard, would knock down the entire edifice of women's studies. "It will take a long time," he says, because "a lot of people are shielded by tenure; and it would help to have a president and a set of deans who took it upon themselves to purge Harvard of these excrescences. But academics tend to be sensitive to begin with, and after the feminists get through with them they are gelded. Harvard is pitifully feminized."

It is ironic, of course, that much of the discrimination against women comes at the hands of the radical feminists themselves. Every woman professor at the Harvard Law School voted against a non-radical (but otherwise qualified) woman candidate for a tenure-track position. (On the other hand, a professor who sought to discipline students for an admittedly tasteless anti-feminist parody said he couldn't care less about freedom of speech: "It's just not my thing.")[92]

In this atmosphere, dissident voices are routinely suppressed. "There's a sense that if you're not exactly where I am in feminism, then you're betraying the cause," complains a woman professor at M.I.T. Another, from Wellesley, says, "Suddenly we're not seen as feminists—because we won't politicize the entire spectrum."[93] Nor is radical feminist political correctness directed only against so-called conservatives. A professor of impeccably liberal credentials is also at risk if he—or she—departs from the radical line in any respect.[94]

Between Scylla and Charybdis: A Poor Man's Response

Men have always had a tough time holding their own with the goddesses. Circe was a beautiful sorceress who turned Odysseus' sailors into swine. Charybdis was struck down by Zeus and changed into a dangerous whirlpool in the Strait of Sicily. Scylla was a beautiful nymph changed into a monster by jealous Circe; terrified by her ugliness, she threw herself into the sea and became a rough rock between Italy and Sicily. She and Charybdis were greatly feared by navigators. Thus, we say of a man coming between two dangers and not knowing where to flee, that he is "between Scylla and Charybdis."

What men need done to women so that men can have intercourse with women is done to women so that men will have intercourse.—ANDREA DWORKIN

I understand a fury in your words But not the words.
—WILLIAM SHAKESPEARE

It is in the academic literature that radical feminists are seen to be most fruitful and to multiply. Proliferation, of course, is characteristic of scholarship generally. Every law school has at least one law review. Professors have to publish to get tenure, or to be recognized as scholars. And as more women go to law school and become professors, there are more feminists writing articles on feminist law. Thus it is to be expected that feminist legal scholars regard the law journals as vital instruments in their crusade, a primary forum where professional opinion is developed. Feminist issues have become a favorite theme in many mainstream law reviews, and more than a few journals devote themselves entirely to the cause: the *Women's Rights Law Reporter* from Rutgers, the *Harvard Women's Law Journal*, the *Yale Journal of Law and Feminism*, the *Journal of Woman and Culture in Society*, the *Berkeley Women's Law Journal*, and the *Law and Inequality Journal*, among others.

The law reviews are so dominated by radicals like MacKinnon and Dworkin and a handful of others, it is easy to get the impression there are no brakes to this bandwagon as it rambles so noisily through the wilderness of scholarship. The few voices in the silent majority are seldom even heard, much less heeded.[95]

Although some of the goals and strategies of feminist legal scholarship may be discernible, much of the literature remains indecipherable to readers not already steeped in radical esoterica. To be fair, at least part of the pettifoggery may be the generic nature of scholarship itself, where one would not expect to find the wisdom of Solomon or the skill of Shakespeare.❀

> ✿So again sayeth Solomon: "A man need not say everything he thinks, nor write everything he says, nor publish everything he writes." But the Wise King (who had a very large number of concubines) also said both "Find a good woman, and you have found a treasure" *(Proverbs* 31:10) and "I have never found a good woman." *(Ecclesiastes 7:28)* A similar mysogeny was evident in the Babylonian Talmud *(Kiddushin, fo. 49b):* "Ten measures of speech descended on the world: women took nine and men one."[96]
>
> Shakespeare also had much to say about women and words. A sampling: "Do you not know I am a woman? When I think, I must speak." *(As You Li ke It, III, iii);* "Do not play in wench-like words with that / Which is so serious." *(Cymbeline, IV, ii);* "You cram these words into my ears against / The stomach of my sense." *(The Tempest, II, I)*

But feminist legal scholarship seems to be written almost exclusively in arch academic prose: it is overwhelmingly windy and wit-less. Perhaps *because* it is so serious, it must be camouflaged in scholarly jargon.

A Profusion of Polemics

Even causes have saturation points—often, there is only so much you can say about a subject before readers become bored or glutted. But feminist scholarship appears to be churned out in geometrically expanding proportions, the process perpetually feeding on itself. Painstaking reference is made to practically everything previously published in the area. As each article, comment, or book review becomes another source to be taken into account, scholarly reaction is generated in the form of even more articles, comments, and book reviews.[97]

Every academic season seems to bring with it a new wave of feminist scholarship about the ever-changing status of women in the workplace, introspective arguments about what is wrong with the nuclear family, and even reviews of recent developments in feminist legal scholarship. Progress is measured, or the lack of it bemoaned, *ad nauseam.* Ultimately, polemics become part and parcel of the literature. The result of all this is an entire body of learning that consists not of ideas, but of words *about* ideas—the cats chasing their own tails.❀

> ❀That may be an indecorous description of feminist legal scholarship, but no more so than from a woman critic who characterizes MacKinnon's logic as "a snake pit of hissing jargon that encircles itself and swallows its own tail."[98]

Bull-Dozing through the Bombast

Perhaps the most self-destructive characteristic of feminist scholarship is its long-winded pretentiousness—a kind of catalytic clack that's become a classic part of the process toward intellectual decay. In their philosophical pursuit of answers to ultimate questions, the radfems get mired in the multi-syllabic muck of over-intellectualization, lacing their ideas with obscure cross-references and mind-numbing bombast, ultimately turning words into meaningless twaddle. The burning bra has become a boombox of babble.❀ In the Academy it's called the MEGO Syndrome, as in Mine Eyes Glazeth Over.

> ❀ Perish the possibility that the writer himself be accused of pretentiousness; here is a glossary that might help this paragraph explain itself:
>
> **Babble:** Idle talk, senseless chatter; from Babel, a biblical city known for its confusion of languages, now (often not capitalized) a place or scene of noise … a confusion of cries, voices. … See "gabble."
>
> **Bombast:** Inflated, pretentious language; implies grandiosity that so outruns the thought that attention is distracted from the matter.
>
> **Boombox:** Not in the author's old Webster's New Collegiate; perhaps, "a noise machine in the form of a radio/tape-deck that serves to replace the chip on one's shoulder."
>
> **Clack:** Loud, continual, empty chatter; prattle.
>
> **Twaddle:** Silly talk, gabble; see "prattle."
>
> A more gentle literary critic might suggest that feminist legal scholarship suffers from the "Buddenbrooks Effect." In Thomas Mann's novel Buddenbrooks, the hero is a strong, practical man-of-affairs who accumulates a fortune. Three generations later, though, his family produces an other-worldly and ineffectual musical genius, not quite over the line to madness.

Here's a leading feminist scholar attempting to explain herself:

> The affirmation of the feminine may be impossible as other than the reversion to the old stereotypes. Undecidability cannot be wiped out in an appeal to knowledge if there is no ontological given to the feminine we can appeal to as our truth. We cannot know for sure, "Yes, this is definitely different. Now we are affirming Woman as other than the signifier of their desire." But the possibility that we might be approaching a new choreography of sexual difference with every new step we take can also not be wiped out. The unexpected pleasure of the Other who remains with us, who keeps up the pace, is always a possibility. Affirmed as the feminine, the threshold might be the opening to a new alliance.[99]

Can this fairly be called scholarship? Such near-incomprehensible exposition is slathered like sludge throughout much of feminist legal scholarship. Another example, this one a description of postmodernism in the *Harvard Law Review:*

> Postmodernism and poststructuralism are often used interchangeably, although each term has a somewhat unique genealogy. Postmodernism, originally used to describe a movement in art and architecture, has been used by Jean-Francois Lyotard and Fredric Jameson to describe the general character of the present age. For Lyotard, whose concern is primarily epistomological, the postmodern condition has resulted from the collapse of faith in the traditional "Grand Narratives" that have legitimated knowledge since the Enlightenment.

Does this passage mean that we have lost both our faith in the sciences and our confidence in ourselves? If so, then the message is as trite as its trappings are pretentious. If it means more, then what?

The titles alone in feminist scholarship can be self-absorbedly off-putting:

"Mind's Opportunity: Birthing a Poststructuralist Feminist Jurisprudence" [100]

"Feminism Historicized: Medieval Misogynist Stereotypes in Contemporary Feminist Jurisprudence" [101]

"Feminism, Marxism, Method and the State: An Agenda for Theory" [102]

"The Dialectic of Rights and Politics: Perspectives from the Women's Movement" [103]

"Liberal Jurisprudence and Abstracted Visions of Human Nature: A Feminist Critique of Rawls' Theory of Justice" [104]

In some quarters, what were once called the "women's questions" have become existential inquiries: "Do we know anything, and if we do how do we know, and how do we know that what we know or think we know is right?" Thus the fundamental philosophy of the radical faminists results in a manifesto for deconstructionism: (a) nothing really exists; (b) if anything did exist it could not be known; and (c) if anything did exist and could be known, it cannot be communicated.

Ah, (c)! At least the radfems are clear about that.

To be sure, changing *anything* by way of law-review articles is problematic: even lawyers don't read them, let alone the world's other movers-and-shakers. It is in just such a virtual vacuum, however, that radical feminist scholarship persists and flourishes, becoming ever more flighty in pursuit of rights and trifles.

Thus we are presented with everything from an exhaustive article about the sexist nature of a casebook on contracts to multitudinous autobiographia—described by MacKinnon as "the major technique of analysis, structure of organization, method of practices and theory of social change in the women's movement."[105]

The sexist-contract-casebook theorist's predictable conclusion—that the law is gender-biased—is based wholly on this piece of evidence: the majority of the buyers and sellers in the contracts casebook she examines (as well as the parties and the judges) are male. One result of this alleged bias is a vast predominance of male pronouns and pronominal adjectives—a cardinal violation of the rules in Feminist Newspeak. In the cases in which women do appear, they play "womanly" roles, such as nurse and homemaker. One woman found to have broken a contract, the author points out, was treated as greedy and fickle by the male judge. Moreover, the casebook already reflects male reasoning—abstract and analytical, organized by doctrinal categories—as opposed to taking the more feminine "problems" approach, emphasizing relational aspects. Finally, the book is branded too legalistic; that is, it stresses "neutral" principles and suppresses ethical, social, and moral issues masked by "legal reasoning" from precedent. Needless to say, such narrowly focused analyses have had very little impact on the compilation of casebooks, much less on anything else.[106]

This genre follows the feminist faith that men must be taught more about women, in order that men's thinking can be better informed and their attitudes made more sensitive as to how women feel about the world and the law. Such consciousness-raising is accomplished by having women write about their individual experiences. The theory seems to be that things will change for the better only if enough women go public with their hurt.✸

> ✸The rare feminist article written by a male is little different in its orientation. In a recent example from this can-you-believe-it? category—"Is the Maryland Director and Officer Liability Statute a Male-Oriented Ethical Model?"—the author answers "yes," because the statute permits officers and directors to limit their liability (except in cases of overt dishonesty or receipt of inappropriate benefits) and because it does not refer to a duty of loyalty; the law is thus said to be based on a contractual model rather than a trust model that would presume the autonomy and equality of all parties, and is therefore male-oriented because it is more concerned with power than it is with honesty and nurturing relationships.[107]

Such open-heartedness, however, makes the literature more lugubrious than enlightening, the sheer mass of individual narratives nearly impossible to bull-doze through without feverishly seeking escape.

The moderate feminists are outshouted by their radical sisters' more intense and provocative prose. But at least MacKinnon's world view is relatively succinct and understandable:

> Women know the world is out there. Women know the world is out there because it hits us in the face. Literally. We are raped, battered, pornographed, defined by force, by a world that begins, at least, entirely outside us. No matter what we think about it, how we try to think it out of existence or into a different shape for us to inhabit, the world remains real. Try some time. It exists independent of our will. We can tell that it is there, because no matter what we do, we can't get out of it.[108]

Res ipsa loquitur. That's Latin for *"Nuf said."*

Humor from Hell

Feminist legal scholarship is not without humor, even if much of it is unintentional. The amusement derives largely from ironic paradox. Take, for example, the savageness of the rhetoric used in pursuit of the transformation of values to achieve a kinder, gentler, more nurturing, caring world. Andrea Dworkin's persona in her latest opus, *Mercy,* wants to smash men's faces in, to declare war, to have the courage to kill.✿

✿On reading the MacKinnon passage quoted above, a psychologist friend delivered his opinion that she "needs cognitive therapy, which diagnosis I duly reported in the *Journal of Legal Education.* Ms. MacKinnon responded that I need the "cognitive therapy of a fist in the face"—eerily reminiscent of Andrea Dworkin's desire to "smash men's faces in." Apparently this kind of gender violence (by women against men) does not fall within the radical feminists' definition of pornography.

So much for nurturing, compassion, empathy. To Ms.

Dworkin, there's no such thing as "the fair sex"—unless the term means that the well-armed little ladies will refrain from shooting their oppressors in the backs instead of indulging in a more fairly feminine *(macho?)* full-frontal assault.

Radical feminists use the academic enterprise, with all its trappings of rationality, to attack the law for its rational, neutral, and analytical aspirations. But they are contortionists when attempting to explain why, for example, heterosexual lovemaking is not (or should not be) fun, or why the older *Bluebook* served to suppress gender identification and thus deny female authors credit for their scholarship (because of its prescribed form of citing an author's first initial and last name).[109]

Humor is likewise anathema to this variety of feminism. One male professor reported very mixed reactions to what he perceived to be an innocuous joke about the Garden of Eden. Adam, lonely and bored, complains to G-d, who offers him a companion but says it will cost him "an arm and a leg." Shocked, Adam whimpers, "what can I get for a rib?" A female colleague and her husband strongly objected to the story, whose impact, they claimed, can only be "destructive." Two other colleagues refused to take his calls soliciting their reactions.[110]

Feminists are not likely to find Freud funny either. The founder of psychoanalysis once said that "a wife is like an umbrella—sooner or later one takes a cab." Even Freud would have recognized the risks of such humor. "One does not say aloud that man is naturally polygamous—unless one feels driven to tell the truth."[111]

Most perversely, perhaps, is that the articles themselves seem to be controlled by some bizarre academic imperative for exceeding the recommended daily allowance of tortured English prose.

Want proof? Here is more from MacKinnon:

> With few exceptions, feminism applied to law has provided no critique of the state of its own, and little insight into specific legal concepts from the standpoint of women's experience of second-class citizenship. Particularly in its upper reaches, much of what has passed for feminism in law has been the attempt to get for men what little has been reserved for women or to get for some women some of the plunder that some men have previously divided (unequally) among themselves. This is not to argue that women should be excluded from the spoils of dominance on the basis of sex, exactly. Rather, it is to say that it is antithetical to what women have learned and gained, by sacrifice chosen and unchosen, through sheer hanging on by bloody fingernails, to have the equality we fought for turned into equal access to the means of exploitation, equal access to force with impunity, equal access to sex with the less powerful, equal access to privilege of irrelevance. As male academics have been able to afford to talk in ways that mean nothing, so also women; as male pornographers have been permitted to subordinate women sexually through pictures and words, so also women. In the words of Andrea Dworkin, if this is feminism, it deserves to die. ... I think the fatal error of the legal arm of feminism has been its failure to understand that the mainspring of sex inequality is misogyny and the mainspring of misogyny is sexual sadism. The misogyny of liberal legalism included. In fact, it is the woman who has not been sexually abused who deviates.[112]

Descending from the Etherworld: Some Humble Suggestions

Women govern us; let us try to make them more perfect.

— RICHARD SHERIDAN

It is only the nature of their education that puts a woman at such disadvantage, and keeps up the notion that they are our inferiors in ability. The best sources of knowledge are shut off from them, and the surprise is that they manage to keep so abreast of us as they do.—JUSTICE JOSEPH STORY

Justice Story notwithstanding, if feminist legal scholars feel the need to continue pressing their causes in the academic journals, they would do well to follow a few simple precepts of persuasive writing: They should not explain all of their thought processes in such excessively detailed free-falls of association: Readers of neither sex are likely to be riveted by abstract personal narratives of women whom they don't know from Eve. They should avoid rash generalizations about men, if for no other reason that men should be at least a major part of their intended audience. They should seek to persuade with clarity and precision, telling men why a certain type of new order (not one in which women smash men's faces in) will be good for *them* as well. In sum, the old saw is still pertinent: More can be won with honey than with vinegar.

A healthy sense of humor would also be helpful. As sinners, after all, male and female were we created alike. Let us all celebrate our similarities as well as our differences. Most men, like Mr. Justice Story, admire women and want to understand them. We've come a long way since Mr. Justice Holmes, who once put it this way: "The brain women never interest us like the heart women; white roses please less than red."[113]

For their part, men (especially male academics) must stop trembling at the feet of radical feminists, and overcome the apathy (or chauvinism, or chivalry, or chagrin, or whatever it is) that causes them to avoid confronting Big Sisters' effronteries to the intellect. They should meet illogical arguments with the voice of reason. They should scorn the absurd. They should recognize (and resent) bullying that masquerades as scholarship.

In a nutshell, the attention of reasonable men and women everywhere must be earned—and can be, if the case is made with more measured moderation and less hysterical rhetoric—with more good writing, instead of that which is impossible to understand, and with more good ideas, instead of ideas that are impossible to implement.

The next generation of enlightened sisters may already have begun to advise the current feminist scholars: Lighten up. Let us understand you. *Get a life.*❀

> ❀This expression, as explained to the author by his then-teenage daughter (who fancies herself a feminist), means "stop saying stupid things, get off your tushy and do something with yourself." (In all fairness it should be explained that she had just uttered "Get a life" to her younger brothers—both of whom, it was already obvious, were destined to become men.)

III

Political Correctness Askew
Excesses in the Pursuit of Minds and Manners

Political Correctness, n., the avoidance of forms of expression or action that exclude, marginalise or insult racial and cultural minorities. —OXFORD ENGLISH DICTIONARY

All I want of you is a little seevility, and that of the commonest goddamnedest kind. —Z. W. PEASE, *THE HISTORY OF NEW BEDFORD*

Forgive us all our peccadillos.

With the fullness of time, when all has been said and done in both the heat of the moment and the cooler perspective of experience, radical feminism may prove to be more a hairline fracture than a major fault line in the history of higher education. Moreover, its broader operating manifesto—what has come to be called "Political Correctness"—may be revealed as little more than passionate folly, merely another skirmish in the eternal battle for the minds, hearts, and souls of humankind.✿

> ✿Once "mankind," a term now considered sexist—along with "manhole" (correctly, maintenance hatch), "manpower" (human resources), "man-made" (artificial), and "manslaughter" (person-slaughter, not to be confused with "man's laughter").[1]

There is nothing new under the sun, said the wise King Solomon; *life is full of futility.*[2] And, indeed, such have been the lessons of history. There may be nothing new about PC, either, except perhaps the realization of futility in trying to define it.

Nevertheless, at the turn of the new century, the atmosphere of Political Correctness that presently permeates campuses small and large and all over the country is, in its pervasiveness, the single most powerful cause of widespread trembling in the Ivory Tower.

Good Intentions and Bad Words: PC Perils and Their Precursors

Good intentions to redress legitimate grievances are part of the American psyche. Although we have yet to reach perfect democracy, we never stop seeking it. And nowhere have the good intentions been more apparent than with the traditional goals of higher education, from equality in the classroom to the ennobling of the human spirit.

But even after 150 years of social engineering—the Civil War, Reconstruction, separate-but-equal doctrines, desegregation, the civil-rights movement, open-admissions policies, and affirmative-action programs—education is unequal and the human spirit somewhat less than elevated by the Academy. True integration in American universities is still largely an unrealized ideal. Although incidents of racism, anti-Semitism, sexism and homophobia are experienced more in the workplace than in the classroom, they also occur regularly on school campuses at all levels.[3] Close to a million students report being harassed every year, and many of the cases go well beyond the bounds of simple speech.[4]

Speech, however, is the crux of the conflict between Political Correctness and the Constitution. "Oppressive language does more than represent violence," says novelist and race critic Toni Morrison. "It must be rejected, altered and exposed."[5] That philosophy has been embraced in a large number of American universities by way of stringent speech and conduct codes. According to a survey by the Freedom Forum First Amendment Center, almost 250 such codes forbid "verbal abuse and harassment," and over a hundred prohibit "advocacy of offensive or outrageous viewpoints."[6]

Like religion, though, and despite dictionary definitions, modern-day manifestations of PC mean very different things to very different people.

Take manners, for example. Perhaps responding to the recent poll which found that 73 percent of Americans think our manners are worse today than they were several decades ago, and that 43 percent say it's worth placing limits on freedom of speech in order to enforce civility, the state senate in Louisiana recently passed a bill that requires elementary-school students to say "yes, sir" or "no, ma'am" whenever answering a teacher.[7]

But at today's universities, the inculcation of good manners is a minor goal. At first promoters of PC on campus argued that incidents of hate crimes and sexual harassment could be diminished by the introduction of affirmative-action programs, curricular reform, and speech codes—which in turn would increase gender and ethnic diversity among students and faculty, expand knowledge of other cultures, and heighten sensitivity toward minority groups.[8]

Alas, time and experience have amply illustrated the pervasive and negative effect that runaway manifestations of Political Correctness have had, and not only in the higher realms of Academia. Such changes, particularly when they served to supplant (instead of complement) traditional norms, have led to politicization of the universities[9] and a lowering of standards needed to graduate.[10]

Nowadays the presence of PC has gone beyond the universities, and is felt in everything from parlor-games to food-shopping, from spectator sports to legislative drafting, from choosing an overcoat to schmoozing in the office. Thus players of the board game Scrabble can no longer score points with certain words; politically-correct butcher-shops shouldn't sell veal;[11] football teams called Redskins are considered racist; lawmakers must comb their codes to remove all masculine pronouns;[12] PC fashion-setters continue to shun fur coats and alligator shoes;[13] and jokes at the water-cooler have to be gender-neutral.[14] ❀

> ❀The Maryland General Assembly spent some two million dollars of taxpayers' money to rid its Annotated Code of all gender-specific pronouns, particularly the patriarchal he and his. There's no telling how much it will cost the State of Maryland to change the translation of the motto on its official seal—*Fatti Maschii, Parole Femine*—from the original *Manly Deeds, Womanly Words* to the newly advocated and politically-correct *Strong Deeds, Gentle Words*.

The latest official Scrabble Dictionary has correctly deleted such racist epithets as "wop,""spic," and "nigger." Also expunged, though, are words like "gyp," "welsh," "redneck," and "squaw—said to offend, respectively, Romany-Americans (formerly called gypsies), people from Wales, residents of Appalachia, and Native Americans. Such well-mannered civility raises sticky questions among seasoned Scrabblers (not the least of which may be that "gypsies" is worth at least 89 points if placed on a triple-word-score square). Tournament-level players are permitted to escape this kind of troublesome semantic dilemma by using an unabridged version of the official Scrabble Dictionary.[15]

Likewise taboo are Indians and Braves. A Harvard University history professor was charged with racism for using "Indian" instead of "Native American" in a lecture. (He blamed "tenured radical[s]" hostile to any speech not "properly on the left," and "minority students . . . placed through affirmative action in institutions where they're not doing very well.") Similarly, various women's sports teams have abandoned their old names as sexist (such as Maryland's erstwhile "Lady Terps") although others have no such qualms (e.g., Tennessee's "Lady Vols"). The rap on the University of Pennsylvania's "Fighting Quakers," however, may have more to do with the oxymoronically-challenged than with political correctness.[16]

Biblical values, meanwhile, cascade around us in gay confusion. The military's current policy on sexual orientation ("don't ask, don't tell") is a case in point. It used to be okay for Uncle Sam to want you—so long as you didn't want Uncle Sam. Now, no one knows for sure.[17]

In the past several years, countless words have been spoken and written on the subject of Political Correctness, from a diatribe by the Prince of Wales[18] to a commencement address by the President of the United States,[19] from inner-office memoranda to best-selling books.[20] Indeed PC has become the cliche of the decade, perhaps journalism's most over-used and under-examined catchword."✦

> ✦As recently as fifteen years ago, the term "political correctness" was barely used in the media; by mid 2001, it had appeared in over 31,500 articles in major newspapers.

117

In the past few years as well, revisionist PC historians have caused at least four different exhibits to close at the Smithsonian Museum and the Library of Congress. Slavery, Sigmund Freud, the Atomic Bomb, the War in Vietnam—each offended some group. The clash of ideas engendered by the PC movement has produced a philosophical furor over whether the group is more important than the individual, whether the sensibilities of minorities and women should be elevated over the freedom of expression, and whether "equality" should prevail over robust discourse. The debate has raised fundamental questions about nearly every aspect of culture and education.

Meanwhile, American schools of education appear to have redirected their mission from pursuing intellectual goals to promoting political ones. In so doing they have replaced their responsibility for insuring a regular supply of knowledgeable elementary- and high-school teachers with a "constructivist" approach to learning, which is based on what students' interests are, not on established curricula. The resulting shortage in competent teachers is painfully evident.[21]

Whence the intrusion of Political Correctness into the American psyche? Although the term was used in mid-century by the communist *apparachik* to describe party-faithful comrades, it did not become part of the general vernacular until the 'Sixties—and even then was the exclusive province of academics and intellectuals. Then, PC was generally considered a favorable concept, usually aimed at "raising consciousness about parts of our vocabulary that are saturated with implicit racism and sexism."✿

✿The two are not necessarily the same. Although most academics fancy themselves intellectuals, others might find that description difficult to uphold when attending a typical faculty meeting.[22]

Somewhere along the way, however, the line between consciousness-raising and common sense has been grievously breached.

Perhaps the most convulsive in a series of campus uprisings in the late 1960's was the takeover by students at Harvard in April 1969. What became an almost reflexive habit of capitulating to student demands began most centrally with the virtual abolition of the university's Reserve Officer Training Corps. This, decreed the students, was "a life and death issue for the people of the world whose lands are occupied by U.S. troops."

Almost a half-century later, the competing views have come to the fore. Author Roger Rosenblatt, a Harvard alumnus, says that at the time he found himself in favor of allowing ROTC to remain on campus as an option for anyone seeking the military life or needing it to complete an education. "In a worthwhile war, who would not wish to be led by a more thoughtful and educated first lieutenant?"

Samuel Huntington, a Harvard professor, offers a similar opinion: "One of the reasons for My Lai was that there weren't enough people there with judgment and values. It is most unfortunate to see our political and economic and intellectual elites totally divorced from our military elites."

And novelist John Updike wrote:

> The protest, from my perspective, was in large part a snobbish dismissal of [President Lyndon] Johnson by the Eastern establishment; Cambridge professors and Manhattan lawyers and their guitar-strumming children thought they could run the country and the world better than this lugubrious bohunk from Texas. These privileged members of a privileged nation believed that their pleasant position could be maintained without anything visibly ugly happening in the world. They were full of aesthetic disdain for

their own defenders ... spitting on cops who were trying to keep their property—the USA and its many amenities— intact.[23]

In time, many liberals came to use "politically correct" in a self-mocking way, applying the term to those who had become obsessed with semantics or disdaining it completely as exclusive to the radical agenda. Conservatives, meanwhile, were converting the phrase to their own purposes, in the process poking fun at the Left's fanaticism over words.✿

> ✿Ambrose Bierce defined a Conservative as someone "who is enamored of existing evils, as distinguished from the liberal, who wishes to replace them with others." John Stuart Mill called conservatives "the stupid party," backward-looking and obstinately resisting innovation.

Nowadays—with politics, as always, making for strange bedfellows—both ends of the political spectrum regard PC talk as "an effort to save souls through language."[24]

The saviors, as it turns out, often become harassers, imposing their own values on everyone else. Political Correctness has become a force all the more subtle and pernicious, as a *London Times* editorial put it, "because it pretends to liberalism and tolerance: the greater inclusion of women and minorities, the acknowledgment of their worth and achievements, the refusal to condemn an idea simply because of its novelty."✿

> ✿Although blue-collar workers themselves do not seem to care what they're called, on the endangered list are "mailman," "disfigured," "WASP," "stepmother," and "middle-aged." Women should not be called "babes, bitches, biddies, or bra-burners." The *Los Angeles Times* form book has deleted the words "deaf," "handicapped," and "illegal aliens."[25]

This particular phenomenon of foolishness, however, takes on a different meaning altogether when viewed in the context of Constitutional law. Here we encounter numerous self-appointed arbiters of propriety who, while occasionally well-intentioned, regard their own idea of what's correct as the one that must be enforced by law or litigation. Emily Post is no longer the governess of Political Correctness, having been replaced by Catherine MacKinnon.[26]

What were once noble and defensible goals—brotherhood, good manners, sensitivity toward others (in short, *civility*)—have been forged into bludgeons of moral imperatives. Instead of being urged into membership in the Very Nice Society, we are coerced into joining the Party of Social Awareness.❀ Instead of looking for common ground, we are forced to focus on past injuries. Instead of blending ethnicity fairly into a melting pot, we have allowed multiculturalism to boil over into a seething cauldron of conflict.

> ❀In fact there is a Very Nice Society at Cambridge University in England, whose sole aim is to promote extreme agreeability. It has no dues nor membership requirements, as I discovered while on sabbatical at Cambridge in 1985 (where I found that the Society's activities are, indeed, very nice). As it turns out Prince Charles is also a member in good standing, the revelation of which created "a definite air of BFD ... And if the Prince ... is uncertain as to what that particular set of capital letters stands for ... the first word is 'big' and the third word is 'deal'. The second word is almost certainly outlawed by The Very Nice Society."[27]

Even if the norm sought were nothing more than civility, it would still have to pass Constitutional muster. Manners, after all, cannot be coerced—at least not in America, where our concept of civil liberties protects the right to be offensive. Most efforts toward that end, whether legislative or judicial, have rightly been held to violate the First Amendment's guarantees of individual liberty and conscience.[28]

Too often, of course, the goal is not civility at all, but its more insidious cousin—power. That purpose, especially when it is camouflaged in the subtler garb of Political Correctness, frequently results in the abuse of fundamental rights—not to mention the trampling of traditional values. Here one can reflect on both the truth and irony of the old adage that "freedom requires eternal vigilance."

Though the pursuit of civility and the protection of Constitutional rights need not be mutually exclusive, they have come into conflict with increasing frequency. When that happens the appropriate standard to be applied need be neither vague nor unfathomable, but requires little more than application of the simple wisdom embodied in the language of the Founding Fathers. What was politically correct for them, after all, was vigorous political debate in a free and open marketplace of ideas.❁ That which is abhorrent will fester if suppressed, according to traditional First Amendment theory. Noxious speech is one price we have to pay for freedom of expression.

> ❁As Justice Holmes put it, "The ultimate good desired is better reached by free trade in ideas ... the best test of truth is the power of the thought to get itself accepted in the competition of the market . ... That at any rate is the theory of our Constitution. It is an experiment, as all life is an experiment.[29]

Examining the origin, evolution, and modern context of Political Correctness—and why it is so widely invoked by opposing elements along the political spectrum—inevitably brings us back to the Academy from whence it has so fully sprung.

Although fathoming the depths of the PC debate is a challenging task, it becomes a necessarily important undertaking if we are to accord the First Amendment the unique and thoughtful deference that it most assuredly deserves. We have seen the corrosive effects of coerced scholarship and radical feminism on today's Ivory Tower. The pages that follow examine in a broader way the PC cases and controversies roiling the modern university, address how they conflict with (or should be governed by) Constitutional principles, and suggest appropriate responses available to a democratic society seeking a fair balance between the rights of the individual and the welfare of the larger group.

The Academy and the Cutting Edge: Current Cases and Controversies

> The professor's crime, it seems, was that his book was not written in the "inclusive" language that is gender-neutral; he had not taken into account the modern principles that feminist historians have brought to the subject; and he had failed to appreciate the importance of social history. ... In short, he was a right-wing chauvinist, insensitive to the new politically-correct culture. If this case had blown up at a liberal arts college in California three years ago, British academics would have given a bemused shrug. Oxford, it has been assumed, is impregnable to the assaults of fad and foible.— LONDON TIMES *(on a decision by Oxford University Press not to publish a work it had commissioned)*[30]

The familiar maxim bears repeating: the reason that academic politics are so sordid is that the stakes are so low.[31]

That may be so when faculties debate the size and shape of blue books for exam-takers, but not when they decide what should be included in and excluded from the curriculum.

There the critical theorists and the ideology they promulgate and enforce are very much in evidence. In the first decade of the Twenty-first Century, political correctness is a most serious matter in the Ivory Tower.

"If thought corrupts language," said George Orwell, "language can also corrupt thought."

And, indeed, the Newspeak now being promulgated at most universities has officially if not unalterably rendered the English language askew. What began as an effort to diminish racism and sexism has turned into an orgy of Orwellian Newspeak. People are no longer "handicapped" or even "disabled," but *physically challenged.*[32] School menu-planners have become *nutritionists*, garbagemen *sanitation workers,* janitors *maintenance engineers.*

In less than half a century, dark-skinned Americans have traveled almost full circle in the name of PC: from "colored people" to "negroes" to "blacks" to "Afro-Americans" to "African-Americans" and, most currently, to "people of color." Such arcania but scratch the surface of the word- and thought-policing that has evolved almost helter-skelter over the past two decades.❁

> ❁When, one might ask, will the National Association for the Advancement of Colored People show some PC sensitivity and become the National Association for the Advancement of People of Color?

As noted earlier, perhaps most powerful among the neo-linguists have been radical feminists, who have turned chair-men into chairs, manholes into personholes, and history into herstory.[33] Thanks to PC, practically all girls and ladies have become self-made women—or *wimmin, wimyun,* or *womyn,* each of which is now an accepted usage according to the - preeminent Oxford English Dictionary, together with their singular counterparts *wofem, womban, womaon, womyn, woperson,* and *person of gender.*[34] ✤

> ✤The history of "herstory" is rather short. The earliest use of the term, according to the O.E.D., was in 1970, when feminists first decided they needed a new word to describe events from a non-male perspective. The O.E.D. does not provide the apparently ancient etymology of "he-said-she-said" disputations.

"Manholes," on the other hand, are now correctly *maintenance hatches,* "manpower" should be *human resources,* "man-made" means *artificial,* and "manslaughter" is actually *personslaughter.* Sometimes even boys are non-surgically re-gendered—or emasculated, depending upon your PC perspective: children now alternate gender in every other paragraph of *Dr. Spock's Baby and Child Care.*[35]

Such absurdist language-tinkering is endemic in the Academy. Perhaps the most inane example is a knee-jerk objection to use of the word "mankind"—even in the Declaration of Independence.[36]

Other language dictates and demands can have more serious consequences. California State University placed an ad seeking a "dynamic" English teacher. But after a feminist professor complained that *dynamic* implied a teaching style most likely possessed by males, the copy was amended (the offending word changed to *excellent*).[37]

Unfortunately, we in the Academy have miles to go before we begin expending less energy (and time and money) on what we call people, and more on what we do for them.

The New Pigs:
Classicists, Patriarchs and Eurocentrists

Though scarcely reported by the media, hundreds of American colleges and universities—from the backwoods of Appalachia to the august quadrangles of the Ivy League—are currently engaged in entrenched warfare over the nature and development of the curriculum. At many of them, traditional teachings of Western civilization have been supplanted with compulsory feminist-oriented and "Third-World" courses, many of them made requirements for graduation.[38]

Though in the beginning the academic PC movement infected only language, its proponents later began to identify and proscribe "politically-incorrect" conduct and curricula. Along the way "deconstructionism,"[39] "multiculturalism,"[40] and "sensitivity training"[41] were created and applauded, while "Eurocentrism,"[42] "traditionalism,"[43] and even modern science[44] were denounced. Students are subjected to mandatory intensive "prejudice reduction workshops,"[45] and professors are hounded by "sexual harassment task forces."[46]

The conflict between campus advocates of Political Correctness and the First Amendment has not always been so out in the open. Before World War II, the university was governed by a strict, not always democratic, hierarchy. Faculties were said to have "a faith in reason and knowledge, in the rational, dispassionate search for truth, and in the dissemination of knowledge for the sake of knowledge." Students and professors were not equals, and not all subjects were studied. Just as World War II brought women into the workforce, the post-war GI Bill supplied the universities with large numbers of students. While America was reconfiguring gender roles, Academia reconsidered its curriculum. An influx of funds came from both government and private sources, which in turn generated projects, programs, institutes, and centers— few of them related to the conventional academic functions of traditional teaching and research.[47]

Much of the grant money was aimed at the social sciences, which many viewed as the means by which society's shortcomings could best be addressed. Over time the socially-conscious university became a politically-conscious one, and the age-old struggle between Right and Left became significantly more subtle. The civil rights movement created "identity politics"—the crusades for women's rights, gay and lesbian liberation, and ethnic pride.[48] Critical race theorists believe that there is no knowledge which exists independent of culture. At least that *might* be what they believe. Here's Derrick Bell, one of the original "CRATS," describing the movement: "Critical Race Theory is an experientially grounded, oppositionally expressed, and transformatively aspirational concern with race and other socially constructed hierarchies."✿

> ✿Was I too knowingly smug when I smiled at my research assistant's plaintive cry of ignorance, "What the hell does that mean?"[49]

Now such movements are firmly entrenched in the university cosmos. Each demands not only that its views be brought into classrooms via the curriculum, and brought to bear upon faculty appointments and official pronouncements on political affairs.[50] It is part of what Camille Paglia calls "militant identity politics," which claims that "no culture can be understood except by its natives, as if DNA gives insight. All scrutiny by outsiders is supposedly biased. Any thing not 'nice' is edited out of history and culture—except, of course, when it can be blamed on white males."[51]

The movement has its own "postmodern" (or "pomo") jargon, which suggests that we inhabit social constructs and must view men and women as distinct entities, and indulges in "metanarratives" which provide stories through which we organize the way we look at the world.[52] Postmodernism seeks to "democratize" critical inquiry—according to one disenchanted professor, "leveling it to that of ignoramuses, who in their hubris assert that 'our opinion is just as good as yours,' regardless of the methods or standards employed. In this world there is no such thing as 'knowledge,' only 'knowledges,' which are nothing more than social constructs."[53]

In the spring of 1999 at the University of California (Berkeley), radicals agitated for more positions in the school's Ethnic Studies Department, despite that program's longstanding inability to attract healthy enrollments. After 135 students were arrested for taking over a campus building, six went on a hunger strike. The university gave in, authorizing eight additional full-time faculty positions, seed money for an "Institute of Race and Gender Studies" and—astounding as it may seem—funds for a mural depicting the student takeover.[54]

What cannot be achieved by group demonstrations, sit-ins, and marches is increasingly accomplished by way of sophisticated lobbying techniques aimed at legislation and litigation.[55] The universities have either allowed themselves to become masterfully manipulated or, perhaps worse, they have unwittingly played favorites.[56] From this perspective, artificially rigid speech and behavior codes, dramatically changed core-curriculum requirements,[57] altered tenure qualifications[58] —all contributions to the "politically correct" agenda—have infringed upon academic freedom, if not substantially curtailed it.

The current PC environment also encourages professorial bickering on a new level. The University of California once again is on the cutting edge. Responding to the growing ethnic diversity in its student body and what it perceived as an increased need for multi-cultural understanding, the university introduced a new World Culture course taught by five professors from diverse backgrounds. Unfortunately, some of the professors felt that their area of study was not being treated as "equally" as others. During a lecture on Islamic culture, one of the instructors, a former Jesuit from Spain, commented on the role of women in Islam. Another professor—a self-described "scholar of color"—objected, stating that he was "deeply offended" by the Jesuit's treatment of the subject. He requested half of the next lecture period in which to respond, saying he was concerned with the fact that the lecturer, while apparently criticizing Islamic culture, had not "acknowledged faults within our own culture."[59]

Adam Smith (author of *The Wealth of Nations*) described the university is a "sanctuary in which exploded systems and obsolete prejudices find shelter and protection after they have been hunted out of every corner of the world." Indeed, if the chief concern of multiculturalists were to foster greater opportunity for a diverse student body to examine pre- or non-Western ways of life under the guidance of competent and unprejudiced scholars, few would object. Modern multiculturalism is not only highly selective in its choice of cultures to be taught, but it repudiates and excludes existing Western civilization. Its proponents are less concerned with exposing students to the serious study of other cultures than with persuading them of a certain interpretation of their own. In so doing there is a distinct tendency to exaggerate the relative sinfulness of the West, as if racism and sexism and imperialism were distinctively western vices. Thus for multiculturalists the highest purpose of higher education is not diversity, but liberating students from their presumed bondage to Western culture. As such multiculturalism has become not ecumenical, but adversarial.[60]

Western Civilization from Maryland to Stanford

Western culture, at least as it is reflected in American or Enlightenment values, is now variously scorned by both Left and Right.[61] Traditionalists who deign to challenge the complete removal of "Eurocentric" classes and Western-based courses, as contrary to the purpose of fostering education, have become voices in the academic wilderness.[62] So have those who question the value (and cost) of requiring students to take "ethnocentric" classes, or who claim that "sensitivity training" is at best forced politeness and, more often than not, simply futile.❀

> ❀Political correctness can be expensive: the University of Massachusetts funds several cultural centers where students can "mingle with their own kind," not to mention many other programs designed to heighten and emphasize the diversity of the population on the 1,200-acre campus. Says the editor of the University of Massachusetts student newspaper: "As at many other schools, it's not clear whether college sensitivity inflames or redresses racial tension. There's been two decades of political correctness here and things only get worse."

Meanwhile, there has been an almost universal abandonment of required courses in history, philosophy, math, and other disciplines (from an average of 9.9 mandated courses in 1914 to 2.5 in 1993).[63]

Some public university systems claim to follow rigorous guidelines, but in fact do not. For instance, the University of Maryland's undergraduate catalog states that—

> Participation in a democratic society requires more than the central instruction provided by one major field of study in our world of rapid economic, social, and technological change, a strong and broadly-based education is essential. General education helps students achieve the intellectual integration and awareness they need to meet challenges in their personal, social, political, and professional lives. General education courses introduce the great ideas and controversies in human thought and experience. These courses provide the breadth, perspective, and rigor that allow [Maryland] graduates to claim to be "educated people."

However, Maryland's flagship campus at College Park mandates no general western or world civilization course, nor does it require a general humanities/literature sequence to introduce undergraduates to the great ideas, books, and fine arts of western culture. Instead, it allows students to meet graduation requirements by taking courses that are narrow and esoteric. To fulfill their physical science requirement, non-science students may take "How Things Work," "Nuclear Physics and Society," "Natural Hazards," and "Collisions in Space." Students can fulfill their humanities requirements with "Philosophy of Rural Life," "Introduction to Landscape Architecture," "Philosophy of Sports," "Popular Culture in America," and "World Popular Music and Gender." Contrary to its catalog statement, College Park does not have an offering in either Western Civilization or Great Books—though it does offer certification in women's studies, African-American studies, and Asian-American studies (as opposed to African or Asian studies *per se,* which presumably would dictate a more traditional approach to what are, after all, traditional societies).

In many respects, such courses can be regarded simply as educational junk food, providing a quick credit-hour fix. They cannot be linked to other classes, and in many cases—for example, "The History of Rock and Roll"—they offer no more than what can be learned from popular magazines. "Why should students receive credit for an education modeled on the inanities of popular culture?" asks the Calvert Institute for Policy Research, a privately-funded group in Maryland. "Why should parents be expected to pay for it?"[64]

The extent of the problem varies from state to state but, generally speaking, the more a university attempts to cast itself as a research institution, the worse the prospects that a student will obtain a genuine liberal-arts education.

Moreover, the new educational policies almost always require that feminist and ethnic studies permeate the primary curriculum, and be incorporated into all other disciplines as a way of "correcting the insidious distortion of the liberal-arts curriculum which serves to support 'Euro-American' hegemony."[65]

Traditional values have been turned on their head at elite private institutions as well.

Stanford University is a good illustration of the sea changes wrought by political correctness run askew. Often referred to as the "Harvard of the West," Stanford saw fit to replace its standard course in Western Civilization with a new one called "Cultures, Ideas and Values." A faculty committee charged with overseeing the transition focused largely on political issues. Minority literature, for example, was now to be taught by minority professors. Booklists were formulated according to how they typified a cultural group rather than on the basis of literary quality. Required student projects reflected a similar bias: credit was awarded for a documentary on a Grateful Dead rock concert, a history of women's athletics in America, and a video of the course itself. The result, observed one (non-minority) professor, is "a very problematic ghettoizing of knowledge."

> ❀ Students were at least partly responsible for the change, having protested the traditional course with chants of "Hey hey, ho ho, Western Culture's got to go!"

Pop culture has also gained increasing curricular legitimacy. Thus does Stanford now offer a course called "Black Hair as Culture and History." Even though the university sits in cutting-edge California, one might expect an institution of its reputation to have objective standards that might prune such courses from a coherent curriculum. Instead (as one alumnus put it), many courses, "each supporting some professor's personal agenda, have sprung up like weeds in the garden of higher education and have choked off genuine liberal arts learning." At this point Stanford could justify "The Home Economics of the Farkleberry Tart."

Just as junk food has little nutritional value, when everything is deemed educationally important—when even hairstyles are worthy of study—the result is intellectual emptiness. ❀

> ❀ The syllabus for the course included "The African Conception of Beauty and the Place of the Face, Head, and Hair in the Conception of Beauty"; "Early Black Hair in America"; "The Birth of Straightened Hair"; "New Ideas on Black Hair in the 1960s and the Rise of the 'Afro' (with Some Cornrows and Some Braiding)"; "The Great Debate: The Legacy of the 1960s; Black Hair as Identity"; "The 1980s-1990s as Festival of Black Hairstyles: Fade-O-Rama, Braiding and Dreadlocks"; "The Economic and Status Importance of Black Hair"; and "Visits from Hairstylists."[66]

A new history course examining "Social Movements of the 1960's in California" studies grassroots political activism through student involvement in civil rights and gay liberation campaigns. A course in comparative literature, analyzing the "resexualization of lesbian history" through the study of Sappho and other readings, probes for "male and female representations of lesbian desire"—including Shakespeare's *As You Like It,* which is identified as a "loci classicus of lesbianism."

Half of the class time in a Stanford course on Nineteenth Century American history focuses on women—because (it is stated) women comprised half of the population at the time. "Religion in America" deals with the peyote cult and Kodiak sect and views Christianity from a feminist or gay perspective —on the assigned reading list: *Jesus Acted Up: A Gay and Lesbian Manifesto*—but says not a word about the Catholic Church. Similarly, students taking "The History of Rights in the United States" never study the Declaration of Independence, although they engage in a vigorous argument on behalf of special minority privileges. Students of Anthropology I at Stanford discover a connection between their adherence to the anti-Western party line and their final grades.[67]

Stanford, of course, is not alone as a premier institution of higher learning which rolls with the politically correct dictates of the time. Harvard, Yale, Princeton, Pennsylvania, and Johns Hopkins, among others, have all seen fit to alter their curricula. Yale University declined a twenty million dollar gift from an alumnus rather than honor his request to use the money for a course of studies in Western Civilization. Yet Yale also insists that Orthodox Jewish students must live in coed dormitories rather than the more modest accommodations they requested. Dartmouth offers a class entitled "Introduction to Gay and Lesbian Studies." A professor at Duke justifies anti-Western dictatorships by declaring that "Stalinism is disappearing not because it failed, but because it succeeded, and fulfilled its historical mission to force the rapid industrialization of an underdeveloped country."[68]

Casting aside the foundations of Western civilization occurs not just at large, trendy, or elite campuses, but at small state and private colleges and universities as well.

Bowdoin College in Maine offers a course entitled "Music and Gender," in which a women's studies class discusses the questions, "Is Beethoven's Ninth Symphony a marvel of abstract architecture, culminating in a gender-free hymn to human solidarity – or does it model the processes of rape? Why do we expect drummers in both jazz and rock bands to be male?"[69]

Middle Tennessee State University created a "Committee for Curricular Transformation," which in short order distributed a "gender consciousness-raising questionnaire." One of its eighty-six questions asked "whether women and men mentioned in the course material were (a) treated separately and not compared; (b) described both separately and comparatively; (c) described both separately and comparatively, stressing interrelationships, or (d) described both separately and comparatively, stressing interrelationships and changes over time."[70]

> ❀ Some cutting-edge schools have created a new discipline called "masculinity studies"—as at Hobart and William Smith Colleges, which now has a "Center for the Study of Women and Men."[71]

Core courses at the University of Massachusetts/Amherst were "reconceptualized" to stress race and the New World Order—introducing, for example, "Women of Color" as a new requirement.✿

> ✿Newly franchised groups of the disadvantaged—including "Gays and Lesbians of Color"—have become increasingly common.

"This is an anti-racist classroom," intoned a (white) teaching assistant on the first day of class. She then assigned the students (all white) to write an essay about their first encounter with a person of another color. Those who questioned her were told they were "in denial" about their racism. In 1996 the same university introduced a new faculty-evaluation form that questioned the extent to which professors' teaching, research, or service made any "significant contributions to multi-culturalism." When asked the meaning of "multi-cultural," few administrators or faculty could define the term.[72] "Let's face it," said a black woman professor at a meeting to create a new women's studies curriculum, "there are two kinds of people in the world, oppressors and the oppressed, and these correspond to white and non-white."

Nobody around the table challenged her.

Drawing the Liberal-Arts Battle-Lines

The group best-positioned to sound alarms about the corrosive effects of political correctness on the quality of higher education is the small but articulate National Association of Scholars (NAS), which regularly documents the collapse of the liberal-arts core curriculum.[73] The NAS consists of both liberal and conservative scholars, most of whom take the position that diversity among faculty and students and multi-culturalism in the curriculum are negative influences primarily to the extent that they *reject* or *exclude* traditional values and thought. As one conservative Harvard student put it, "I'm all for diversity—who isn't?—but maybe my idea is diversity of ideas and viewpoints, and the administration is bent on diversity of physical traits." Harvard philosophy professor Harvey Mansfield has a similar lament: "The ideal of diversity-mongers seems to be a cosmopolis of all categories of society's victims, where everyone says the same thing in unison."[74]

In the study of literature, the warring factions are the highly politicized 30,000-member Modern Language Association (MLA) and a newer but much smaller group calling itself the Association of Literary Scholars and Critics (ALSC). The latter's constituency fashion themselves as resistance fighters against the prevailing academic trends of deconstruction, multi-cultural curricula, and gender studies that examine literature solely to expose its racism, colonialism, sexism, and homophobia.[75]

The ALSC substantiates and decries the fact that young graduates who don't speak the language of race, gender, and class studies cannot get college-teaching jobs. John Ellis *(Against Deconstruction, Literature Lost)* writes that politics has become the most important aspect of literature, and oppression the most important aspect of politics. Practitioners of this theory form a kind of literary jet set whose language is indecipherable except to those who speak it—thereby qualifying themselves as insiders. Those who do not are characterized as old-fashioned and unsophisticated outsiders who camouflage their "triviality or absurdity." But literature, argues Ellis, should be something which "enables us to see ourselves in perspective, to become more enlightened citizens and to think more deeply about important issues in our lives." The more the literate public hears of what is happening on campus, the sooner the literary radicals will retreat.🏵

> 🏵The beneficial aspects of adverse publicity can be seen clearly in the negative reaction to Bowling Green State University's refusal to allow one of its tenured professors to teach a course on political correctness, ostensibly because school officials felt it would ridicule the modern trend.

As of 1997, however, only 23 of nation's top 70 universities required English Literature majors to take at least one course on Shakespeare. Meanwhile, courses on Spenser, Chaucer, and Milton have virtually disappeared from the curriculum altogether.[77]

Georgetown University now sports a new curriculum designed to reflect "the power exerted on our lives by such cultural and performative categories as race, class, gender, sexuality, and nationality, and on the ways in which various kinds of representation aid in the construction, reproduction, and subversion of these categories."[78] Thus, English majors at the venerable Jesuit institution no longer need take even one course in Shakespeare (or Chaucer or Milton). Forget the Bard at Stanford as well, where even classic theater has been caught in the PC clutch: *The Tempest* is staged from a "slavery perspective" to teach about the evils of Western imperialism.[79] At Arizona State University, the drama director was dismissed for wanting to stage the non-PC version of a Shakespeare play.[80] English Literature majors at Florida State need not learn anything about Shakespeare—but all students must have enrolled in at least two "multi-cultural studies" programs in order to graduate.[81]🏵

⚙Georgetown's English Department now offers courses called "White Male Writers," "Women, Revolution, and the Media," and "Unspeakable Lives: Gay and Lesbian Narratives." The chairman of the department says, "We want students to be aware that there are problems in Shakespeare's plays with the way women were portrayed. We want to get away from the notion that literature is sacred. That is really a secular version of fundamentalism, the belief that there are magic books that have all the wisdom, all the authority, and if students passively attend to these books, they'll have all the answers." Few questioned his assumptions that Shakespeare has "all the wisdom" or that the critical race-and-gender theorists do not revere their own sacred texts.

The ALSC might be considered a conservative organization, but the MLA brands it a bastion of liberalism whose members are right-wing apologists. The MLA, on the other hand, is peopled by well-spoken deconstructionists, new historicists, queer theorists, radical multi-culturalists, and devotees of "cultural studies." For the race/gender lobby, all social, artistic, and intellectual life must be subjected to a battery of political tests—the "Sovietization of intellectual life, where the value of truth is determined not by its intrinsic qualities but by the degree to which it supports a given political viewpoint or self-determined moralistic position." The gender-race-class critics (called "Gerc-Crits" by the irreverent) are certain that their triad of issues is fundamental and virtually everything else is superficial.

John Ellis recounts a recent incident in which a young woman professor berated a visiting lecturer who had just finished talking about a character in Camus. "How does all of this speak to the trauma she had experienced as a female growing up in Palo Alto?" The class was silent. "Everyone seemed to be afraid to disown what they had been condoning and promoting," observes Ellis, "but also just as afraid of defending it. The young woman's personal obsessions were the beginning and the ending of it all; here were the triviality and narcissism of the new regime, in all its primitive absurdity."[82]

American universities today have thus come to be dominated by people who think that Plato, the Bible, and Shakespeare are "subjective" and "value-laden."[83]

In history, the excesses are even more obvious. Johns Hopkins University amended the reading list in one of its Introduction to American Politics courses—*replacing* the Constitution, the Federalist Papers, and Toqueville's "Democracy in America" with the writings of Malcolm X, Martin Luther King, Jr., and films such as "Do the Right Thing" and "Platoon."[84] The new *National Standards of History* emphasize the complexities of Native American civilizations to the virtual exclusion of the sources of Western cultures: both the Renaissance and the Reformation are barely mentioned. An African school in Timbuktu is described fully, but nothing is said about the great universities of Europe. Religion is largely ignored as well—except as it can be seen to have exploited women. The role of women and minorities in World War II is stressed over that played by white men in the service of their country. The effect, according to one traditional historian, "is to reduce historical work to polemics tricked out with footnotes."[85]

Today's unwritten code of political correctness likewise shuns the study or discussion of "myths" about Christopher Columbus. The University of Cincinnati's student senate demanded that the school declare itself a "Columbus-myth-free campus."[86] In Montgomery County, Maryland, ceremonies marking the 500th anniversary of Columbus' voyage to the New World began with a proclamation that

"Columbus' arrival opened an era marked by the clash of cultures, the exploitation of peoples and the near extinction of civilizations." In the end, it was conceded that Columbus taught the New World about humankind's "potential for both good and evil ... compassion and cruelty."[87]

> ✸This hasn't been difficult for the twenty-five percent of all college seniors who (according to a recent survey) could not come within fifty years of dating Columbus' discovery of America.

The new *National Standards of History* were defended by Joyce Appleby, president of the American Historical Association, as follows:

> Largely political, the tempest over the standards raged over the inclusion of the scholarship in social history that had been the pride of the profession for three decades. Critics found too much about ordinary people in them and not enough about the presidents, scientists, and generals who had previously filled the history classroom. Incorporated into school texts, the new scholarship failed the test of nostalgia. There was too much about an unfamiliar Harriet Tubman and not enough about old familiars like George Washington,. Instead of presenting Thomas Jefferson in relation to James Madison and Alexander Hamilton, the standards showed how to surround him with his daughters, grandchildren, slaves, hired laborers, and ordinary neighbors of Albemarle County, all because now, thanks to pathbreaking research, we now knew a great deal about these people.[88]

A distinct trend can be discerned in favor of writing the histories of minorities and women and against analyzing the history of governments led by white males and their role in society. The great majority of panels at recent conventions of the American Historical Association have been about "culture," "race,""identity," "religion," and "women"—and very few about governments, the institutions that actually exercise the most power over citizens. In their zeal to deconstruct traditional methodology and historical logic, postmodernist historians use language that bears a striking resemblance to the virtually incomprehensible voice of radical feminists. An example:

> It has become a recent commonplace to recognize that regions, like nations, are imagined constructs, that they possess historical specificity, and are imagined differently by different people at various times. It is less well acknowledged, however, that there are also flexible imaginaries that perhaps are related to and extend already existing structures, or that turn against these structures and contest their claims. These flexible imaginaries require looking at specific moments and episodes that have either been repressed by state-centered narratives of history or displaced by nostalgic yearnings for the local in an environment of dominating global and total structures. ....[89]

As historian David Kaiser points out: "Those of us who learned in elementary school that Asia was the largest continent or Earth will be surprised, undoubtedly, to discover that Asia has no actual existence, but is merely a concept that has been 'articulated' by different people at different times, always as part of a certain 'political or historical project.' " [90]

In the humanities and the social sciences, the crux of the problem is that deconstructionist theoreticians dismissively ignore the logic of traditional education. But it is hard to deny that Western culture remains the foundation of contemporary thought—that, regardless of their ethnic origin, Americans live in a Western country, and are governed by Western ideas in politics, economics, science, and technology.

Nevertheless, even though many honest scholars might find it difficult to understand how objectively-verifiable scientific data can be perceived as being politically oppressive, not even the hard sciences have escaped the broad brush-strokes of politically-correct post-modernism.

In 1996 a fashionable academic journal named *Social Text* published an article by New York University physicist Alan Sokal entitled "Transgressing the Boundaries: Toward a Transformative Hermeneutics of Quantum Gravity." The fact that the essay was in truth a purposefully unintelligible, multi-syllabic parody of postmodernist thought—in Prof. Sokal's own words "a melange of truths, half-truths, quarter-truths, falsehoods, non-sequiturs, and syntactically correct sentences that have no meaning whatsoever," through which he sought to demonstrate and unmask the ignorance of many postmod-ernist theorists—was completely lost on the editors of *Social Text*. Perhaps it is understandable that they were unable to evaluate critically, for example, Sokal's claim that "catastrophe theory, with its dialectical emphases on smoothness/disconti-nuity and metamorphosis/unfolding, will indubitably play a major role in the future mathematics; but much theoretical work remains to be done before this approach can become a concrete tool of progressive political praxis." But shouldn't they have source-checked spurious or irrelevant citations such as "Epistemological Reflections of an Old Feminist" or "Desire and the Interpretation of Desire in *Hamlet*"?

When Sokal revealed his hoax—suggesting that his arti-cle had been accepted largely because it was "liberally salted with nonsense" that "sounded good" and "flattered the editors' ideological preconceptions"—many scientists congratulated him for debunking the charlatans and bringing to light a seri-ous deficiency in academic literature, but a number of debun-kees (including some editors at *Social Text*) defended themselves and attacked both the author's methods and motives. The controversy that erupted both within and outside the academy bounded merrily between amusing and scandalous, and is still being debated today.[91]❀

> ❀In a 1998 meeting of the American Public Health Association, Sally Zierler of Brown University's Department of Community Health declared that AIDS is "a biological expression of social inequality," and that the way to reduce the epidemic is to "limit the power of corporations, cap salaries of CEOs, eliminate corporate subsidies, prohibit corporate contributions to politicians and strengthen labor unions."[92]

As suggested earlier, there is no "people's science" to replace existing science, no feminist cosmology to dismiss empirical data, no deconstructionist theory of mathematics, no "Afrocentric protein chemistry." History cannot change the fact that great scientists have mostly been white men. The most that PC advocates can reasonably ask is that groups historically under-represented in science be given diverse role models and greater opportunities. But proponents of affirmative action seldom recognize the advancement of orientals and Jews in scientific fields, most often targeting only blacks as victims.[93]

Humanities and the social sciences may have been debauched by politicization, but because student movements were so untheoretical, natural sciences were not a target and remained relatively unaffected. Nevertheless, as Alan Bloom observes in *The Closing of the American Mind*, now there is a trend in the interpretation of the history of science that says that all scientific theories are mere "constructs" and none has a claim to universal validity. Thus postmodernism turns on the proposition that all the great faiths can be dismissed.[94]

In March 1999, MIT released a much-heralded *mea-culpa* study in which the university admitted to systemic gender discrimination against tenured female science faculty. But an anonymous MIT committee source noted that there was no actual evidence, confidential or otherwise, to support the study's conclusions. Judith Kleinfeld of the University of Alaska at Fairbanks wrote a critique of the MIT study that was published by the independent Women's Forum. "It's a political manifesto masquerading as science," she said, which "falls below basic standards for scientific evidence in the social sciences," and which allows "a few senior women to be judge and jury of their own complaints." Cathy Young, author of *Ceasefire! Why Women and Men Must Join Forces to Achieve True Equality,* observed that "It may well be true that women in science still encounter some prejudice, but the MIT study certainly doesn't prove it. Such claims can easily become an excuse for selective favoritism toward women." Added Camille Paglia: "The MIT document is studded with touch-feely locutions that should have been red flags to any scrupulous journalist."[95]

This isn't a phenomenon unique to MIT. Similar committees on the status of women are being funded on campuses across the nation.

Though Western cultural inheritance may not be perfect, it is also difficult to dispute or diminish its successes. It has managed to abolish many kinds of human cruelty, given us forms of democratic government that actually work, and created a record of human thought in literature and philosophy that offers range, depth, and complexity. "Far from debasing human beings," says one traditionalist, "it has enhanced their dignity in a thousand different ways. We can build on it, extend it, modify it; but if we allow the politically correct to pull it down with their characteristic utopian promises about what they can replace it with, we have only ourselves to blame."[96]

Fortunately, there is no conflict between the sound study of humanities and what is good for society in general and women and minorities in particular. Properly understood, the liberal arts are substantial and practical. The skills they yield are the same as those measured by scholastic-aptitude and IQ tests. They are considered the best predictors of success in almost any enterprise. Many businesses and other institutions select their employees largely on the basis of such aptitudes. But curricula based almost solely on race/gender/class perspectives are devoid of historical context, and channel students' energies more toward resentment than constructive reform.[97]

Do we really want to abolish traditional standards of performance because we cannot agree on them? Should everyone be passed into the professional school of his or her choice because we are uncertain about the degree to which cultural biases may have dictated their rejection? Perhaps entrance into the professions should be based on factors other than exams, but until such criteria can be objectively identified we must live with what we have.❀

> ❀Critical race theorists argue that because the bar exam has a "discriminatory impact along racial, ethnic, and gender lines," and because it is at best "nothing more than a law school synthesizing experience, more akin to a law school comprehensive examination than a professional entrance examination," bar examiners should redouble their efforts to make the exam fair and valid.[98]

In any event, it is not clear that the adoption of middle-class values is a bad thing for society. Perhaps we are too quick to apologize for such values, and too reluctant to ignore the possibility that, far from being the ruination of the black community, they might be the key to its salvation—and to that, in turn, of everyone.

There is certainly nothing wrong with re-evaluating history. Offering new interpretations of old events—in fact, challenging entrenched dogma of all kinds—is what the academic enterprise is about. But *discarding* past culture wholesale because it is deemed "patriarchal"—*excluding* all that is "Eurocentric," *rejecting* whatever is "white"—can hardly be understood as the honest scholar's quest for Truth.

Attacks on Traditional Teaching

Many of today's professors are fearful of their students, their deans, and their radical colleagues. They strain for the right words or phrases or ideas so as not to offend or agitate would-be disciples, superiors, or their more politically powerful peers. Nowadays, a slip may cost them their careers.

This may have always been the case with tenure decisions made by administrators and colleagues, but it's something new when student evaluations, which may be negatively influenced by a professor's political position, can be employed by superiors as leverage in non-tenure reappointment consideration.

Thus textbooks, notes, and extensive syllabi are used extensively in an implied contract with the professor's student-customers. While there is nothing intrinsically wrong with such materials, too often they replace original thinking and subdue classroom dynamics. Moreover, professors have learned from experience that their popularity is more secure—enrollments healthier, course evaluations more positive—when they are less demanding in their assignments. They are more likely to play it safe by substituting shorter works to be read, fewer papers to be written, and less homework to be completed."✿

> ✿In truth students have always tried to manipulate professors. (Socrates once wrote that "Adolescents have bad manners and contempt for authority, contradict their parents, and tyrannize their teachers.") In a classic latter-day experiment, students were told to nod approvingly whenever their instructor—the unknowing subject—stepped back, while nodding disapprovingly whenever the instructor stepped forward. By the end of the hour, the professor found himself cowering in a corner, entirely unaware of how he'd got there. Students in a second experiment were told to give the nod whenever the professor put his index finger to his lips. By the end of the class, his finger was swinging back and forth as regularly as a metronome.[100]

As students have become more assertive, their would-be mentors have become more intimidated. Here's the way one literature professor put it:

> What's an instructor to do when faced with the student who ostentatiously reads the sports pages during the lecture hour . . . or the student who won't shut up . . . or the student who derides the professor as racist or sexist or homophobic) . . . or the student who loudly announces: "We're paying $25,000 to be here, so you'd better be really good." And what of the subtler boundary tests, the students who are perpetually late or who use questions to change the subject. If ignored, such behavior can wreck a classroom. If mishandled, it can escalate into profitless confrontation.[101]

Politically-correct overreactions by administrators, on the other hand, can and do cause greater harm to character and career. Anecdotal evidence might be our best (if not only) proof to examine the threat.[102] Consider the following stories, and ask how the troubling results might have been different had the prevailing standards been either traditional civility or

Constitutionality, instead of what was arbitrarily viewed as politically correct.

For Constitutional scholars, the abiding concern about PC has always been the stifling effect that coerced civility can have on both free speech and academic freedom. Where can and should the line be drawn? As each of the cases below clearly illustrates, the line to be drawn is between speech and conduct.

The Law of Sexual Harassment: "Hostile Environments" and Academic Hornswoggles

Much of the fear and trembling in the modern Ivory Tower is caused by a singular form of cultural terrorism: the threat of being charged with sexual harassment.

The proper and civil responses to harassment of any kind would be to redress it within the bounds of the law, while remaining fully within Constitutional principles of civil liberties (freedom of speech, press, religion, and assembly) and civil rights (due process and equal protection). In recent years, there has been a noticeable upsurge in allegations of sexual harassment on campus, due in part to the large number of colleges and universities that have imposed sweeping speech and language codes[103]—which in turn reflect exceedingly broad interpretations of what constitutes a "hostile environment."

At Pennsylvania State University, for example, an English instructor claimed she was being sexually harassed by the presence of Goya's famous painting *Naked Maja* in a university lecture hall. "Any nude picture of a woman," she said, "encourages males to make remarks about body parts." Although the painting had been hanging on the same classroom wall for at least a decade, it was removed as a result of her complaint.[104]

At the University of Michigan, a male student taking "Introduction to American Politics" was chastised for writing a paper in which he conjured up a polling example featuring "Dave Stud."[105] The paper was initially reviewed by a female teaching assistant, who found it to be sexually biased and contrary to the department's "Checklist for Non-sexist Writing."[106] Her concerns were forwarded to the professor teaching the course (also a woman), who agreed that the passage constituted verbal assault and harassment. She warned the student against similar conduct in the future. Rather than run the risk, he decided to drop the course.

Of greatest concern, though, is what happens to professors themselves who are accused of sexual harassment.

Take the case of James Maas, who had been teaching at Cornell for about thirty years, during which he had won numerous teaching awards. His "Psychology 101" may be the largest undergraduate course in the country—attracting close to 1000 students a semester. In 1994, Prof. Maas was called before Cornell's "Professional Ethics Committee" to defend himself against charges of sexual harassment. The allegations, brought by four former students, centered around his "overly friendly and affectionate behavior"— which, it turned out, were hugs and occasional social kisses, most often in front of class or family.

After an investigation which (Prof. Maas was assured) was "confidential," he was found guilty. Although he never conceded any wrongdoing, Prof. Maas accepted a token punishment with the understanding that the matter would be kept quiet. During the entire spring semester of 1995, however, the *Cornell Daily Sun* ran stories and cartoons depicting him as a sexual aggressor and took the university to task for not firing him. The affair soon found its way into *The New York Times, Time Magazine, The Chronicle of Higher Education,* and at least one wire service.

Prof. Maas may have been willing to live with Cornell's administrative slap on the wrist had it been kept in-house as promised. But once he felt that his reputation had been grievously and unfairly damaged, he sued the university for $1.5 million.[107]

Cornell, in fact, keeps a "locked box" of informal complaints lodged against faculty. Professors are not informed that such a file exists, much less told about potential grievances bubbling up against them. If a student decides to press formal charges against an offending professor—even years after the fact—the box is opened and its contents examined.[108]

For many professors who feel the chill of PC and guard their every comment and gesture, Maas-like hugs would be out of the question. Others find themselves already caught in webs spun by students and administrators zealously on the lookout for hostile environments, quietly resign themselves to various forms of censure and fade back into academic anonymity. Those who deign to challenge the system face years of litigation, which they are less prepared to undertake (psychologically or financially) than the impersonal institution on the other side.[109]

Professor Graydon Snyder of the Chicago Theological Seminary, for example, had to spend close to $75,000 of his own money to restore his reputation. His offense? Referring to an obscure Talmudic passage which he used to illustrate the difference between Christianity and Judaism. It was an example he had employed often over three decades of teaching : "A roofer fell from his scaffolding and landed atop a woman passing by below—in the process accidently having sex with her." According to the New Testament, said Prof. Snyder, even if you think only about doing the act you've committed, it's a sin. But, according to the Talmud, if you had no intention of doing the act, you're not responsible at all, even if in fact you did it.[110]

For this analytical insight, Prof. Snyder was brought before a "student-faculty sexual-harassment task force"— which in 1992 brought formal charges against him. Although he was fully tenured, the seminary subsequently placed him on probation, ordered him to write an apology and enroll in a sexual-harassment workshop, and forbade him to be alone with students or staff members. In addition, the seminary administrators issued a public reprimand, put notices in every student and faculty mailbox announcing that Prof. Snyder had engaged in sexual harassment, and assigned a school official to monitor his classes.[111]

Prof. Snyder sued the seminary for defamation. "Academic freedom is the principle here," he said through his attorney. "It is important for other professors around the country to know that their every word will not be reviewed by a cultural swat team."[112] Realizing it would not likely prevail on the merits, the seminary offered to settle out of court— provided Prof. Snyder would resign. He refused. Eventually, in early 1996, a settlement was reached, with a clause stipulating that neither side would publicly disclose its terms.[113]

The most notable example of a professor who stood his ground against sexual-harassment charges, and won a very public apology, is J. Donald Silva, a tenured member of the English faculty at the University of New Hampshire. When a student in his technical-writing course asked for an example of a "working definition," Prof. Silva chose what he thought was a useful word-picture: "Belly dancing," he said, is "like a plate of Jell-O with a vibrator underneath." The simile was arguably vulgar, but one Silva had used many times before. This time, though, was different. Within days, he found himself accused of sexual harassment.

Shortly thereafter, Dr. Silva was suspended from his job, ordered to pay the university $2,000 for a replacement teacher, and directed to undergo psychological counseling with a university-approved therapist.[114] But the professor was not ready to end his 35-year teaching career, and certainly not under the stigma of sexual harassment. "I am not sick," he said, "and I am not going to give up my right to trial by jury."[115] He filed suit in federal court, arguing that dismissal of a tenured professor on the basis of statements made in class violates principles of academic freedom, federal statutes, and the First Amendment.[116] He compared the therapy order to brainwashing by a totalitarian regime, as if he had been convicted of a "thought crime."

The University of New Hampshire's policy on sexual harassment defines speech as punishable if it "has the purpose or effect of unreasonably interfering with an individual's work performance or creating a hostile or offensive working or academic environment ... whether intended or not."[117] The offended party's misperception, in other words, can be grounds for sanction.

The court disagreed and ultimately ordered Silva's reinstatement.[118] The university, which had already expended close to $200,000 in legal fees, chose to settle rather than appeal, and paid the professor another $250,000.[119]

A triumph like Dr. Silva's, however, is rare.[120] Most of

those similarly hounded have considerably less gumption for litigation—even though not one speech code tested in court has yet been found constitutional. To the contrary, courts have found that the various codes currently in place breed clear failures of due process: unfounded complaints, suppression of heretical views, and the absence of fair hearings—in short, academic hornswoggles of the worst order.

At the University of Minnesota several years ago, four women students brought sexual-harassment charges against all six members of the Scandinavian Studies Department (including a female professor), complaining of such things as disagreeing with a student in a "non-supportive" way. After an eight-month investigation, all the charges were dismissed as groundless. But the accused faculty members found themselves profoundly shaken by the experience, describing it as "terrifying" and "totally demoralizing."

Michael Kraus, a law professor at George Mason University, suffered a similar fate. During a class in 1993, he gave two examples of conduct that might constitute the tort of assault. One involved a demonstration in front of a Holocaust survivor's home, where a group of neo-Nazis advocated the continued pursuit of Hitler's "Final Solution." The other was about a Ku Klux Klan cross-burning outside the house of a newly-arrived black family, where hooded Klansmen shouted "Kill the Niggers!" Several faculty colleagues and twenty students—none of whom had attended the class—filed a complaint with the dean, demanding that Prof. Kraus apologize. The media were also notified. Three full-scale investigations over a two-year period (one of them by the Civil Rights Division of the United States Department of Education) yielded no evidence of racial discrimination. There was no telling how many hours or dollars Prof. Kraus had to spend defending himself, nor the effect it had on his career.❀

> ❀The Department of Education held a hearing that lasted two full days before dropping the case—although it declined to find Kraus "not guilty."

Both students and professors must be ever more careful about what they say and how they say it, because someone seems always to be watching and listening. At Mankato State University in Minnesota, for example, members of the Women's Studies Department set up a group of student informants to watch out for any sexist, racist, or homophobic language in classroom discussions.

The chilling effects of PC likewise take their toll on intellectual discourse. At Ohio State University's law school, students protested an evidence course they claimed had created "a hostile learning environment" because, in both of the hypothetical case files pursued throughout the professor's chosen text (one involving a rape, the other a fatal accident where the deceased is a girl and the plaintiff her mother) women were the victims. The fact that they were also the parties who invoked the legal process did not seem to ameliorate the criticism.[121]

Similarly, at New York University, students refused to brief one side of a moot-court argument on denial of custody to a lesbian mother, because they thought no legitimate arguments could be made against the mother's claims.

In 1993, after Harvard Law Professor Alan Dershowitz spent two classes discussing men falsely accused of rape, a group of female law students filed formal sexual-harassment charges against him for having created a hostile atmosphere.

According to Prof. Dershowitz, many professors avoid teaching classes involving issues of race, gender, or sexual preference for fear of a PC backlash—a sentiment echoed by Prof. Kraus. For people whose political preferences matter more than professional skills, says Prof. Dershowitz, the question becomes not "How well have you applied law to this case?" but "Which side are you on?"[122]

Unfair claims of discrimination often take on lives of their own, well beyond the ability of the alleged offender even to apologize.

Murray Dolfman, a longtime adjunct professor in legal studies at the University of Pennsylvania's Wharton School, was lecturing about personal service contracts. Telling his class that no one can be forced to work against his or her will, he asked the origin of the phrase "involuntary servitude." When he got no response, he asked if anyone knew the Thirteenth Amendment ("Neither slavery nor involuntary servitude shall exist within the United States"). Prof. Dolfman said, "We will all lose our freedoms if we don't know what they are." He noted that he was descended from the former Jewish slaves in Egypt, who celebrate their emancipation every year at Passover. He remarked that there may be some descendants of ex-slaves in the class who should know about the Thirteenth Amendment.

Several minority students complained to him privately about what they perceived to be his racial insensitivity. He duly apologized for having offended them, and thought the matter finished. Some time later, however, during Black History Month, the "Dolfman Affair" was raised repeatedly to support the claim that racism is pervasive at the University of Pennsylvania. Students disrupted Prof. Dolfman's classes. The university president reprimanded him and initiated an investigation. Although the university's ironically-named "Committee on Academic Freedom and Responsibility" found that Prof. Dolfman had been an exceedingly popular professor, and that there had been no complaints against him in his twenty-two years at Wharton, the president ordered him to apologize once again—which he did. Nevertheless, some two hundred students subsequently occupied the president's office, demanding Prof. Dolfman's dismissal. He was suspended for a semester, and ordered to undertake sensitivity training. Although he was later reinstated, he ultimately ended his thirty-year career at the university, stating that he "had had enough."[123]

At Wellesley, freshwomen attend a mandatory orientation program called "Inter-Cultural Awareness Now" (ICAN). It is intended to root out unconscious racism in order to make one more "sensitive to the pain of others." According to one (female) participant, the event degenerated into a tearful encounter group with women crying as they described the various ways they had been oppressed by sexism, racism, homophobia, etc. "I felt I had been trapped for four hours in a room feeling stigmatized and alienated because I was an American with blonde hair. I had learned only one thing from the session: you have to be a victim to fit in at Wellesley."[124]

Humor and the New Taboos: Bimbos, Biscuits, and Battered Women

Although not a single campus speech code has survived a First-Amendment test and a few have been rescinded or modified, many such rules and regulations continue to be promulgated and enforced. The enforcers are often radical feminist professors and the students they indoctrinate, who frequently shoot down more than idle or boorish racist and sexist comments. Words can and do offend, but the blunderbuss approach of many campus speech codes and their advocates often yield absurd results. Words take on different meanings in different contexts. To PC guardians, however, the determinative test is whether the words have *ever* offended *anyone*.

At Bowdoin College in Maine, all of the following are forbidden: "leering, staring, catcalls, vulgar jokes, language, photographs, or cartoons with sexual overtones." The University of Connecticut's ban on all "inappropriately directed laughter and conspicuous exclusion of students from conversations" is a good illustration of impossible expectations camouflaged as good intentions. UConn also prohibits attributing objections to any perceived slight to "'hypersensitivity' of the targeted individual or group." Thus students would be hard put to shun either a hate-mongering bully or a classmate with bad breath—or even to suggest that someone was overreacting.[125]

At the University of Minnesota, the official definition of sexual harassment may include such a vague offense as displaying "callous insensitivity to the experience of women."[126] Nowadays such insensitivity can be evidenced merely by a professor's choice of language.

At the University of Baltimore School of Law, a student chastised a professor for using the word *whore* to describe some consultants who testify as expert witnesses. Suppose, however, the same professor had {a} asked a hypothetical in class concerning the size of Dolly Parton's chest, {b} used the name "Chas. Tittybelt" on an exam question, or {c} wrote a casebook mentioning a fictional lingerie store called "Tanks for the Mammaries"? ✿✿

> ✿Luckily for the professor, the student, who was president of the school's Gay and Lesbian Student Bar Association, chose not to charge him with sexual harassment. She apparently was satisfied with writing him a long memorandum (wasting both her time, he says, and his).
>
> ✿✿As the reader might have guessed, these anecdotes are true. See note 124.

Many words have perfectly innocent origins, but no self-respecting feminist would permit their use in any venue except perhaps a formal allegation of sexual harassment. Consider, for example, the terms *bimbo, hussy,* or *streetwalker.* In the modern vernacular, they often appear as *dumb bimbo* (referring to a vacuous sexpot),[127] *brazen hussy* (a forward, overbearing matron),[128] and *common streetwalker* (a prostitute).[129] But "bimbo" is derived from the Italian "bambino" (baby). "Hussy" was born into the King's English as the affectionate British diminutive for "housewife." And "streetwalkers" have been considered in quite different lights by different courts.✿

> ✿My familiarity with at least two of these terms stems from several of my own encounters with PC. I once took some flak for suggesting that an out-of-the-closet chauvinist friend name his Maryland-bred filly "Uppity Bimbo." (I liked the rhythm of that name then, and still do. Uppity Bimbo won a few races, too, against male competition.) And early in my law-teaching career, I was chastised by a feminist colleague for illustrating how to use the legal-bibliographical tool *Words & Phrases* by having my students research the word "streetwalker."[130]

While circumspect professors nowadays would likely think twice before using words they know will be taken by some to be offensive, should they be *prevented* from doing so?

Under the new conduct codes, it has also become awkward or impermissible to engage in campus humor (however sophomoric or sophisticated), or romance (however blasé or blatant).

According to adherents of critical legal studies ("Critters," or "Crits," as they have come to be called) — for whom political correctness has become a selectively-applied tool-of-choice to enforce a particular agenda — ethnic and minority humor is taboo, while that aimed at people of higher station (e.g., white males) is acceptable. Included in the former group are housewives, "Jewish-American Princesses," rednecks, and blondes. The excluded targets thus account for roughly 150 million Americans.

Political correctness as espoused by the "Crits" is reflected in much of modern legal scholarship. But if truth is whatever one wants it to be, or if it is the will of the stronger force, then the distinction between scholarship and advocacy collapses. If all law is racially indeterminate, then all legal scholarship becomes a form of advocacy[131]

Humor in the Ivory Tower has taken on a dark and dreary (if not ominous) cast. Freud's famous one-liner ("A wife is like an umbrella—sooner or later one takes a cab.") elicited decidedly negative reactions when a professor presented it in a test-survey of his colleagues. Likewise, there was an uproar when the student newspaper at the University of Baltimore School of Law published a cartoon of a woman on a bakery table being doused and powdered by a baker, the caption underneath reading: "Every fourteen seconds a woman is battered somewhere in the United States." A number of women students were outraged, and staged a rally on the law school's plaza during which the offending cartoonist was roundly excoriated. Less was said about the paper's questionable taste and arguably poor judgment. No one mentioned the rights of free speech and press, or questioned the extent to which the offensive humor might or should have been tolerated.

PC-minded campus groups are inclined to steal or destroy newspapers containing articles they don't like. The thefts are often overlooked by college administrators. After a cartoonist for Ohio State University's student newspaper satirized the Women's Studies program, campus feminists sought to harass him and the paper's other staff. They stole some 15,000 copies of the offending paper. One of the group's leaders all but admitted the theft, but exonerated herself—telling reporters that "it's within my First Amendment rights to steal." After 3000 copies of the Georgetown *Academy*, a conservative student magazine, were purloined, the theft was ignored by one student newspaper *(The Voice)* and applauded by another *(The Hoya)*. When 3000 copies of the California State University/Sacramento newspaper *State Hornet* were stolen, there was no reaction at all from the university president. (Rare exceptions occurred at Skidmore and Yeshiva University, both of which reprimanded *administrators* for stealing newspapers, and reimbursed student editors for their cost.)[132]

> When the group tried to burn their bras on the cartoonist's front porch, they were foiled—because the fabric was fire-retardant.

In 1991, a fraternity at George Mason University staged an "ugly woman contest" as part of a series of events whose proceeds went to charity. Various fraternity members dressed up as caricatures of different types of women. The stereotypes were found offensive enough to justify suspending the fraternity from all activities for the rest of the semester, and levying additional sanctions as well—including the requirement that it develop an educational program addressing cultural differences and the concerns of women.

The fraternity went to court and won—a bitter pill for the aggrieved students and administrators to swallow. But how much of their discomfort stemmed from the traditionally chauvinistic behavior exhibited by college men? Would the same women students have been offended by the film "Coming to America," in which a black preacher, among a course of amens, whinnies out: *Girl, y'looks so good I'd like to put y'on a plate and sop y'up with a biscuit!"?*

But those who advocate the abolition of jokes about women or minorities, their demographic numbers aside, do not address the possibilities that a joke when told by a group against itself (e.g., Jewish students or professors telling "Jewish American Princess" stories) might have therapeutic value; that where the butt of the humor is a non-traditional minority (e.g., blondes or rednecks) it may not have any true negative consequences; or that humor is often a way of opening or continuing important debates about controversial issues (e.g., using Freud's one-liner about wives to explain the Clinton-Lewinsky affair). Some commentators regard *triumph* as the vindication of all jokes—even racist or sexist ones.

Moreover, stereotyping is often an essential element of humor: why should the caricatures of empty-headed women depicted by Lucille Ball in *I Love Lucy* or Gracie Allen in

George and Gracie be any less offensive than George Stevens' television role as the comically shrewd Kingfish in *Amos and Andy?* Yet only the latter left the airwaves due to PC pique.[133]

Likewise, it is not always easy to discern the targets of the ridicule—the narrator, listener, or viewer. Just as not all blacks resent the characters in *Amos & Andy,* few should find fault with the following joke, but many likely would:

> An airline pilot informs his passengers that the plane is in trouble, and he will have to order some people to jump off. To be fair, says the pilot, he will call passengers by groups. "African Americans" are the first called. The lone black father and his son are silent. "Blacks." No response. "Colored people." Silence. "Darkies." The boy turns to his father and asks, "Dad, haven't we been called?" The father answers, "Son, we are Negroes and don't you forget it!"[134]

Over Here, Over There:
Double Standards and the Dangers of Platonic Love

The double-standarded application of situational ethics manifests itself most clearly in rarely reported "reverse discrimination." At California State University in Sacramento, for example, a woman professor regaled her mixed-gender class in psychology with tales of various sexual exploits, illustrated the lecture with close-up photographs of genitalia, extolled the bliss of auto-eroticism, and invited students looking for "the perfect Christmas gift" to stop by her office after class for copies of a sex-toys catalog. A number of students (both male and female) charged the professor with having created a sexually hostile classroom environment in violation of the university's harassment code, which prohibits both explicit sexual statements and pictures. But university administrators declined to press the matter, declining even a reprimand.[135]

> At Wesleyan University, students in a course called College of Letters 289 were required by their (female) professor to create a work of pornography as a final project. One student submitted a short film that focuses on a man's eyes while he masturbates. Another created a piece in which a female student acts out a scene of sexual bondage. The sole response of the university president appears to be a letter he sent to all faculty in which he questioned "the appropriateness of this course in the Wesleyan curriculum."

Also seldom challenged are women's groups, classes, or events that exclude or discriminate against men. Every year, for example, the Ms. Foundation for Women sponsors a "Take our Daughters to Work Day." However, parents of boys complained that their sons were being excluded from the important national event. But many women railed against the inclusion of boys. "Boys," they argue, "are constantly exposed to role models and opportunities that girls just don't enjoy."[136]

The current PC climate has also served to chill campus romance. Antioch University's celebrated "sex code" requires that partners ask specific permission before engaging in any physical contact—for example, "May I kiss you?" and "May I put my hand there?"[137] Amorous Antioch students reportedly circumvent the code by verbally agreeing in advance to "activate the policy."

The pernicious nature of such political correctness is best illustrated by its absurd extremes. Perhaps no better example is the University of Connecticut's aforementioned code banning "inappropriate laughter and conspicuous exclusion of students from conversations." There once was a time when hugging and kissing—the polite embrace or a peck-on-the-cheek—was as much a matter of civility as the tip of a gentleman's hat.

Now, any such behavior, especially when it happens on campus, could well evoke visions of a hostile environment if not actually invite a charge of sexual harassment.❀

> ❀If Cornell's Professor Maas was punished for hugging, post-structuralist literary critic Jane Gallop should have known better: she was accused of sexual harassment by two women students for flirting with them, and kissing one of them on the mouth. At least neither of them had to deal with a politically correct totalitarian government: the international politics faculty at Beijing University was told by the Chinese Education Ministry to focus on Marxism and stop their lucrative sideline of selling women's underwear.

Such pre-emptive feminist strikes are by no means limited to American campuses. Wollongong University in Australia has a policy that forbids not only student-teacher sex, but platonic love as well.[138] The University of Ontario's code of conduct makes sexist humor and language grounds for complaint, providing for hearings which could ultimately lead to a professor's dismissal.[139] At the University of Toronto a professor of chemical engineering was convicted of sexual harassment in 1989 because of his "prolonged and intense staring" during swims in the university pool.[140] At the University of Waterloo, faculty and teaching staff carefully guard their words to avoid anything that might be considered anti-feminist, anti-homosexual, or anti-minority. Some professors fear tjat so much as a mention of an author's sexual orientation during a discussion of his work, that could leave themselves open to attack.[141]

Thus again does it become clear that the most sensible line to be drawn is between speech and conduct.

Free Speech and Super-Sensitives

Other First-Amendment problems are presented when aggrieved parties or their advocates make charges of discrimination based on race or ethnicity, and rely upon the new conduct codes for enforcement of sanctions.

A fraternity at the University of California was disciplined for violating the "high moral and social standards of the Greek community on campus" because it distributed T-shirts showing a cartoon figure of a man holding a beer and wearing a sombrero. The caption around the cartoon read, "It doesn't matter where you came from, as long as you know where you're going." Two campus Hispanic organizations found this to be a racist slur against Spanish people. The fraternity defended itself by explaining that the T-shirt was part of an effort to promote and celebrate a South-of-the-Border party and, as such, had been designed by a Hispanic member of the fraternity. In fact, twenty-two of its forty-seven members were Hispanic. The university nevertheless suspended the offending fraternity for three years and ordered its members to attend sensitivity training sessions.[142]

Perhaps the most infamous example of political correctness gone askew occurred in 1993 at the University of Pennsylvania. Eden Jacobowitz, an Israeli-born undergraduate, shouted, "Shut up, you water buffalo!" at a group of five black sorority sisters who were making loud noises outside his dormitory window late at night. The women took offense at the remark and complained to campus authorities, who charged Jacobowitz with racial harassment under Penn's hate-speech code and threatened him with expulsion. Despite his explanation that the particular epithet he used was the translation of the Hebrew word *beheimah* (slang for "obnoxious person"), a host of scholars was assigned the task of locating the term's racial antecedents. Finding none, the university nonetheless determined that the use of the term "water buffalo" here was racially offensive.

At none of the formal disciplinary hearings against Jacobowitz did Penn allow him to have an attorney present. Finally it offered to drop proceedings against him if he would admit his guilt and allow himself to be "re-educated through a program for living in a diverse community environment." Jacobowitz refused, and hired a lawyer. Eventually, the university cleared him of all charges and paid his legal fees.[143]

What could Penn find wrong with another student's statement (written as part of a mandatory seminar on racism) about her "deep regard for the individual and desire to protect the freedoms of all members of society"? An administrator sent back the statement with the comment that the word "individual" was a red flag which may be considered by many to be racist.

Such verbal hypersensitivity is hardly unique to the Ivy League. An academic bureaucrat at the University of Colorado took offense at the phrases "a chink in his armor" and "a nip in the air." An anonymous professor on the Internet related a story about how, by mentioning in class that "there's more than one way to skin a cat," he'd offended one of his students who happened to own one.[144]

At DePaul University, a private Catholic school, the student newspaper ran an allegedly racist article about a fight at a black fraternity. Politically-correct student activists shredded 3000 copies of the newspaper and took over its offices. The university president of the responded by shutting down the paper for two weeks, providing tutors for the protesters, and appointing an outside consulting firm to monitor future articles involving minorities.[145]

A white professor at the predominantly black Florida A&M University was taken to task for saying this to his class:

> What I want you to be aware of is that in this day and age, a person ... who doesn't take advantage of the opportunities that are there, or who doesn't make opportunities ... may be guilty of what some would call 'a nigger mentality'—the sort of thinking that can keep us all on the back of the bus forever.

Several students contended that the remark was "derogatory," "unethical," and "inappropriate." Although the professor apologized, he was nevertheless suspended for two weeks without pay.[146]

Similarly, the University of Arizona has a "Diversity Action Plan" which deals with discrimination against students because of their "age, color, ethnicity, gender, national origin, physical and mental ability, race, religion, sexual orientation, Vietnam-era veteran status, socio-economic background or individual style." In response to a telephone inquiry, a "diversity specialist" stated that "individual style" would include "nerds and people who dress differently" because the school "didn't want to leave anybody out."[147]

At Harvard University, a new conduct code prohibits "unwelcome" speech whose "effect" might create an "offensive working or educational environment." Even before the code was adopted, two white medical students were formally chastised for having celebrated Halloween by painting their faces black and dressing as Anita Hill and Clarence Thomas. Their punishment: to draft and submit a syllabus and bibliography on medicine in a multi-ethnic society.[148]

A similar incident happened at the University of California at Santa Cruz, which was planning a dinner featuring Asian food. An Asian staff member noticed that the date for the dinner coincided with Pearl Harbor Day. Her suggestion that the menu be changed and the date postponed was adopted. Students then staged demonstrations and wrote letters claiming the administration was racially insensitive, grouping all Asians together and thereby implicitly blaming them for the actions of their distant ancestors. There were several resignations, and lawsuits were filed on both sides.[149]

In each of the above cases, had the distinction been made clearly between offensive speech and conduct—protecting the former, prosecuting the latter—the legal entanglements would have been significantly diminished and, moreover, the goals of sensitivity and inclusiveness may have well been achieved to a greater degree.

Campus Codes and the Constitution: When Political Correctness Meets the Law

Courts ought not to enter this political thicket. —FELIX FRANKFURTER[150]

The most radical PC advocates disdain the First Amendment as "the first refuge of scoundrels," its foundations "built on sand."[151] Perhaps that is why most speech codes pay little heed to established jurisprudence. Though many of them promulgated during the current PC wave have never been tested in court and continue to be broadly implemented— some to the great detriment of professional careers and reputations—others have already been struck down as being unconstitutionally broad or vague in prohibiting speech that would otherwise be protected, or too arbitrary in the manner in which punishments are meted out.[152]

Even a narrowly-drawn, specifically-tailored speech code may be deemed unconstitutional because of its content-based discrimination. In *R.A.V. v. City of St. Paul,* a city ordinance was found wanting because it punished the placing of a "symbol, object, appellation, characterization or graffiti ... which one knows or has reasonable grounds to know arouses anger, alarm or resentment in others on the basis of race, color, creed, religion or gender."[153]

Understanding that content-based regulations are presumptively invalid under the First Amendment, the city of St. Paul had sought to save its ordinance by limiting its application only to those expressions which constitute fighting words, within the meaning of *Chaplinsky v. New Hampshire.*[154] The Court nonetheless held that even fighting words cannot be regulated on the basis of their content.[155]

Thus, any speech code that attempts to restrict speech based on its content is likely to be unconstitutional.

Most states have enacted laws that prohibit harassment based on race, color, religious beliefs, or national origin. Many have statutes specifically aimed at sexual harassment.[156] Such legislation may be distinguished from hate-crime measures, which punish conduct related to bias.[157] Few people, however, are likely to be charged with violating a hate-crimes statute as a result of their politically incorrect speech. Everyday citizens are more prone to encounter the effects of PC on the job, either in the form of universal sensitivity training or a particular hostile-environment claim.[158]

This training can begin very early in one's education. At

least two Maryland schools require children to run for student elections on "multicultural slates"—a practice that, as one nay-saying school board member has pointed out, means class officers are being chosen by classmates on the basis of "what [they] are rather than who [they] are."[159]

It is hard to say exactly how many colleges and universities have enacted speech and conduct codes, but the number appears still to be growing. Practically all of the codes seek to enforce civility by regulating speech. None of them, however, has yet to pass Constitutional muster.

The most notable university codes to be overturned to date have been those at the Universities of Michigan, Wisconsin, and Stanford. In 1989, a federal judge struck down the Michigan code as an unconstitutional restriction on free speech. Among other complaints was one from a graduate student in bio-psychology who said he feared the rules would prevent him from discussing controversial theories abut biological differences among the sexes and races. Even if the speech exceeds all the proper bounds of moderation, said the court, "the consolation must be that the evil likely to spring from the violent discussion will probably be less, and its correction by pubic sentiment more speedy, than if the terrors of the law were brought to bear to prevent the discussion."

In 1991, the University of Wisconsin's speech code was declared unconstitutionally vague and overbroad. The university, which had been one of the first to ban racial and sexual slurs on campus, redrew its code more narrowly, then dropped it entirely in 1992.

Perhaps the most surprising code to fail has been Stanford's. Crafted carefully to avoid any chilling effect on the debate of sensitive topics by forbidding only "fighting words" linked to sex and race, it was nevertheless found wanting. Said the judge simply: "Stanford cannot proscribe speech that merely hurts the feelings of those who hear it."[160]

Many of the ideas the universities condemn may in fact be false and offensive, but it is not the place of the Academy to determine all false and offensive ideas. Most speech codes are essentially subjective. For example, they would not prohibit condemnation of the United States as an oppressor nation, or of capitalism as a form of exploitation, or invectives directed against students and professors seen as agents, apologists, or running dogs of the establishment. But all of them would likely be interpreted to permit burning the American flag, even if it might be acutely offensive to veterans or families of soldiers killed in battle.[161]

The most heated topic of debate may well be the freedom to debate heated topics—even though universities should be places where debate thrives in a raucous, freewheeling and at-times impolite climate. But that purpose sometimes flies in the face of the desire to preserve a tolerant, respectful community. The battle is about where to draw the line.

All too often, the First Amendment's guarantee of free speech is either ignored in the line-drawing or forgotten altogether.

Codes have been used to silence students and teachers with views that lean toward the political right—including religion professors for citing Biblical language about women and homosexuals; English professors for quoting and explaining raunchy passages from Chaucer and Shakespeare; psychology and sociology professors for introducing controversial theories about race and sexuality into course work; and conservative journalists for expressing viewpoints critical of minority groups.

At Yale, after the student-edited conservative weekly *Light and Truth* urged freshmen to skip mandatory sex-education program, dorm advisors confiscated 750 copies of the paper—and were not reprimanded for doing so.

A syllabus for a course in speech communication at the University of Maine warned, "Any language that may be deemed sexist, racist or homophobic, or may be found offensive by any minority group, is prohibited. Use of such language can result in immediate failure of that paper and possible future action." At Colby College (also in Maine), the speech code punishes "any hostile or intimidating remarks, spoken or written (including jokes), or physical gestures directed at a person because of their [sic] race, color, sex, sexual orientation, religion, national or ethnic origin, or disability."

Mount Holyoke's code punishes "unwelcome slurs, jokes, graphic or written materials."❀

> ❀On rare occasions codes are used to protect men. At Montana State University, a portion of the campus speech code prohibiting "sexual intimidation" in the classroom was put to novel use by a male nursinig student. After twice failing a course, he brought charges against the woman head of the nursing department. She had not been his instructor, but had pubicly referred to the male sexual organ as "the worthless male appendage" and had opined that men were most useful as "sperm donors." Making reference to its code, the school agreed to expunge the student's failing grades.[162]

One of the more interesting arguments in support of campus speech codes is that the Supreme Court's landmark decision in Brown v. Board of Education[163] should be read as having gone well beyond simply ordering schools to integrate, but in fact as a command to dismantle "the systematic group defamation of segregation" by way of guaranteeing equal access to education.[164] Today, the argument goes, recurring acts of hate on campus are reminiscent of the pre-*Brown* era and threaten the promise of equality for all.

While the immediate goal of *Brown* may have been to acknowledge that segregated schools were inherently unequal, the Supreme Court left undefined the exact dimensions of its enunciated principle of equal access to education. Is it somehow conceivable that the Court also "mandated the creation of an atmosphere of diversity, participation, and fulfillment of career aspirations beyond the mere ability to enroll in the institutions of learning?"[165]

Such a creative reading of *Brown* is said to address "the more central issue" of an individual's right to equal opportunity in education.[166] The PC debate is thus re-framed as one between two equally impressive constitutional doctrines: Free Speech versus Equal Protection. From this perspective, the argument concludes, the best way to constitutionally protect such competing interests is to balance them.[167] While this kind of analytical approach may be intellectually appealing, it also has serious shortcomings. First, the Supreme Court found only government-sponsored programs to be unconstitutional; it neither required nor authorized the regulation of private conduct.[168] Even if one accepts the argument that Congress can regulate private discriminatory conduct under the Commerce Clause, there is little authority to support the proposition that private discriminatory speech can be controlled under the First Amendment.[169]

Throwing equal protection into the free-speech fire only

creates more smoke. Censoring speech—even that which is outrageous or offensive—is contrary to the underlying principle of equal protection. After all, "every individual is presumptively entitled to be treated by the organized society as a respected, responsible, and participating member."[170] Why should the acceptable topics of discussion be defined by those who deem themselves politically correct? Speech codes enable people to restrict speech when it serves their own agendas. They do just the opposite of what educators should be doing—namely, to address the problem of inequality by diminishing the pressures that political correctness has created. One way to accomplish this is by *increasing* speech on campus, not limiting it.[171]

Even if one were to assume, for the sake of argument, that speech codes could be constitutional, they are undesirable for a number of other reasons. One is that such rules seek only to prevent the results of abusive speech, not the underlying cause. Students come to college with prejudices, fears, doubts, and misconceptions. If they spend four years under repressive regulations, although they might dutifully obey the rules, offend no one, and enjoy politically correct acceptance, they leave with their prejudices, fears, doubts, and misconceptions firmly intact."[172]

In fact, speech codes may exacerbate the very tensions they seek to alleviate. Censorship often makes the banned expressions more attractive. This can lead to greater harm, not less.[173] Even if they could offer temporary relief from racism, sexism, and prejudice, speech codes do not address the root problems.

Similarly, speech codes impede the process of learning. Their coercive restriction of unpopular viewpoints is inconsistent with the idea of a college education, and their concurrent limitation of academic freedom is much too high a price to pay for whatever short-term gains may be obtained through arbitrary codes.[174]

Most important, however, is that there are other ways for colleges and universities to combat the problem of hateful and bigoted speech that do not interfere with students' or faculty members' Constitutionally-protected rights. All educational institutions, both public and private, for that matter, should teach civility and tolerance. All should lead by example. That too few do may be a sign of the times, but an indication as well to wake up and smell the politically-correct coffee. Some of it is stale, much of it unconstitutional.

Sex under Title Seven

Title Seven (VII) of the Civil Rights Act of 1964 made it an unlawful employment practice to "discriminate against any individual with respect to his compensation, terms, conditions, or privileges of employment, because of such individual's race, color, religion, sex or national origin."[175] Although its legislative history indicates that gender was added "in a failed parliamentary maneuver aimed at defeating the entire bill," Title VII has been interpreted in such a way that eliminating gender discrimination on the job is viewed as a compelling government interest.[176]

Two theories of recovery are available under Title VII: for harassment that is *quid pro quo*—the demand of a sexual favor in return for something like promotion—and for that which creates a "hostile environment." It is generally agreed that *quid pro quo* harassment, although speech-related, was never protected by the First Amendment.[177] Recovery under the theory of hostile environment, however, is much more Constitutionally problematic.

The guidelines of the Equal Employment Opportunity Commission (EEOC) concerning implementation of Title VII provide that "unwelcome sexual advances, requests for sexual favors, and *other verbal or physical conduct of a sexual nature* constitute harassment when . . . such conduct has the purpose or effect of unreasonably interfering with an individual's work performance *or creating an intimidating, hostile, or offensive working environment.*"[178]

What is "verbal conduct of a sexual nature"? What if an overly sensitive person has been offended by an unintentionally offensive speaker? Who is to decide what is offensive, and what is a hostile environment? According to the guidelines, even if the *effect* of the speech in question is an interference with an individual's work performance, a federal action can be brought.

A hostile environment can thus be generated by classroom discussion of a controversial subject, the assignment of an "offensive" text, or use of "off-color" language or hypotheticals. Although punishment of such purely verbal activity appears to run directly afoul of the First Amendment, there have been few cases testing its constitutionality.

In fact, the EEOC guidelines have been used by students, administrators, and faculty on many campuses to establish harassment surveillance and enforcement bureaucracies and to enforce campus speech and conduct codes. Under the watchful gaze of "abuse awareness counselors," the accused are routinely denied due process—that is, the right to counsel, to confront accusers, and to present exculpatory evidence. Anti-harassment tribunals mete out stiff penalties on the basis of little or no investigation.[179]

Those who support the hostile-environment concept argue that sexist speech in the workplace amounts to equality-depriving conduct. Epithets and innuendo are said to have meaning beyond dictionary definitions; their use conjures up a painful historical context of powerlessness, subjugation, and the lack of legal and social identity, except as prostitutes or as men's chattel. Their true power lies in their ability to evoke the present-day realities of rape, incest, and domestic violence. Such utterances are often perceived as threats; women are forever uncertain whether they will escalate into more harassing words or a physical assault.[180]

Although even among women this view is far from universal, the risk of liability under Title VII has become substantially greater.✿

> ✿ "I may not be an expert on sexual stereotyping," says one of my research assistants, "but as a woman I feel compelled to respond to these assumptions. When someone says something to me that is sexually offensive—by this I mean a comment that criticizes me merely because of the fact that I am a woman—I do not automatically associate the person's comment with 'an entire history of subjugation.' Nor do I associate sexist comments with rape, incest, and domestic violence. These are not part of every woman's present-day realities. When confronted with sexually offensive speech, I do not think that that person perceives me as a prostitute, but that that person is ignorant. Those who assume that all women take sexually harassing words as a threat do themselves a disservice."

In *Meritor Savings Bank v. Vinson*, the Supreme Court treated the EEOC guidelines (which give employees the right to "work in an environment free from discriminatory intimidation, ridicule, and insult") as authoritative.[181] Since *Meritor*, hostile-work-environment claims have become one of the fastest-growing fields of employment discrimination law.[182]

This is especially true in the area of academic freedom. There are, to be sure, types of verbal expression that amount to harassing conduct—such as sustained and calculated group defamation—and that kind of behavior may well create an actionable hostile environment.[183] But the guidelines, especially as enforced by the Office for Civil Rights (an investigatory agency under the Department of Education), sweep much more broadly.

The defendant in *Meritor*, however, did not present a First-Amendment defense, and the Supreme Court did not rule on the free-speech issue. Indeed Title VII has not yet faced a serious constitutional challenge. As the Ninth Circuit has noted, "Title VII ... has for over a decade restricted harassing speech in the workplace, but ... [b]ecause First Amendment defenses were rarely raised, harassment law evolved with little concern for free speech."[184]

Recent Supreme Court decisions have likewise found no First-Amendment problems in holding employers vicariously or strictly liable for the sexual harassment of their employees by supervisory personnel.[185]

The first and only reported case dealing with the conflict between the First Amendment and Title VII was *Robinson v. Jacksonville Shipyards, Inc.* The court concluded that there was no First Amendment problem because (a) the employer was not expressing itself through language used by its employees; (b) speech creating a hostile environment is actually conduct similar to speech which constitutes a crime; (c) limitation of such discriminatory speech is nothing more than a constitutional regulation based on time, place, and manner; (d) workers are part of a captive audience that should be protected from offensive language; and (e) the speech in question must be weighed against the government's interest in cleansing the workplace of impediments to the women's equality.

Each of these arguments, however, is flawed: (a) employees are usually within the scope and course of their employment when making offensive comments, and even if they were not, both employer and employee have free-speech rights; (b) a speech crime (e.g., blackmail) is criminal not solely because of its content but because of its unlawful effect (e.g., extortion); (c) time, place, and manner restrictions are valid only if they are neutral as to the content of the speech; (d) Supreme Court jurisprudence to date has applied the captive-audience theory only to the home, and not to the workplace (where, to the contrary, free-speech rights have been repeatedly recognized); and (e) a proper balancing argument would require that the state's interests be weighed against *all* expression suppressed by the law in question—not just speech subjectively deemed offensive.[186]

Application of Title VII to speech-based hostile-environment claims is the first icy patch on the slippery slope to repression of unpopular ideas. Indeed misuse of the federal law has already occurred. In 1990, for example, an employee won a religious-harassment suit against his (private) employer based on the religious content of the company's newsletter and the Biblical verses printed on its paychecks.

How and where should the line be drawn between protected "political" speech and offensive "sexist" remarks? All speech should be considered political unless it is specifically targeted at an individual or group with the intention to harass, or it amounts in fact to harassing conduct (such as a pattern of phone calls in the middle of the night).

But the Office of Civil Rights is highly reflective of the current university environment (or vice versa). Its enforcement of sexual-harassment guidelines poses a powerful and potentially lethal threat to the traditional American idea that individual rights and responsibilities are more important than group insults. Many who would never engage in racial or sexual harassment are being forced to defend themselves against frivolous or vengeful claims.[187] Even if formal charges under Title VII are never brought, campus PC encourages other constitutionally questionable procedures.[188] (OCR attorneys do not rule out the possibility of an investigation based on the assignment of Huckleberry Finn or a classroom discussion of affirmative action.)[189]

The Academy has thus become a decidedly unwelcome nesting place for those with different points of view. As those with highly sensitive PC antennae, particularly radical feminists, have assumed greater degrees of power, the standards describing sexual harassment have become ever more vague. The conflict between perceived offensive conduct and free speech is often much sharper on campus than in the ordinary employment context. Academic freedom is clearly at risk.[190]

The rules regarding harassment deter not only genuine misconduct but also harmless (and even desirable) speech, which in higher education is central both to the purpose of the institution and to the employee's profession and performance. Faced with legal uncertainty, many professors will avoid any speech that might be remotely interpreted as creating a hostile environment. The chilling effect can be widespread. My aforementioned friend, pilloried for suggesting that a lesbian candidate for the faculty at a small women's college "might not be a good role model," is still suffering from that comment a decade after it was made. At the University of Michigan, a student was sanctioned for saying in a social work research class that "homosexuality was a disease that could be psychologically treated." (The issue, of course, is less the accuracy of the statement than that its utterance should be punishable.)[191]

On the other hand, an English professor was fired for wearing a "Support Gay Rights" button. And an instructor at Bethel College in Minnesota was dismissed for expressing his belief that all sexual relationships, including homosexual ones, required commitment.. The Baptist General Conference passed a resolution that "those who believe that homosexual behavior is a biblically acceptable lifestyle are not qualified to serve in the leadership of the conference or to teach in its education institutions." The University of Iowa requires professors "to warn students about any materials which include explicit representations of human sexual acts that could reasonably be expected to be offensive."✿

> ✿An English professor at San Bernardino Valley College assigned his students to write a paper defining pornography; a female student requested an alternative assignment and was refused. The college supported the student. The professor sued. The court ruled that a state college can limit the classroom speech of its faculty in order to prevent the creation of a hostile, sexually discriminating environment.

Such a regulation might be reasonable enough, but in today's academic environment even staring at a stranger has been cited by some radical feminists as "a well-established cultural taboo."[192]

Once again, the clear line to be drawn between academic freedom and actionable harassment is the same as that between speech and conduct.

Affirmative Action Programs

Affirmative action programs, though widely accepted and applied as a means for achieving equality of educational opportunity, have fallen into disfavor even among liberal constitutional scholars—but such ideas die hard in an atmosphere suffused by political correctness.[193]

Perhaps President John F. Kennedy's most noteworthy executive order required employers who were government contractors to "take affirmative action to ensure that the applicants are employed, and that employees are treated during employment without regard to race, creed, color, or national origin." But that is virtually the antithesis of what "affirmative action" has come to mean today.

In their recent book *The Shape of the River,* Derek Bok and William Bowen (former presidents of Harvard and Princeton) assert that "the data" have shown preferential treatment for blacks and Hispanics in college admissions to be a great success. But that conclusion is strongly refuted by Stephan and Abigail Thernstrom, coauthors of *America in Black and White,* who regard the Bok/Bowen treatise as elitists' thumbing their noses at the public majority.[194]

Others feel it is no coincidence that black excellence, even superiority, is so visible in those areas where we live by high expectations and enforced consequences—sports, music, entertainment, literature—and that the "inclusion" we most need now is in the realm of intellectual respect, which can be gained through only by way of merit."[195]

Lino Graglia, a University of Texas law professor, was widely condemned for speculating that the gap in academic achievement between Blacks and Hispanics, and between Whites and Asians, might be attributable to cultural differences in attitudes toward education. "Blacks and Mexican-Americans are not academically competitive with whites in selective institutions. It is the result primarily of cultural effects." The College Board, however, a longtime supporter of race-based preferences, seems to agree: its report concluded that improving educational outcomes among black and Hispanic children requires a dramatic shift away from group-preference policies, which cover up real disparities, to promoting individual achievement and development.[196]

Harvard philosophy professor Harvey Mansfield is an outspoken critic of affirmative action, which he characterizes as "a bad idea wrapped up in one great mistake, self-esteem." He describes the late 1960's as a time of catastrophe for Harvard and the nation, when everything became "directed toward the goal of social justice rather than truth and learning." These days, he says, "Harvard is very trendy. It does not want to be isolated, aloof in an ivory tower. That's a big mistake we're making. We should be much further from political and social questions. The purpose of the university is not to produce solutions for these questions but to think and raise questions and to challenge." He observes the paradox that the counterculture of the late 1960's became the establishment culture of Harvard—"even though many of them are very liberal or very far to the left and oppose the idea of establishment."

Many of Mansfield's colleagues, of course, argue that all he seeks to save is "a tradition of patriarchy and white male dominance."[197]

Taboo or Not Taboo?
PC and the Politics of Teaching

I have always been of the mind that in a democracy manners are the only effective weapons against the bowie-knife.
—J.R. LOWELL

Civility costs nothing.—PROVERB

Political Correctness has served to blur significantly the lines between Left and Right, but some generalizations remain apt. Liberals still advocate inclusiveness: the gates of opportunity in the socio-economic framework should be opened to all who choose to enter, regardless of whether those who would seize the opportunity have the skill to master the course. No one should feel excluded or unwanted.[198]

Conservatives, on the other hand, seek the order of the status quo—a strict hierarchy in which every member has a place, depending on individual qualifications. The ability to perform is more important than the desire to participate. Those unable to unlock the gates of opportunity should not have to have them opened by others. In this view, open-admissions policies and affirmative-action programs make college accessible to students, especially blacks and minorities, who would otherwise not meet the regular requirements.[199]

At their extremes neither side necessarily speaks for the great numbers of people who seldom take to the courts, the airwaves, or the op-ed pages.

Mainstream women may be the most under-represented. "I feel more able to deal with old goats chasing me around the desk," says novelist Erica Jong, "than with the ideology commandoes who want to scrutinize my writing to make sure I never say a non-P.C. thing." Besides radical feminists, so too have deconstructionists, critical race theorists, and critical legal studies "story-tellers" alienated large numbers of their colleagues in the Academy. Alienation, in fact, appear to be their *mission.* "Everybody should get anti-racist, anti-sexist, anti-heterosexist training," says one.[200] "The strategy I am proposing," says another, "involves fighting with your elders and betters—sassing them, maybe; undermining them, maybe; hurting their feelings, certainly."[201]

And still another:

> We can disrupt faculty meetings with various acts of civil or, preferably, uncivil disobedience. We can engage in subversion by memorandum. The possibilities are limited only by the available concepts of the absurd. Our challenge is to put ourselves on the line, to engage in acts of 'macho self-immolation,' to become moral terrorists, to 'whack-off' in faculty meetings, to construct a praxis which is meaningful, public, and dangerous.[202]

Though few laymen read academic journals, and much of the deconstructionist sniping is done in the relatively harmless wasteland that sometimes passes for scholarship,[203] the radical theories are often reflected in the curriculum, in the conservative PC campaigns conducted in the mass media—and ultimately in the regulatory actions of the government.

After a survey found that many Bowling Green State University students felt classes were highly politicized by faculty members on the far left, sociology professor Richard Zeller proposed a course on "Political Correctness." His book list included Dinesh D'Souza's *Illiberal Education,* Richard Herrnstein and Charles Murray's *The Bell Curve,* and

Christina Hoff Summers' *Who Stole Feminism?* The proposal was turned down flat by the departments of sociology, American studies, ethnic studies, and psychology—even though Zeller said he doesn't agree with all those writers have to say and expressed commitment to teaching about PC in an even-handed way.[204]

Similarly, students were excluded from a conference at Columbia University entitled "A Place at the Table: Conservative Ideas in Higher Education." Thus what the speakers had to say was effectively silenced—which would seem to fly in the face of the university's published policy: "Columbia University prides itself on being a community committed to free and open discourse and to tolerance of differing views."[205]

Political considerations increasingly affect curricular decisions. In 1993, the University of Oklahoma School of Law sought to establish an endowed chair in honor of Anita Hill for the study of sexual harassment and other women's issues. Although funds for the chair were subsequently provided by the university's board of regents, both the law school's dean and the university's president resigned because their defense of the project offended important donors. ❀ Similarly, Cuban-American legislators threatened funding to the University of Florida after two professors from the University of Havana were invited to a symposium on Caribbean economics.[206]

> ❀Conservative state legislators likened the position to the "Jeffrey Dahmer Chair in the School of Cooking" and the "Adolph Hitler Chair for Creative Population Control."

Other courses as well are approved, taught, and/or evaluated on political grounds. For example, most introductory psychology courses deal with intelligence and mental abilities. An honest treatment of this material should suggest that intelligence is determined by both environmental and genetic factors—that different ethnic and racial groups score differently on standardized tests—and should then analyze the factors that contribute to this empirical data. But faculty members who teach objectively from such a perspective may find their academic careers in serious jeopardy.

At the University of British Columbia, for example, student evaluation forms ask whether the instructor used materials "that were demeaning to members of certain racial or cultural groups" or to women or men. Especially in view of the fact that many students might find it difficult to separate the scientific evidence from the instructor's own opinions, many faculty members (particularly those seeking tenure or promotion) might well avoid teaching about certain sensitive issues for fear that their politically unpopular conclusions will lead some students to label them as sexist or racist.

Media and the Politics of Profit

Political correctness may be woven into the fabric of the current university motif, but it is decidedly on the defensive in the pop culture reflected by the media—who are likely motivated less by ideology than by the lure of profit.[207]

Particularly noticeable has been the enlistment of the media by the Conservative Right. Consider, for example, how Swarthmore College's "rape policy" was handled by *U.S. News and World Report.* In 1990, the magazine published an article declaring that the college, "driven by feminist ideology," had expanded the definition of date rape to include "inappropriate innuendo."[208] In fact the source of that phrase was an out-of-

date, student-authored discussion guide which suggested topics for date-rape prevention workshops. It was never a reflection of official school policy. Nevertheless, *U.S. News* printed
the piece about innuendo, unadorned by accuracy. No correction or apology was ever offered, nor was a letter of clarifica-
tion ever published.[209] To the contrary, the magazine stood by
as its "inappropriate innuendo" story was picked up by the
Washington Times, Reason, Playboy, New York Magazine, and
Time.[210]

PC-bashing has proven as contagious as it is fun and
popular. Witness the phenomenon of Rush Limbaugh, who
has a three-hour talk radio show with thirteen-million listen-
ers, and whose book, *The Way Things Ought To Be,* was a massive
best-seller. As a British commentator observed, "His capacity
to outrage is mesmerizing. He's the virtuoso of bile, senior
wrangler of twisted prejudice, but he's also discovered that hatred
delivered with humour is insidiously disarming."[211] Limbaugh
attributes his success to the fact that he conveys "a unique conservative message." Still, he is candid enough to concede that
he is not out to save America, only to profit from it.[212]

The polemical power of conservative PC-bashing is
dependent upon confusing its meaning. In the media, Liberal
notions about race, gender and power are characterized as official compulsion and censorship, while Conservative ideology
is dressed up in the noble rhetoric of the First Amendment.
Thus any new idea, however moderately progressive it may be,
is likely to be condemned as "politically correct" and therefore
suspect.[213]

Although the media's motivation for airing Conservative,
PC-bashing talk shows may be mostly a matter of ratings, the
reason for right-wing criticism is more subtle. On the surface,

conservatives often claim they are merely protecting free speech.[214] But it is not difficult to discern the political agendas lurking barely beneath the surface. The PC debate has become a fight for political power, between old enemies (or at least the loudest voices among Liberals and Conservatives) who have merely forged new weapons.[215]

Political correctness, when it is used as a synonym for social sensitivity and manners (as opposed to coerced agendas promulgated by particular interest groups) can be a positive force. On the other hand, self-righteousness unfettered by self-control is generally self-defeating. As Mark Twain so astutely put it: "Good breeding consists of concealing how much we think of ourselves and how little we think of other persons."

Conclusion

The bright students will not stand for political correctness.
—WILLIAM F. BUCKLEY

When all is said and done, listening carefully to *all* points of view is still the best path toward reason. Reaching that goal requires open-mindedness in the search for truth.

In most American universities today, however, that process is a lost art. Career-minded administrators and intimidated faculty are less likely to defend the principles of liberty, equal justice under law, and individual dignity than they are to appease self-appointed arbiters of political correctness pushing radical changes in the curriculum. Neither indifferent trustees, nor unknowing parents seeking a return on their investments, nor alumni living in the past are able to slow the transformation taking place in the Ivory Tower.

It is often the students themselves who are the first to see the academic forest for the trees—the first to recognize that coerced scholarship is counter-productive, that radical feminist professors distort the meaning of liberal education, and that speech and conduct codes will not end campus racism and may in fact exacerbate the very tensions they seek to alleviate.[1] But even students, molded as they are by their mentors, are swept up by trends. Unfortunately, those astute enough to comprehend the negative implications of the new academic orders are in a distinct minority.

This book is not about why Johnny (and Jane) can't read, but about why they can't read Shakespeare or the history of western civilization. It is about why they are both subjected to a radically changing curriculum—taught that, because Johnny has oppressed Jane throughout the ages, he must firmly and finally be put in his place, as must the patriarchal system that has so wrongfully perpetuated western biases. It is about why they show increasingly less respect for traditional-minded professors, who in turn have come to tremble before their increasingly strident colleagues pressing political causes and exclusionary courses.

The foregoing pages have thus sought to explore the manifold excesses in the modern Ivory Tower, moving from one in representative particular (legal scholarship, specifically the relationship between coerced and ever-proliferating law-review articles and tenure) to another more generally pervasive (radical feminism, and its impact on modern faculties), and culminating in an examination of the most cosmic contemporary intemperance (political correctness, and its corrosive effects on the entire academic enterprise).

Understanding the dimensions of the problems should be the first step toward solving them. And while such solutions are not always easy, there are some hopeful signs of a return to normalcy based on reason and common sense. The pendulum appears to swing slower among educators, but an increasing number of them are beginning to articulate a backlash. More now feel that coercive restriction of unpopular viewpoints is inconsistent with the idea of a university education, and that limitation of academic freedom is much too high a price to pay for whatever short-term gains to be obtained through arbitrary codes that enforce superficial civility.

The non-academic world has been slow to recognize that there are other ways for universities to combat the problem of hateful and bigoted speech—ways that do not interfere with students' Constitutionally protected rights of expression. All public and private educational institutions should teach civility and tolerance, and lead by example. Equally important (if not more so) is the need to understand the extent to which western culture is being systematically suppressed—history being rewritten, traditional curricula arbitrarily abandoned, classic subject matter declared taboo.

Classical art or music or literature should not be discouraged simply because there were few great black or women artists or composers or novelists—although legitimate questions can be addressed, such as why there were so few, what criteria are used to decide greatness, and who determines the criteria.[2]

So what can be done to halt the deterioration of the traditional liberal-arts curriculum, or to reverse it?

It is too easy to place fault solely on faculty. Professors reflect social values as much as they create them. Their failures are ours, as much as their successes. The more that the literate public hears about what is happening on campus, the sooner the literary radicals will retreat.✸ Fortunately, there is no conflict between the sound study of humanities and what is good for society in general and women and minorities in particular. But curricula based almost solely on race/gender/class perspectives are devoid of historical context, and channel students' energies more toward resentment than constructive reform.[3]

> ✸The beneficial aspects of adverse publicity, for example, can be seen clearly in the negative reaction to Bowling Green State University's refusal to allow a tenured professor to teach a course on political correctness

Both academic freedom and the rights of individuals have been violated by misguided efforts to combat sexual and racial harassment. Not surprisingly, a chill has descended on academic discussions of sensitive but legitimate topics. Worse, procedures have been widely adopted that violate the canons of due process. The brightest line to be drawn is between speech and conduct. The First Amendment and its jurisprudence have been proven over a long period of time to be the best guarantee of individual liberty. But offensive speech that clearly becomes conduct—a pattern of verbal harassment, for example, over an extended period of time—should be forcefully redressed.

No campus speech code promulgated to date has come close to meeting First Amendment requirements. Some that have been tested in court and found wanting (such as those at the Universities of Pennsylvania and Wisconsin) have been abandoned altogether. Others have been dropped without formal challenge. Still others (like those at Harvard and Stanford) are now so tempered with constitutional guarantees that they are little more than redundant statements of suggested civility and required deference to free speech.

Perhaps the best balance of these competing tensions, at least as they exist on university campuses, is the National Association of Scholars' policy on academic freedom. Seeking "reasoned scholarship in a free society," the NAS guidelines call for precise definitions. Sexual harassment, for example, should be confined to "individual behavior that is *manifestly* sexual and that *clearly* violates the rights of others." There should also be a reasonable statute of limitations on bringing sexual-harassment charges; separation of the offices of investigator, prosecutor, judge, and jury; observation of the established requirements for due process; assurance that the accused has the opportunity to make an adequate defense; punishment of those who knowingly lodge false accusations; and forceful action against proven harassers, by dismissal if necessary.[4]

Discrimination and harassment are certainly too abundant in American society, just as are ignorance and prejudice. But much of what is being done to combat those evils in the name of Political Correctness is fueled by a new culture of victimization—nurtured by the desire of special-interest groups for more political power.

The hypersensitivities they encourage are so delicately calibrated that racism can be detected in the inflection of a voice, sexism in a classroom's seating pattern, or patriarchal oppression in a Shakespearean sonnet.[5]

Such groups may be spurred by a strong inclination to atone for a variety of perceived wrongs, both past and present. They fervently wish to see the formerly powerless come to force amends from the formerly powerful. But instead of using this new opportunity for the greater good of all, those who should be advocates of civility have become zealots of PC, wielding censorship, intimidation, and brainwashing as battle-axes in ideological warfare. Instead of promoting tolerance of different opinions through education and good example, they seek merely to ensure that all ways of thinking pay homage to their own.

Too often, the call for "sensitivity" is in truth the pursuit of power, pure and simple—the high-minded rhetoric little more than camouflage. The lesson for all of us, perhaps, is to listen more carefully before reacting to the extremes on both right and left, if for no other reason than to add a healthy balance of common sense to the debate.[6]

In the long run, tolerating offensive speech should be a small price to pay to ensure the vital ideals of academic freedom and liberty of conscience. If the debate is about equality, the lesson for all of us, perhaps, is that allowing everyone to speak their minds—and teach their subject matter, using whatever words they want—assures a healthy measure of common sense in response.

If eternal vigilance is the price of freedom, then we must be especially alert that the trustees of the academic enterprise are forever honest in perpetuating the vigorous exchange of ideas, values, and convictions; that they be determined in their preservation of fairness, due process, and equality before the law; and that they are consistent and critical in their pursuit of truth. To raise standards, to strengthen respect for learning, to put radical political agendas in reasonable perspective, that quest must once again become the primary goal of higher education.

Then will the Ivory Tower cease in its trembling.

Then will its keepers regain their sense of noble mission.

Then will they and their disciples be truly free.

Notes

Introduction

[1] Kenneth Lasson, *On Letters & Law Reviews: A Jaded Rejoinder*, 24 CONN. L. REV. 201, 205 (1991).

[2] *See generally* Alan Kors and Harvey Silverglate, THE SHADOW UNIVERSITY: THE BETRAYAL OF LIBERTY ON AMERICA'S CAMPUSES (1998).

[3] The first quote was by James Bryant Conant, the second by Nathan Pusey. Carlin Romano, *The Troves of Academe*, THE NATION (6/12/00).

[4] This phenomenon was made abundantly clear in the 1960s. *See* Kevin Driscoll, *Literature In An Ivory Tower of Babel*, WASHINGTON TIMES, 11/9/97 at B6.

[5] Clifford Orwin, *All Quiet on the Post-Western Front?*, THE PUBLIC INTEREST, March 1996 at 3.

[6] *See* Diane Ravitch and Chester E. Finn, Jr., WHAT DO OUR 17-YEAR OLDS KNOW? A REPORT ON THE FIRST NATIONAL ASSESSMENT OF HISTORY AND LITERATURE (1987), and National Association of Scholars, *The Dissolution of General Education, 1914-1993*, at 43 (1996).

[7] *Literature Lost* (1997) at 228. *See also* Bradford Wilson, *NEH and the Death of Culture*, WASHINGTON TIMES, 11/28/97 at A23.

[8] *See* Victoria Stearns, *With Prices Unaffordable and Educational Quality Down, College Isn't What It Once Was*, BUFFALO NEWS, 5/21/97 at 2B, and Editorial, *OSU Should Start Using Teachers To Do Teaching*, COLUMBUS (OHIO) DISPATCH, 3.31.99 at 10A. *See also* Ernest Benjamin, *Declining Faculty Availability to Students Is the Problem—But Tenure Is Not the Explanation*, AMERICAN BEHAVIORAL SCIENTIST (February 1988).

[9] 103 HARVARD LAW REVIEW 926 (1990).

[10] 42 JOURNAL OF LEGAL EDUCATION 1 (1992).

[11] 63 TENNESSEE LAW REVIEW 689 (1996).

[12] For perhaps an excess of excesses, *see Lawyering Askew: Excesses in the Pursuit of Fees and Justice,* 74 BOSTON UNIVERSITY LAW REVIEW 301 (1994).

[13] The two letters excerpted in the text appeared in *Scholarship Admired: Responses to Professor Lasson,* 103 HARVARD LAW REVIEW 926 (1990). Mr. McGrath, who clerked for a Supreme Court justice after graduating from Columbia Law School, noted that "positionality" and "knowability" did not pass his WordPerfect 5.1 spell check. "And I do not know to which or whose end 'standpoint epistemology' refers," he added, "but it sounds great even if meaningless."

Mr. Kilgour added that I "might be amused to see" the draft of his letter. I was. Here it is:

> *Why should I continue my subscription to the* Review *when I seldom read it? After the headnotes and racy titles, my will weakens and eyes glaze over. At first I thought I was the problem. Maybe it was just age or perhaps the cocktail before dinner. On the other hand there were signs pointing to the possibility that the stuff was simply too murky to read. One such sign was that I had no better luck getting past the headnotes in the morning, head bright and clear. Another was that now and then I encountered an article I could actually read straight through, no skimming and no glazed eyes. So I checked back to see what made these articles readable when so many others were not. To my surprise, almost all the readable articles had appeared in those In Memoriam issues where you get old friends to write about their departed buddies. Admittedly this was not scholarship. On the other hand, most of the authors were scholars.*

> *This little bit of amateur research led to the question: how come scholars can write readable obituaries but can't write readable articles on matters of true substance? Maybe it is easy to write clear, concise prose about the death of a friend, but when it comes to a deep subject like the curvature of constitutional space, one doesn't want the reader to understand at first go; one expects the reader to work hard, and even to learn from physics.*

[14] Somewhat piqued, one of the women on our faculty wondered in print why I hadn't asked *her* to decipher what I found to be an impenetrable piece of feminist prose. See Odeana Neal, *The Making of a Law Teacher,* 6 BERKELEY WOMEN'S L.J. 129 (1990-91).

[15] 42 JOURNAL OF LEGAL EDUCATION 465 (1993).

[16] 142 SOLICITORS JOURNAL S38(2), December 11, 1998.

[17] *See* Tamar Jacoby, *Time to Outlaw Racial Slurs?*, NEWSWEEK, June 6, 1988 at 59.

[18] See Susan H. Williams and David C. Williams, *A Feminist Theory of Malebashing*, 4 MICH. J. GENDER & LAW 35 at (1996).

[19] As quoted by Jonathan Rauch, *In Defense of Prejudice: Why Incendiary Speech Must Be Protected*, HARPER'S MAGAZINE, May, 1995, at p.37.

[20] Survey by the Freedom Forum First Amendment Center, quoted in Bill Marvel & Barbara Kessler, *A Culture War: Political Correctness Provokes Backlash*, DALLAS MORNING NEWS, April 24, 1994, at p. 1A.

[21] Even the politically-correct OXFORD ENGLISH DICTIONARY finds it difficult to rid itself entirely of traditional standards, refusing to label "manhole" as *offens.* (offensive). See Mark Lawson, *The Word Is Out*, MANCHESTER GUARDIAN (July 5, 1995) at p. T2. See also HENRY BEARD AND CHRISTOPHER CERF, THE OFFICIAL POLITICALLY CORRECT DICTIONARY AND HANDBOOK (1992).

[22] Steve Kogan, *No Freedom but in Harness*, ACADEMIC QUESTIONS (Fall 1997) at 38.

[23] *Searching for Equality*, RITES: THE WOMEN'S CENTER PUBLICATION AT CHICO STATE UNIVERSITY, *quoted in* 12 ACADEMIC QUESTIONS 62 (Winter 1998-99).

[24] *See* Stanley Coren, *When Teaching Is Evaluated on Political Grounds*, ACADEMIC QUESTIONS (Summer 1993) at 73.

[25] To some, it seems odd that feminism should be included under the heading of multi-culturalism, in view of the fact that women do not have a distinctive culture—nor do they form a discrete minority, the effects of past discrimination against whom are inherited by subsequent generations. *See* Daniel Bonevac, *Manifestations of Illiberalism in Philosophy*, 12 ACADEMIC QUESTIONS 14 (Winter 1998-1999).

[26] Walter A. McDougall, *An Ideological Agenda for History*, ACADEMIC QUESTIONS at 30.

[27] Paul Gross and Norman Levitt, *The Natural Sciences: Trouble Ahead? Yes*, ACADEMIC QUESTIONS (Spring 1994) at 14-15 and 20. *See also* Sally Satel, *PC, M.D.: How Political Correctness is Corrupting Medicine*, Basic Books (2001).

[28] William Simon, *PC Has A Price*, 9 ACADEMIC QUESTIONS (Spring 1996) at 49.

[29]David Sacks and Peter Thiel, *Multiculturalism and the Decline of Stanford*, 8 ACADEMIC QUESTIONS (Fall 1995) at 58. For details on the course in black hair, see pages 131-132. Yale offers some fifty courses in homosexual studies. Jeff Jacoby, *On College Campuses, All Is Not Lost,* BOSTON GLOBE, May 27, 1997 at A15.

[30]*See* Dinesh D'Souza, *Illiberal Education: The Politics of Race and Sex on Campus* (Free Press, 1991). *See also* Daniel Bonevac, *Manifestations of Illiberalism in Philosophy*, 12 ACADEMIC QUESTIONS 14 (Winter 1998-1999).

[31]Paul A. Cantor, *A Welcome for Postcolonial Literature*, 12 ACADEMIC QUESTIONS 23 (Winter 1998-99).

[32]A variation of the language caught by the acute ear of Professor Stephen Kats, Trent University, Peterborough, Ontario, as quoted in the April 1998 issue of THE QUARTERLY REVIEW OF DOUBLESPEAK, published by the National Council of Teachers of English.

[33]Cynthia G. Bowman, *Street Harassment and the Informal Ghettoization of Women*, 106 HARVARD L.REV. 517 (1993). *See also* Michael S. Greve, *Do "Hostile Environment" Charges Chill Academic Freedom?*, ABA JOURNAL, Feb, 1994 at 40.

[34]Transcript #99051805-j04, *ABC World News Tonight with Peter Jennings*, May 18, 1999. *See also* Carlin Romano, *The Troves of Academe*, THE NATION (6/12/00).

[35]At the University of South Carolina, a graduate seminar in women's studies required students to adhere to a set of discussion guidelines that asked them to "acknowledge that racism, classism, sexism, heterosexism, and other institutionalized forms of oppression exist." At the University of California/Berkeley, a course description for "The Politics and Poetics of Palestinian Resistance" encouraged "conservative thinkers ... to seek other sections." At Arizona State University, a course on Navajo history restricted enrollment to American Indian students." Thomas Bartlett, *Guidelines for Discussion, or Thought Control?*, CHRONICLE OF HIGHER EDUCATION, 9/27/02.

[36]For more recent instances of academic excesses, *see generally* notices published by the Foundation for Individual Rights in Education (F.I.R.E.) at http://www.thefire.org; the American Council of Trustees and Alumni at info@goacta.org; and the National Association of Scholars at nas@nas.org.

I

Scholarship Amok

[1]The saying is attributed to Solomon by the Talmudic scholar Yisroel Salanter (1810-1883) in KOHELES/ECCLESIASTES 202 (Artscroll Tanach Series ed. 1976). *See also Ecclesiastes* 12:12 ("The making of many books is without limit.")

[2]N *See, e.g.* Editorial, *OSSU Should Start Using Teachers To Do Teaching*, COLUMBUS DISPATCH (3/31/99)(noting that undergrads are subjected to large classes taught by nonfaculty).

[3]"Even at liberal arts colleges that emphasize teaching, at least in their brochures, it is increasingly necessary to keep putting things in print. . . . At one time 'publish or perish' was the watchword at big research universities, but today it is the holy grail from Harvard to Podunk A & M." DENVER ROCKY MOUNTAIN NEWS, 12/24/97; Terence Monmaney, *Researchers Feel the Crunch from VA Shutdown*, LOS ANGELES TIMES (4/3/99)(describing the publish-or-perish world of international academic medicine).

[4]*See* John Elston, *The Case Against Legal Scholarship or, If the Professor Must Publish, Must the Profession Perish?*, 39 J. LEGAL EDUC. 343 (1989).

[5]Fred Rodell (1907-1980) in *Goodbye to Law Reviews*, 23 VA. L. REV. 38 (1936). *See also* Wright, *Goodbye to Fred Rodell*, 89 YALE L.J. 1455 (1980).

[6]INDEX TO LEGAL PERIODICALS (1937).

[7]CURRENT LAW INDEX (1988).

[8]Rodell, *Goodbye to Law Reviews—Revisited*, 48 VA.L.REV. 279 at 286.

[9]Rodell, *supra* note 5 at 45.

[10]*See* Symposium Edition, *Political Correctness in the 1990's and Beyond*, 23 NORTHERN KENTUCKY LAW REVIEW 472 (1996) and George Will, *Storm at the Faculty Club*, WASHINGTON POST, 4/20/97, C7. See also three articles in the February 1998 issue of AMERICAN BEHAVIORAL SCIENTIST: David Leslie, *Redefining Tenure*; Anne Rice and R. Eugene, *Making Tenure Viable: Listening to Early Career Faculty*; and Ernest Benjamin, *Declining Faculty Availability to Students Is the Problem—But Tenure Is Not the Explanation*.

[11] *One of the more recent is "term tenure" (e.g., 12 years) to junior faculty, ending upon promotion to full professor. A two-tier faculty system—tenured or tenure-track professors, and everybody else—is increasingly common.*

[12] *See* Michael Barbaro, *Yale U. Authors Find Academic Audience More Receptive than Other Profs,* YALE DAILY NEWS, 3/14/99; Robin Wilson, *Provosts Push A Radical Plan to Change The Way Faculty Research Is Evaluated,* CHRONICLE OF HIGHER EDUCATION, 6/26/98; and Will, *supra* note 10.

[13] *Ecclesiastes* 1:18.

[14] See, e.g., ASS'N OF AMERICAN LAW SCHOOLS BY-LAWS §6.8, *Faculty Development* (1997).

[15] *See* Cane, *The Role of Law Review in Legal Education,* 31 J. LEGAL EDUC. 215 (1981).

[16] 1 HARV. L. REV. 35 (1887).

[17] *SEE* SHAPIRO, *THE MOST-CITED LAW REVIEW ARTICLES,* 73 CALIF. L. REV.1540, 1549-51 (1985). In addition, *Harvard* is still the only review in America that is self-sustaining, unsubsidized by a university or bar association. *See* Cane, *supra* note 15, at 215.

[18] 7 B.C. THIRD WORLD L.J. 1 (1987).

[19] 1987 J. PLAN. & ENVTL. L. 484.

[20] 62 MODERN L . REV. 100 (1999).

[21] 77 NORTH CAROLINA L. REV. 523 (1999).

[22] Bohannon, Hon. Richard L. and William C. Plouffe, Jr., 7 TULSA J. COMP. & INT 1 (1999).

[23] 68 B. U. L. REV. 733 (1988).

[24] 39 SYRACUSE L. REV. 1455 (1988); *see also New South Carolina Dog Bite Rule,* 38 S.C. L. Rev. 236 (1986).

[25] 32 N. IR. LEGAL Q. 284 (1981); *see also Rediscovering Traditional Tort Typologies To Determine Media Liability for Physical Injuries: From the* Mickey Mouse Club *to* Hustler Magazine, 10 HASTINGS COMM/ENT L.J. 969 (1988).

[26] 11 HARV. WOMEN'S L.J. 53 (1988).

[27] 23 EUROPEAN LAW REVIEW 488 (1998).

[28] 10 CARDOZO L. REV. 1389 (1989).

[29] 1986 WIS. L. REV. 527.

[30] 5 INT'L REV. L. & ECON. 199 (1985).

[31] 13 CRIM. JUST. & BEHAV. 419 (1986).

[32] 22 IDAHO L. REV. 629 (1986).

[33] "Toward A [Something or Other]" appeared in 5,297 titles in the past [24] years; "Model" in 6,563; "Theory" in 7,698. Lexis also provides refinements which, like eating peanuts, are fun and hard to stop doing, such as: "Toward a Model . . ." in 18 recent titles; "Toward a Theory of . . ." in 70. "Give Me A Break!" was the partial title of a piece in the PENNSYLVANIA LAW REVIEW. Anyone who can find its specific citation is entitled to an autographed copy of the author's next READER'S DIGEST article, *You and Your Sabbatical: Have Fun!* My thanks to University of Baltimore Law Librarians Will Tress and Robert Pool for their generous instruction on Lexis esoterica. Tress holds the current world records (both semester and career) for the fewest "inappropriate command" rebukes from a legal database.

[34] The original title was "The Economy of Shit in English Renaissance Studies." THE NEW REPUBLIC (4/12/99). *See also* William Penny, *The Municipal Solid Waste Landfill Presumptive Remedy,* 13 NATURAL RESOURCES & ENVIRONMENT 471(3), Winter 1999.

[35] 7 HETERODOXY 3 (March 1999).

[36] Professor John Lynch, faculty advisor to the *University of Baltimore Law Review.*

[37] *Rodell, supra* note 2, at 40. Even law professors' intentional efforts at humor are likely to engender more groans than belly-laughs. *See, e.g., On the Lighter Side,* 39 J. LEGAL EDUC. 47-54 (1989); *On the Lighter Side,* 38 J. LEGAL EDUC. 359-68 (1988); *see also* Leibman & White, *supra* note 39; at 423 ("[M]ost attempts by legal writers to employ irony and hyperbole range from ill-advised to pathetic.").

[38] Some see as a fundamental weakness the fact that law reviews are mostly student-run. See J. SELIGMAN, THE HIGH CITADEL 183-85 (1978).

[39] *See* UNIVERSITY OF BALTIMORE SCHOOL OF LAW, FACULTY HANDBOOK at J-6 (1979-1980). "Mechanical requirements cast in terms of a specific number of

articles of a particular form or in particular journals are likely to cause more harm than good." Cramton, *"The Most Remarkable Institution": The American Law Review"*, 36 J. LEGAL EDUC. 1, 11 (1986).

[40] *See* Kaye, *One Judge's View of Academic Law Review Writing*, 39 J. LEGAL EDUC. 313, 320 (1989) (pointing out the lack of "value and pertinence" of law reviews to judicial decision-making).

[41] *See* Michael McClintock, *The Declining Use of Legal Scholarship by Courts: An Empirical Study*, 51 Oklahoma L. Rev. 659, and Peter Schuck, *Why Don't Law Professors Do More Empirical Research?*, 39 J. LEGAL EDUC. 323, 336 (1989).

[42] *See* Elson, *The Case Against Legal Scholarship or, If the Professor Must Publish, Must the Profession Perish?*, 39 J. LEGAL EDUC. 343, 344-45 (1989); Rodell, *supra* note 5, at 45. *But cf.* Strong, *The* Iowa Law Review *at Age Fifty*, 50 IOWA L. REV. 12, 13 (1964) (supporting the existence of law reviews).

[43] *See* Austin, *Footnotes As Product Differentiation*, 40 VAND. L. REV. 1131, 1152 (1987).

[44] *See, e.g.,* Nowak, *Woe Unto You, Law Reviews!*, 27 ARIZ. L. REV. 317, 322-23 (1985).

[45] *See* GTE Sylvania Inc. v. Continental T.V., Inc., 537 F.2d 980, 1018 (9th Cir. 1976) (Chambers, J., concurring and dissenting).

[46] *See* Getman, *Voices*, 66 TEX. L. REV. 577, 580-81 (1988).

[47] *See* Miller, *The Myth of Objectivity in Legal Research and Writing*, 18 CATH. U.L. REV. 290, 294-95 (1969).

[48] *See* Tushnet, *Legal Scholarship: Its Causes and Cures*, 90 Yale L.J. 1205, 1205 (1981); *see also* Jensen, *The Law Review Manuscript Glut: The Need for Guidelines*, 39 J. LEGAL EDUC. 383, 385 (1989) ("The legal publication system is, to put it bluntly, absurd."); Leibman & White, *How the Student-Edited Law Journals Make Their Publication Decisions*, 39 J. LEGAL EDUC. 387, 418 (1989) (discussing weaknesses in the law-review model and ways to correct those weaknesses). "[I]f a publication medium is perceived by its users to be biased, capricious, narrow, rigid, and unqualified, they will seek alternatives, even if the perceptions are mostly or totally unfounded." *Id.*

[49] *See* Douglas, *Law Reviews and Full Disclosure*, 40 WASH. L. REV. 227, 229-31 (1965).

[50]Cramton, *supra* note 39, at 8. For another intelligent critique, see Cramton, *Demystifying Legal Scholarship*, 75 GEO. L.J. 1 (1986). *See also* Antoline, *A Burst of Specialty Alternatives,* STUDENT LAW., May 1989, at 26-30 (discussing the proliferation of "alternative journals"); Jensen, *supra* note 48, at 384 (mentioning a "glut" of legal articles); Leibman & White, *supra* note 48, at 418 (describing a "flood of paper and ink at the medium- and high-impact journals").

[51]36 J. LEGAL EDUC. 21, 21 (1986) (footnotes omitted); *see also Gresham's Law of Legal Scholarship*, 3 CONST. COMMENTARY 307, 309 (1986) (suggesting that the principle of "adverse selection" operates in legal scholarship to ensure that "law review literature will be dominated by articles taking silly positions"). For an especially thoughtful, well-articulated—and unheeded—piece, see Bard, *Scholarship*, 31 J. LEGAL EDUC. 242 (1981).

Scholarship is legal academe's temple jade: we sing its glories and genuflect before it, bedizen it with jewels, and then demean it by pretending to make it the gate keeper of the profession. It becomes the price we must pay to be a law professor, rather than the prime privilege of that calling. And, most justly, it reciprocates in kind, by forcing us to accept as scholarship work that is little more than ritualized diligence.

Id. at 242; *see also* Murray, *Publish and Perish—By Suffocation*, 27 J. LEGAL EDUC. 566, 566 (1975) (quoting George Eliot, who offered this sadly under-used benediction: "Blessed is the man who, having nothing to say, abstains from giving in words evidence of the fact."); Cane, *supra* note 9, at 221 nn. 35-39 and accompanying text (arguing that law reviews form the basis of an "old boy" network that propagates itself from generation to generation). For a particularly bitter, and thus more easily dismissed, attack on the system, see Elson, *supra* note 42.

[52]Rodell, *supra* note 5 at 43.

[53]*Id.*

[54]Rodell, *supra* note 5 at 288.

[55]*See, e.g.,* Martin, *The Law Review Citadel: Rodell Revisited*, 71 IOWA L. REV. 1093, 1104 (1986); *see also* Hewitt, *Altered States: Evolution or Revolution in Journal-Based Communications*, 25 AMERICAN LIBR. 497, 497-500 (1989); Westwood, *The Law Review Should Become the Law School*, 31 Va. L. Rev. 913 (1945).

[56]WEBSTER'S NINTH NEW COLLEGIATE DICTIONARY 1051 (1988) [hereinafter WEBSTER'S DICTIONARY].

[57]Jacobellis v. Ohio, 378 U.S. 184, 197 (1964) (Stewart, J., concurring).

[58] *See, e.g.,* UNIVERSITY OF BALTIMORE SCHOOL OF LAW, FACULTY HANDBOOK at H-1.6, H-1.7 (1989-1990) [hereinafter BALTIMORE FACULTY HANDBOOK]; *cf.* UNIVERSITY OF MARYLAND SCHOOL OF LAW, FACULTY HANDBOOK at B.2-1 (1985) (noting that "[a] candidate for tenure is required to have engaged in significant research and to have produced a significant product or products"). An exceptionally liberal policy, along the lines of that recommended in this Commentary, may be found in SANTA CLARA UNIVERSITY, FACULTY HANDBOOK (1987), which notes that the criteria for promotion and tenure include an evaluation of the candidate's creative work, including "recognized accomplishment or significant production in the arts of painting, sculpture, music, drama, fiction, poetry, dance, journalism, or the like." *Id. ¶ 3.6.2*

[59] *U. BALTIMORE FACULTY HANDBOOK, supra* note 58 at H-1.6

[60] *Id.* at H-1.6, H-1.7.

[61] *Id.* at H-1.7.

[62] *Id.*

[63] *Id.*

[64] Barrett, *To Read This Story in Full, Don't Forget To See the Footnotes,* Wall St. J., May 10, 1988, at 25, col. 2.

[65] *See supra* A NOTE ON THE NOTES. For a good example of authors' disdain for editors compelling the flying of footnote, see Gabel & Kennedy, *Roll Over Beethoven,* 36 STAN. L. REV. 1 (1984).

[66] *See Oser, Numerous Notes No Shot in Foot,* Nat'l L.J., Jan. 16, 1989, at 35, col. 1; *see also* Jacobs, *An Analysis of Section 16 of the Securities Exchange Act of 1934,* 32 N.Y.L. SCH. L. REV. 209 (1987) (accompanying Jacobs' 4824 footnotes with 491 pages of text); Choper, *Consequences of Supreme Court Decisions Upholding Individual Constitutional Rights,* 83 MICH. L. REV. 1 (1984) (accompanying Choper's 1611 footnotes with 208 pages of text); Project, *Sixteenth Annual Review of Criminal Procedure: United States Supreme Court and Courts of Appeal* 1985-1986, 75 GEO. L.J. 713 (1987) (accompanying the Georgetown staff's 3917 footnotes with 585 pages of text). The alleged record-holder for judicial opinions is United States v. E.I. Dupont de Nemours & Co., 118 F. Supp. 41 (D. Del. 1953), with 1715 footnotes. *See Kaplan, the Article in a Law Review That Included the Most Footnotes Is …,* Nat'l L.J. Mar. 18, 1985, at 4, col. 3. Jensen's *tour de force* appeared in 50 J. LEG. ED. (March 2000).

[67] A remarkably similar law-and-economics graph was recently sighted in Gillete & Hopkins, *Federal User Fees: A Legal and Economic Analysis,* 67 B.U.L. REV. 795,

810 (1987). Such charts are as incomprehensible to lawyers as higher mathematics or advanced psychology are to laypersons. *See, e.g.,* Grossman, *Stability in n-Dimensional Differential-Delay Equations*, 40 J. MATHEMATICAL ANALYSIS APPLICATIONS 541 (1972); G. ZURIFF, BEHAVIORISM: A CONCEPTUAL RECONSTRUCTION (1985). Grossman and Zuriff are close friends of the author. *See infra* note 69.

[68]With all due respect to Rodell, *supra* note 5, at 40, I think my version is better.

[69]*See* Martin, *supra* note 55, at 1097. They also allow a writer to cite self, family, friends, and colleagues. *See, e.g., supra* notes 67 and *infra* notes 116-123.

[70]304 U.S. 144, 152 n.4 (1938); *see also* Balkin, *The Footnote*, 83 NW. U.L. REV. 275 (1988) (noting the importance of Carolene Products' footnote four from a deconstructionist's point of view).

[71]310 U.S. 150, 224 n.59 (1940).

[72]392 U.S. 1, 19 n. 16 (1968).

[73]Austin, *supra* note 43.

[74]Austin, *supra* note 43, at 1153.

[75]*Id.* at 1135.

[76]*Id.* at 1153.

[77]123 U. PA. L. REV. 1474 (1975).

[78]18 AM. CRIM. L. REV. 441 (1981).

[79]*See* Austin, *supra* note 43 at 1155.

[80]*Id.* at 1133.

[81]Mikva, *Goodbye to Footnotes*, 56 U. COLO. L. REV. 647, 647 (1985) (quoting Professor Rodell).

[82]D. MELLINKOFF, LEGAL WRITING: SENSE AND NONSENSE 94 (1982).

[83]*Id.*

[84]Rodell, *supra* note 5 at 41.

[85]Arthur Goldberg, *The Rise and Fall (We Hope) of Footnotes*, 69 A.B.A. J. 255, 255

(1983).

[86]Mikva, *supra* note 81 at 647-48.

[87]Barrett, *supra* note 64, at 1 n.2, col. 3 (quoting Coward).

[88]*See* A UNIFORM SYSTEM OF CITATION, rule 2.2(c) (145th ed. 1986).

[89]*See* Austin, *supra* note 43, at 1144-45.

[90]*See, e.g.,* Essays and Correspondence sections of volumes 84 to 88 (present) of the *Michigan Law Review.*

[91]WEBSTER'S DICTIONARY, *supra* note 56 at 82.

[92]BALTIMORE FACULTY HANDBOOK, *supra* note 58 at H-1.6.

[93]*See* Stanley Coren, *When Teaching Is Evaluated on Political Grounds,* ACADEMIC QUESTIONS (Summer 1993) at 73.

[94]Shenefelt, *Disposable Scholarship*, WASHINGTON POST, 9/12/89, at A21.

[95]*See, e.g.,* Rodell, *supra* note 5, at 289; *see also* Wright, *supra* note 5, at 1460 (observing Rodell's belief that he was denied an endowed chair because he wrote for non-academic publications).

[96]*Ecclesiastes* 5:1.

[97]*See* Getman, *supra* note 46 at 581.

[98]*See* Rodell, *supra* note 5 at 289.

[99]*See* Benson, *The End of Legalese: The Game Is Over*, 13 N.Y.U. REV. L. & SOC. CHANGE 519, 520-22 (1984-1985); Shenefelt, *supra* note 87.

[100]Christine Littleton, *Reconstructing Sexual Equality*, 75 CALIF. L. REV. 1279, 1329 (1987).

[101]*See* Elson, *supra* note 34 at 347-99.

[102]*See supra* note 24.

[103]Getman, *supra* note 46 at 580.

[104]*See id.* at 588.

[105]Wright, *supra* note 5 at 1458.

[106]*See* Getman, *supra* note 46 at 581.

[107]*Adjudication Is Not Interpretation: Some Reservations About the Law-As-Literature Movement*, 54 Tenn. L. Rev. 203, 208-09 (1987).

[108]*The Critical Legal Studies Movement*, 96 Harv. L. Rev. 561, 645 (1983).

[109]For an example of good use of explanatory notes, see Fisher & Lande, *Efficiency Considerations in Merger Enforcement*, 71 Calif. L. Rev. 1580, 1600-02 nn. 87-100 (1983).

[110]West, *Jurisprudence and Gender*, 55 U. Chi. L. Rev. 1, 2-3 (1988). For an attempt to decipher the legal feminists' agenda, see Bowles, *'Feminist Scholarship' and 'Women's Studies': Implications for University Presses*, 19 Scholarly Publishing 163 (1988); and Lewis, *Feminist Scholars Spurring a Rethinking of Law*, N.Y. Times, Sept. 30, 1988, at B9, col. 3. (See Part II of this book for a lengthier discussion of feminist scholarship.)

[111]*Letter to a Young Clergyman (Jan. 9, 1720), reprinted in* J. Bartlett, Familiar Quotations 322 (15th ed. 1980).

[112]*Why Study Pacific Salmon Law? supra* note 32, and *If Spot Bites the Neighbor, Should Dick and Jane Go to Jail? supra* note 24.

[113]*See* Wright, *supra* note 5, at 1457-58. Even some law professors who fancy themselves good writers have lapses now and then. *See, e.g.,* Lasson, *Group Libel Versus Free Speech: When Big Brother Should Butt In*, 23 Duq. L. Rev. 77, 112 (1984). *But see* Lessard, *What Do people Do All Day* (Book Review), Washington Monthly, Mar. 1972, at 41, 47 (comparing "Lasson's clean simple prose" with "[Ralph] Nader's cliche-ridden and windy" writing).

[114]*Ecclesiastes* 1:2.

[115]Again, the fact that this is hardly a new plea should underscore both its importance and the likelihood that it will go unheeded. As Bard states:

Scholarship is neither served nor celebrated by using it as the fine mesh to sift out some of our colleagues. Scholarship cannot be coerced, only cultivated. No one can stop a real scholar. And no useful end is served by squeezing some pages out of unwilling writers, who are enthusiastic teachers . . . .

Bard, *supra* note 43, at 245; *see* Rodell, *supra* note 5 and accompanying text.

[116](Like, say, my father—whose single small book on the fourth amendment has been cited frequently by the Supreme Court.) *See* N. LASSON, THE HISTORY AND DEVELOPMENT OF THE FOURTH AMENDMENT TO THE UNITED STATES CONSTITUTION (1937). *See, e.g.,* United States v. Leon, 468 U.S. 897, 934 n .4 (1984); Oliver v. United States, 466 U.S. 170, 177 (1984); Bush v. Lucas, 462 U.S. 367, 375 (1983). LEXIS refers to a host of others.

[117] 6 GEORGE MASON L. REV. 35 (1997).

[118] 36 WASHBURN L. J. 18 (1996).

[119] 17 NOVA L. REV. 857 (1993). (1990).

[120] 9 JOURNAL OF LAW AND RELIGION 471 (1993).

[121] 24 CONNECTICUT L. REV. 201 (1991).

[122] 3 ST. THOMAS L. REV. 49 (1991).

[123] 7 HARVARD BLACKLETTER JOURNAL 139 (1990).

II

Feminism Awry

[1] *See* Bulfinch's Mythology 290 (New York, 1934). For this and other pertinent mythological references, I am indebted to Jim Chen, former executive editor of the *Harvard Law Review*. That many of the notes herein may be gruff, pointed, or pithy is entirely intentional, in hopes that some of them might actually be read. *See* Note on the Notes. *See also* Jean Shinoda Bolen, *Goddesses in Everywoman: A New Psychology of Women* (San Francisco, 1984).

[2] Cf. the new Random House Webster's College Dictionary 1532 (New York, 1991), which offers an alternative spelling for "women" ("womyn"), and the Oxford English Dictionary 20:358 (Oxford, England, 1989), which allows "wimmin"—all to avoid any reference to "men." Choice of the right words can be confusing even to those who wish to be politically correct. Compare, for example, Mary Joe Frug, A Postmodern Feminist Legal Manifesto (An Unfinished Draft), 105 Harv. L. Rev. 1045, 1075 (1992) ("only when the word 'woman' cannot be coherently understood ... will oppression by sex be fatally undermined"), with Rosalie Maggio, *The Nonsexist Word Finder: A Dictionary of Gender-Free Usage* 154 (Boston, 1989) ("'woman' is a respected, acceptable term that can be used anywhere, any time, any place, as long as the context in which it appears is not sexist or exclusive.") Homosexuals and lesbians, for another example, argue both for and against use of various terms to describe their sexual orientation (which may lead some irreverent language lovers to ask: Are we living in the Gay Nineties, or what?).

[3] To be fair, not all arguments supporting a "reasonable woman" standard are based on the notion that men are oppressive. See, e.g., Kathryn Abrams, Hearing the Call of Stories, 79 Cal. L. Rev. 971 (1991); Bridget A. Clarke, Comment, *Making the Woman's Experience Relevant to Rape: The Admissibility of Rape Trauma Syndrome in California*, 39 UCLA L. REV. 251 (1991); Nancy S. Ehrenreich, *Pluralist Myths and Powerless Men: The Ideology of Reasonableness in Sexual Harassment Law*, 99 YALE L.J. 1177 (1990).

[4] Four states have statutory requirements for gender-neutral language: Maryland, Oregon, Washington, and Wisconsin. In seventeen states, there is similar explicit policy but no such law: Alaska, Arizona, Colorado, Connecticut, Hawaii, Illinois, Indiana, Michigan, Minnesota, Montana, Nebraska, New Jersey, North Dakota, Ohio, South Dakota, Texas, and Utah. In one state (Idaho), there is a statutory directive that the singular include the plural and the masculine include the feminine. *National Conference of State Legislatures* (1991). Various committees have

also been appointed to review administrative rules and regulations. *See, e.g., Report of the Special Joint Committee on Gender Bias in the Courts* (Annapolis, 1989). But cf. 1 U.S.C. § 1 (1988), which adheres to usage of the traditional indefinite masculine pronoun but explicitly makes it include women.

[5]Paul Greenberg, "American Satire, From Bland to Worse," Chicago Tribune, Nov. 18, 1991, at 19. See also Jeanne L. Schroeder, *Abduction From the Seraglio*: Feminist Methodologies and the Logic of Imagination, 70 TEX. L. REV. 109, 110 (1991) ("the title to Mozart's opera [*Cosi fan Tutti*] may be taken as a description of the plight of women in masculinist society").

[6]John Leo, *PC Follies: The Year in Review*, U.S. NEWS & WORLD REPORT, Jan. 27, 1992, at 22.

[7]*See* Kennedy, How the Law School Fails: A Polemic, 1 YALE REV. L. & SOC. ACTION 71 (1970).

[8]*See* Camille Paglia, *The Joy of Presbyterian Sex*, NEW REPUBLIC, Dec. 2, 1991, at 24. For the argument that women are out of place in politics, *see* Edgar Berman, *The Politician Primeval* 84-85 (New York, 1974). A pertinently impertinent excerpt:

It might be said that if God had wanted women to be politicians, he would have made them with thicker skins, grosser tastes, an unparalleled egomania, and the inclination and capacity to absorb a fifth of Old Forester in any one tough campaign day without the benefit of Lydia Pinkham's Compound.

Whether by cosmic design or chance, in the three billion years of animal history, only a handful of the million or so species (the South African phalarope and the striped hyena among others) are dominated by the female. If our present-day human phalaropophiles think they can buck this formidable fact and change their own natural endowments by edict, confrontation, petition, or constitutional amendment, they are smoking testosterone-cut hashish and bulling it through just like any male would flat on his back at the count of nine.

See also Brigitte Berger, *Academic Feminism and the "Left,"* ACADEMIC QUESTIONS, Spring 1988, at 9.

[9]*See also* Paglia, *supra* note 8, ("[The movement] is a new tyranny of the group, pretending to speak for individuals as it crushes them").

[10]"And therefore it has nothing to do with us." Sally Quinn, *Who Killed Feminism? Hypocritical Movement Leaders Betrayed Their Own Cause*, WASHINGTON POST, Jan. 19, 1992, at C1. For this and other anti-feminist commentary, Quinn was summarily labeled "a waterbug on the surface of life" by Gloria Steinem, a

mother of the movement. John Elvin, *Inside the Beltway*, WASHINGTON TIMES, April 27, 1992, at A6.

Phyllis Schlafly, another leading anti-feminist, says, "The feminist movement has *not* improved women's lot, [and] the polls reflect the fact. The fact that the majority of women do not want to identify with feminists I think is obvious." *Quoted* in A. M. Chaplin, *Where Now Feminism*, Baltimore Sun Mag., Dec. 8, 1991, at 8.

In response to the question, "Do you consider yourself a feminist or not?" 34% of women said yes and 57% said no (Gallup-Newsweek poll). In a 1989 Yankelovich-Time-CNN poll, 77% of women said the movement had "made things better for women since the 1960s," while 8% said it had made things worse, and 10% saw no difference. Eighty-two percent said it was true that the movement was still improving lives of women, 12% said it was not. Thirty-five percent said the movement looks down on women without jobs; 57% disagreed. Twenty-four percent said the movement was anti-family; 65% disagreed. Forty-four percent had a favorable impression of feminists; 62% said they felt feminists had been helpful overall to women. In a 1970 Harris-Virginia Slims poll, 40% of women favored "most of the efforts to strengthen and change women's status in society." By 1974, 42% opposed and 57% favored such efforts; by 1985, 73% were in favor; by 1989, 77%. Chaplin, *supra* note 10 at 12.

[11]A *Women Lawyer's Journal* began publication in 1911, but it was more concerned with the activities of women lawyers in the bar association that sponsored it than with legal issues. Neva B. Talley, *Women Lawyers of Yesterday, Today and Tomorrow*, 46 WOMEN LAWYERS L.J., Summer 1960, as 21. Feminist legal scholars are sprung from loins of much more recent vintage. What we know as "feminist law" probably started in the late 1960s. See Leo Kanowitz, *Women and the Law* (Albuquerque, 1969); Karen Decrow, *Sexist Justice* (New York, 1974); 1 HARV. WOMEN'S L.J. (1978).

[12]"Feminist jurisprudence" has abounded in the journals over the past ten years; a computer search limited to those words yields several hundred articles. Law librarians in Southern California who compiled a bibliography of books and articles on "women in the law" produced 70 pages of titles. There is also a *zaftig*, two-volume bibliography of such literature. *See* Cardozo, *Women's Annotated Legal Bibliography* (1988).

[13]*See* the *AALS Director of Law Teachers* 1991-92, at 1139-40 (1991). Carolyn Heilbrun & Judith Resnick, *Convergences: Law, Literature and Feminism*, 99 YALE L.J. 1913, 1925 & n.36 (1990).

[14]The intimidation factor is real. More than one fully tenured and promoted law professor has told me that, although he may have more strongly negative views

than I do about radical feminism, he would not assert them publicly for fear of being ostracized by the Academy—i.e., unable to obtain a teaching position elsewhere. Perhaps that is the primary reason criticism of modern-day feminists is often more harsh from women than from me. Paglia (*supra* note 8), a professor at the University of the Arts in Philadelphia, has observed that women's studies "is a jumble of vulgarians, bunglers, whiners, French faddists, apparatchiks, doughface party-liners, pie-in-the-sky utopianists, and bullying, sanctimonious sermonizers." Greenberg, *supra* note 5 at 19. Brigitte Berger, a professor of sociology at Wellesley College, notes that professional feminists are "unfettered by any serious intellectual resistance" and are "driven by their presuppositions toward ever more radical conceptualizations." See Berger, *supra* note 8, at 13. See especially a scathing review of Catharine MacKinnon, *Feminism Unmodified*, by Maureen Mullarkey (not a pseudonym) in *The Nation*, May 30, 1987, at 720.

Male critics of radical feminism are led by Michael Levin, a professor of philosophy at the City College of New York. In his book *Feminism and Freedom* (New Brunswick, N.J., 1987), he argues that feminists deny innate sex differences have anything to do with the basic structure of society, and that this denial leads them to interpret observable differences between male and female roles as the result of discrimination and restrictive social conditioning rather than as the free expression of basic preferences. Levin concludes that feminist proposals for remedying this imaginary oppression serve systematically to thwart individual liberty. Elsewhere he describes "a grand gesture of intellectual affirmative action" in which "the predominantly male academic establishment continues to allow feminists to get away with anything." Michael Levin, *Gender and History*, 5 CONST. COMM. 201, 202 (1988) (reviewing Catharine A. MacKinnon, *Feminism Unmodified*). In his view, the deference to feminist excess "may be partly due to misplaced chivalry and an understandable reluctance to provoke further feminist anger, but it derives primarily from guilt about the massive oppression supposedly suffered by women." *Id.* at 202. *See also* Daniel A. Farber, *The Case Against Brilliance*, 70 MINN. L. REV. 917 (1986), and *Brilliance Revisited*, 72 MINN. L. REV. 367 (1987); David Bryden, *Between Two Constitutions: Feminism and Pornography*, 2 CONST. COMM. 147 (1985). Cf. Critical race theory, *infra* note 54 and accompanying text.

For a jaundiced-eye view of the feminist movement in general, see Edgar Berman, *The Compleat Chauvinist: A Survival Guide for the Bedeviled Male* (New York, 1982).

The scarcity of criticism by men may also be because men's brains deteriorate faster than women's, or that they lose their verbal abilities sooner. *Results of Study by Brain Behavior* Laboratory at University of Pennsylvania, N.Y. TIMES, April 2, 1991, at C2.

[15]Berger, *supra* note 8 at 7-15.

[16]Berger, *supra* note 8, at 10, 15. "Academic feminism provides instructive insights into what can happen to an enterprise, when its guardians do not take care to root out the first cropping of intellectual mischief, either because it appears too silly to bother with, or in the misguided hope that it will eventually die out on its own." *Id.* at 7.

[17]Maureen Mullarkey, *Mullarkey Replies*, THE NATION, Aug. 1/8, 1987, at 93.

[18]*Id.*

[19]The thesis may be simple, but it will likely be misconstrued by some as proof of the argument put forward in Susan Faludi's much ballyhooed book, *Backlash: The Undeclared War Against American Women* (New York, 1991), that lawmakers, the media, and others have consciously sought to diminish the gains of the women's movement by making women feel guilty about their career achievements. *See* Bernard Weinraub, *Say Hello to the Nanny from Hell*, N.Y. Times, Jan. 5, 1992, at M13.

[20]GREEK MYTHOLOGY (Paul Hamlyn Ltd., London 1967).

[21]Katharine T. Bartlett, *Feminist Legal Methods*, 103 HARV. L. REV. 829, 833 (1990).

[22]Mary Joe Frug, *Re-Reading Contracts: A Feminist Analysis of a Contracts Casebook*, 34 AM. U. L. REV. 1065, 1066-68 (1985).

[23]Catharine MacKinnon, *Feminism Unmodified* 59 (Cambridge, Mass., 1987) [hereinafter F.U.]. *See also* Abigail Thernstrom, *Rough Justice*, NEW REPUBLIC, Nov. 11, 1991, at 24.

[24]Stewart, J., concurring in Jacobellis v. Ohio, 378 U.S. 184, 197 (1964). Some feminists see pornography everywhere (except, of course, in their own prose). *See infra* notes 65-68 and accompanying text.

[25]For example, a National Conference on Women in Legal Education was co-sponsored by the Association of American Law Schools, the American Bar Association Committee on Women and the Profession, and the ABA Section on Legal Education and Admission to the Bar. Many state courts have approved gender-bias studies, as recommended by the Conference of Chief Justices in 1988. Since 1979, there has been a National Association of Women Judges (current membership more than 800). Perhaps most symptomatic of the new sensitivity about sexual harassment are popular television programs. Following the nomination hearings of Clarence Thomas, specific episodes treated the issue on "Designing Women," "A Different World," and "The Trials of Rosie O'Neill." There is even a Henson Productions dinosaur character named Sexual Harris PARADE MAGAZINE, Dec. 29, 1991, at 16.

[26]See Bartlett, *supra* note 21 at 833 n.7 (1990).

[27]Try either Joan C. Williams, *Dissolving the Sameness/Difference Debate: A Post-Modern Path Beyond Existentialism in Feminist and Critical Race Theory*, 2 DUKE L.J. 296 (1991), or the critique of Barbara Flagg, Women's Narratives, Women's Story, 59 U. Cin. L. Rev. 147 (1990) (reviewing MacKinnon's *Toward a Feminist Theory of the State*).

[28]Theodore Ziolowski, *The Ph.D. Squid*, 59 AM. SCHOLAR, Spring 1990, at 177.

[29]*See generally* Alice S. Rossi, *Feminists in Politics: A Panel Analysis of the First National Women's Conference* at x-xi (New York, 1982). *See specifically* Taunya Lovell Banks, *Toilets as a Feminist Issue*, 6 BERKELEY WOMEN'S L.J. 263 (1990-91).

[30]*See supra* note 1 and *infra* notes 59-62 and accompanying text.

[31]Once in a while, a male voice is heard as well to suggest that abortion is not a question for the courts. *See, e.g.,* Justice Scalia's concurrence in Webster v. Reproductive Health Services, 109 S. Ct. 3040, 3065 (1989). Witness, too, the developing schism in feminist ranks over whether to support prohibition of abortions that have been motivated by sex selection (that is, with a disparate impact on female fetuses). See Martha Bayles, *Feminism and Abortion*, ATLANTIC MONTHLY, April 1990, at 79.

[32]See Berger, *supra* note 8 at 10-11.

[33]Julia Brophy & Carol Smart, *Women in the Law: Explorations in Law, Family and Sexuality* (London, 1985).

[34]Carrie Menkel-Meadow, The Comparative Sociology of Women Lawyers, 24 OSGOODE HALL L.J. 897 (1986).

[35]Rosabeth Moss Kanter, *Reflections on Women in the Legal Profession: A Sociological Perspective*, 1 HARV. WOMEN'S L.J. 1 (1978).

[36]Elizabeth Villiers Gemmet, *Law and Literature: An Unnecessarily Suspect Class in the Liberal Arts Component of the Law School Curriculum*, 23 VAL. U. L. REV. 267 (1989).

[37]Heilbrun & Resnick, *supra* note 13. See also Frug, *supra* note 22. *Cf.* Richard Delgado, *The Imperial Scholar: Reflections on a Review of Civil Rights Literature*, 132 U. Pa. L. Rev. 561 (1984), which makes similar arguments about minority scholars. Of course, it is important (for promotion and tenure purposes) to be cited in mainstream law reviews, and (for pedagogical purposes) to have diversity on reading lists, but proving some sort of conspiratorial motive for excluding women is purely conjectural.

[38]Lisa G. Lerman, *Mediation of Wife Abuse Cases: The Adverse Impact of Informal Dispute Resolution on Women*, 7 HARV. WOMEN'S L.J. 57 (1984).

[39]Heather Ruth Wishik, *To Question Everything: The Inquiries of Feminist Jurisprudence*, 1 BERKELEY WOMEN'S L.J. 64, 72-77 (1985) (questions are upper-case headings in original).

[40]Paula Hyman, as quoted in a review by Midge Decter (COMMENTARY, Jan. 1992, at 61-63) of a book by Letty Cottin Pogrebin entitled *Deborah, Golda, and Me* (1991).

[41]It might be more difficult to categorize some of the founders of the feminist movement, such as Betty Friedan, whose political agenda is somewhat vague in the context of her postmodern sisters. According to at least one biography, under her maiden name (Betty Goldstein) she was a believer in and professional propagandist for the Communist Party for nearly thirty years prior to publication of her groundbreaking book *The Feminist Mystique*. See David Horowitz, 7 HETERODOXY 14 *(March 1999).*

[42]*See* Quinn, *supra* note 10 at C2; CHICAGO TRIBUNE, Nov. 14, 1991, at 14. *See also* M. J. Willoughby, *Rendering Each Woman Her Due*, 38 U. KAN. L. REV. 169 at 179 n.14, 173 n.16 (1989) (citing *Domestic Violence on Trial: Psychological and Legal Dimensions of Family Violence*, ed. Daniel Jay Sonkin, 72 (New York, 1987)); and Califano v. Goldfarb, 430 U.S. 199 (1977).

[43]*See* Felice A. Schwartz, *Management Women and the New Facts of Life*, HARV. BUS. REV. (Jan.-Feb. 1989) (acknowledging that women want both jobs and family, and conceding that they are less likely than men to work continuously from college graduation to retirement); John Leo, *The Trouble With Feminism*, U.S. NEWS & WORLD REP., Feb. 10, 1992, at 19; Quinn, *supra* note 12. Even Blondie Bumstead, after sixty years as a loyal housewife making Dagwood sandwiches, left hearth and home to become a working woman. L.A. TIMES, Sept. 2, 1991 (View Section) at 1.

[44]Berger, *supra* note 8 at 10.

[45]*See* Kathryn Abrams, *Gender Discrimination and the Transformation of Workplace Norms*, 42 VAND. L. REV. 1183 (1989); Leslie Bender, *Sex Discrimination or Gender Inequality*, 57 FORDHAM L. REV. 941, 944 n.11 (1989).

[46]Alice Steinbach, *Statistics on Women Cause Static*, BALTIMORE SUN, April 19, 1992, at H1.

[47]Illustrative titles: Carol Gilligan, *In a Different Voice: Psychological Theory in Women's Development* (Cambridge, Mass., 1982); Mary Field Belenky, Blythe

McVicker Clinchy, Nancy Rule Goldberger & Jill Mattuck Tarule, *Women's Ways of Knowing: The Development of Self, Voice, and Mind* (New York, 1986); Carrie Menkel-Meadow, *Portia in a Different Voice: Speculations on a Woman's Lawyering Process*, 1 Berkeley Women's L.J. 39 (1985).

[48]Robin West, *Jurisprudence and Gender*, 55 U. Chi. L. Rev. 1, 28 (1988).

[49]*Id.* at 15 and *passim.*

[50]*See, e.g.*, 105 Harv. L. Rev. 8 (1992).

[51]A. M. Chaplin, *Where Now Feminism?* Baltimore Sun Mag., Dec. 8, 1991, at 12. Schlafly, president of an organization called the Eagle Forum, is a longtime foe of feminists such as Dworkin and MacKinnon.

[52]West, *supra* note 48 at 13 (*emphasis implied*). Although the quoted declaration would undoubtedly offend feminists if it were made by a male (see *supra* note 9), it is unlikely that the scholar who wrote it has ever been inside a men's locker room or college fraternity-house, where a traditional rallying cry is, 'Let's go out and get l——!"

[53]See *supra* note 1 and accompanying text.

[54]*See* West, *supra* note 48, at 46 (citing Dworkin). *See also* Encyclopaedia Britannica 11:794, 18:918 (Chicago, 1986); Time, Dec. 2, 1991, at 78-79; Quinn, *supra* note 10; and Leo, *supra* note 6.

[55]Here is a typical passage from Dworkin:

He has to push in past boundaries. There is the outline of a body, distinct, separate, its integrity an illusion, a tragic deception, because unseen there is a slit between the legs, and he has to push into it. There is never a real privacy of the body that can co-exist with intercourse: with being entered. The vagina itself is muscle and muscles have to be pushed apart. The thrusting is persistent invasion. She is opened up, split down the center. She is occupied—physically, internally, in her privacy. ...

She is a human being, is supposed to have a privacy that is absolute; except that she, a woman, has a hole between her legs that men can, must, do enter. This hole, her hole, is synonymous with entry. A man has an anus that can be entered, but his anus is not synonymous with entry. A woman has an anus that can be entered, but her anus is not synonymous with entry. The slit between her legs, so simple, so hidden—frankly, so innocent—for instance for the child who looks with a mirror to see if it *could* be true—is there an entrance to her body down there? ... —that slit which means entry into her—intercourse—appears to be the key to women's lower human status. By definition . . . She is intended to have lesser privacy, a lesser integrity of the body, a lesser sense of self . . . [and] this lesser privacy, this lesser integrity, this lesser self, establishes her lesser significance. . . . She is defined by how she is made, that hole, which is synonymous with entry; and intercourse, the act fundamental in existence, has consequences to her being that may be intrinsic, not socially imposed. Andrea Dworkin, *Intercourse* 122-23 (New York, 1987).

MacKinnon is no less reserved. In F.U., she asks, "Who listens to a woman with a penis in her mouth?" MacKinnon, *supra* note 23 at 193. She also wonders "whether a good fuck is any compensation for getting fucked" and says that "[a]bortion offers women the liberal feminist dream of being real women—that is, available to be freely fucked." *Id.* at 144-45. More: "Women in pornography, when you tickle us, we get turned on; when you scratch us, we start to come; when you kill us, we orgasm until death." *Id.* at 227.

"It is pretty crude to set out deliberately to horrify people. . . . Mrs. Post tells us that no lady ever uses slang or swears." Alice-Leone Moats, *No Nice Girl Swears* 7-8 (New York, 1933).

[56]Levin, *supra* note 14 at 207-08.

[57]F.U. at 187. Levin adds that "MacKinnon's hysteria might be understandable if her statistics were trustworthy" and proceeds to demonstrate how they are not. Levin, *supra* note 16, at 207. For a largely sympathetic review of F.U., *see* Cass Sunstein, 101 Harv. L. Rev. 826 (1988).

[58]F.U. at 187. Compare MacKinnon's outraged response to the rape acquittal of William Kennedy Smith (New York Times, Dec. 15, 1991, at E15) with this view from Camille Paglia: "Women should accept that men are biologically programmed as the aggressor and they should stop blaming society and crying assault. Instead, they should revert to the precautions women have always taken to avoid 'being taken advantage of.' A girl who gets drunk at a party or goes upstairs with a fellow-student is a fool." *Quoted in* Charles Bremmer, *Feminist Fall Out in the Rape Debate*, London Times, Feb. 2, 1991 (Overseas News).

[59]Mullarkey, *supra* note 17 at 93.

[60]*See* Suzanne Fields, *Porn by Gender*, Wash. Times, March 5, 1992, at B1; Mullarkey, *supra* note 16; and N.Y. Times, Feb. 28, 1992, at B7.

[61]F.U. at 209.

[62]Harvey Porlock, *On the Critical List*, LONDON SUNDAY TIMES, April 28, 1991 (Features Section). To refresh your memory of Dworkin's own purple prose, you might try rereading note 55 *supra*.

[63]Mullarkey, *supra* note 17.

[64]Levin, *supra* note 14.

[65]Mullarkey, *supra* note 17.

[66]*Id.*

[67]*Elizabeth Mehren, Feminist vs. Feminist*, L.A. TIMES, April 30, 1992, at E1.

[68]Mullarkey, *supra* note 17.

[69]F.U., *supra* note 23 at 137.

[70]The Englishman was J. F. Saville, an English dramatist (1783-1853).

[71]*See* M. G. Lord, *This Pinup Drives Eggheads Wild*, NEWSDAY, Oct. 6, 1991, at 36; BALTIMORE SUN, June 23, 1991, G1, 6, 7. Another well-known feminist author, Susan Brownmiller, says Wolf's *Beauty Myth* is nothing new. "I wrote that book and published it in 1984—it was called *Femininity*. And while I think her points are valid I felt I covered all that material and did it very well." *Id.*

[72]*Robin West, Progressive and Conservative Constitutionalism*, 88 MICH. L. REV. 641, 693 (1990).

[73]Margarita Levin, *Caring New World: Feminism and Science*, 57 Am. Scholar 106 (1988).

[74]John Mortimer, *The First Rumpole Omnibus* 11 (New York, 1983). The Irish playwright was George Farquar, as quoted in Tryon Edwards, *The New Dictionary of Thoughts* 733, rev. ed. (New York, 1960).

[75]*See* West, *supra* note 48, at 46.

[76]*See* Judith Kleinfeld, *Why Smart People Believe Schools Shortchange Girls*, GENDER ISSUES (Winter/Spring 1998).

[77]*See* Adrienne Stone, *The Public Interest and the Power of the Feminist Critique of Law School: Women's Empowerment of Legal Education and its Implications for the Fate of Public Interest Commitment*, AMERICAN UNIVERSITY JOURNAL OF GENDER AND THE LAW 536 (1997). "Feminists do not want to ameliorate the existing con-

ditions just to make patriarchal structures more tolerable and long-lived. You have to get rid of the whole enterprise." *See also* Anita Bernstein, *A Feminist Revisit to the First-Year Curriculum,* 46 JOURNAL OF LEGAL EDUCATION 217 at 220 (1996); and Carol Smart, *The Ties That Bind: Law, Marriage and the Reproduction of Patriarchal Relations* 222-23 (London, 1984). Readers confused by deconstructionism must read Daniel A. Farber, *The Deconstructed Grocery List,* 7 CONST. COMM. 213 (1990).

[78]Daniel Bonevac, *Manifestations of Illiberalism in Philosophy,* 12 ACADEMIC QUESTIONS 14 at 17 (Winter 1998-99).

[79]Cf. George Stephanopoulis' description of William Jefferson Clinton in *All Too Human* (1998).

[80]*See, e.g.,* Susan H. Williams and David C. Williams, *A Feminist Theory of Malebashing,* 4 MICH. J. GENDER & LAW 35 at (1996).

[81]*See* Berger, *supra* note 8, at 14.

[82]N.Y. TIMES MAG., Oct. 6, 1991. See also Levin, *supra* note 14, at 214; Jim Chen, *Something Old, Something New, Something Borrowed, Something Blue,* 58 U. CHI. L. REV. 1527, 1535 (MacKinnon is cited in at least five separate examples provided by the latest edition of the *Bluebook*).

[83]Paul Gross, *On the "Gendering" of Science,* 5 ACAD. QUESTIONS, Spring 1992, at 10.

[84]Robert Lerner, Althea K. Nagai & Stanley Rothman, *Filler Feminism in High School History,* 5 ACAD. QUESTIONS, Winter 1991-1992, at 28.

[85]Levin, *supra* note 14.

[86]David Sacks and Peter Thiel, *The Diversity Myth: "Multiculturalism" and the Politics of Intolerance at Stanford* 75-79 (1995).

[87]*Hall of Shame,* 8 INSIGHT, April 20, 1992, at 28.

[88]Prof. Daly's cause was championed by Gloria Steinem and Eleanor Smeal (former president of NOW). Cathy Young, *When Teaching Feminism, Preach Inclusiveness,* BALTIMORE SUN, August 30, 1999. Prof. Daly sued Boston College for dismissing her, and lost. *See Minimum Daly Requirement, II,* HETERODOXY (April-May, 1999) at 3.

[89]Mehren, *supra* note 67.

[90]Barry Gross, *Salem in Minnesota,* 5 ACAD. QUESTIONS, Spring 1992, at 67.

[91]*See* Janet Tassel, *The 30 Years' War*, HARVARD MAGAZINE (September 1999)].

[92]Fox Butterfield, *Parody Puts Harvard Law Faculty in Sexism Battle*, N.Y. TIMES, April 27, 1992, at A10.

[93]Mehren, *supra* note 67.

[94]*See* Editor's Note, *PC's Liberal Victims: Two Case Studies*, ACADEMIC QUESTIONS (Spring 1993) at 59.

[95]*See* Daniel A. Farber, *Gresham's Law of Legal Scholarship*, 3 CONST. COMM. 307 (1986).

[96]Attributed to Solomon by Rav Yisroel Salanter (1810-83), *in* Meir Zlotowitz, *Koheles- Ecclesiastes* 202 (Brooklyn, N.Y., 1976). *See also* Babylonian Talmud (Kiddushin, fo. 49b).

[97]*See* Levin, *supra* note 14 at 202 and Berger, *supra* note 8 at 11 and accompanying text.

[98]*See* Mullarkey, *supra* note 17 at 722.

[99]Drucilla Cornell, *Beyond Accommodation: Ethical Feminism, Deconstruction, and the Law* (New York, 1991). *See also* Katharine T. Bartlett, *Feminist Legal Methods*, 103 HARV. L. REV. 829, 877 n.210 (1990).

[100]38 SYRACUSE L. REV. 1129, 1170-73 (1987) (by Marie Ashe).

[101]75 IOWA L. REV. 1135 (1990) (by Jeane L. Schroeder).

[102]7 SIGNS 515 (1982) (by Catharine A. MacKinnon).

[103]61 N.Y.U. L. REV. 589 (1986) (by Elizabeth M. Schneider).

[104]16 N.M. L. REV. 613- 618-24 (1986) (by Mari J. Matsuda).

[105]F.U., *supra* note 23 at 57, 515, 519 n.2.

[106]The reference is to Frug, *supra* note 22 at 1094-97 (1985).

[107]Paul Zwier, *Is the Maryland director and Officer Liability Statute a Male-Oriented Ethical Model?*, 18 U. BALT. L. REV. 368 (1989).

[108]F.U., *supra* note 24 at 57.

[109]Bartlett, *supra* note 21 at 829. But the feminist lobby appears to have won this little skirmish: for enlightenment in this regard, readers who have gotten this far are urged to see Jim Chen's reviews of the latest *Bluebook* (cited *supra* note 82).

[110]Dan Subotnick, *The Joke in Critical Race Theory: De Gustibus Disputandum* Est?, 15 Touro L. Rev. 105 (1998) at 119.

[111]J. N. Ibsister, *Freud* 141 (1985). *See also* Subotnik, *supra* note 110 at 115-116.

[112]F.U. *supra* note 23 at 4-5.

[113]*The New Dictionary of Thoughts*, at 737.

III

Political Correctness Askew

[1] *See* THE NONSEXIST WORD FINDER: A DICTIONARY OF GENDER-FREE USAGE 88 (1988).

[2] Ecclesiastes 1:9. Solomon himself was a model of majestic rectitude, although modern feminists might divine a hostile environment among the extensive collection of women in his court.

[3] Harassment less often results in legal action on the campus than in the workplace. A survey of Fortune 500 companies found that 90 percent had received sexual harassment complaints; more than 30% of those companies had been sued, 25 percent more than once. *See* BILLIE WRIGHT DZIECH & LINDA WEINER, THE LECHEROUS PROFESSOR xiv (Preface to the Second Edition 1990). *See also* Carolyn M. Mitchell, *The Political Correctness Doctrine: Redefining Speech on College Campuses*, 13 WHITTIER L. REV. 805 (1992) (stating that hate crimes "instigated by intolerance for race, religion, ancestry or sexual orientation are increasing in great numbers"). Mitchell also points out that hate crimes are "spill[ing] over into America's university campuses. *Id.*

[4] At the University of Massachusetts, for example, a black resident-advisor was punched in the chest by a visitor after the RA had asked him and his friends to stop drinking. The RA awoke the next morning to find racist slurs written in the hallway and feces outside his room. The white students who had signed-in the visitor were forced to vacate their dormitory rooms, although they were allowed to continue attending classes. Stephen Goode, *Campus Radicalism Lacks Mass Appeal*, INSIGHT MAGAZINE, Feb. 1, 1993, at p. 12. Such incidents have become endemic: for example, flyers distributed at Northwest Missouri State University stating, "The Knights of the Klu Klux Klan are watching you"; the letters "KKK" carved on the dormitory room of two black students at the University of North Carolina; Asian-American students spat upon at the University of Conncecticut. The figure represents about 7% of the approximately 15.5 million students currently attending U.S. colleges and universities. U.S. Census Bureau, *Statistical Abstract of the United States, 1999*. The incidents are both sexist and racist.]

[5] As quoted by Jonathan Rauch, *In Defense of Prejudice: Why Incendiary Speech Must Be Protected*, HARPER'S MAGAZINE, May, 1995, at p. 37.

[6] Bill Marvel & Barbara Kessler, *A Culture War: Political Correctness Provokes Backlash*, DALLAS MORNING NEWS, April 24, 1994, at p. 1A.

[7]Transcript #99051706-j04, *ABC World News Tonight with Peter Jennings*, May 17, 1999.

[8]See Mitchell, supra note 3 at 805-06.

[9]"The effect of this multipronged assault of affirmative action—in student admissions and faculty appointments—has been the Balkanization of the university. The traditional ideal of the university, as a community where professors and students are united in a common enterprise for a common purpose, has been replaced by the idea of a loose, almost amorphous, federation made up of distinct groups pursuing their special interests and agendas." Himmelfarb, *What to do About Education 1: The Universities,* COMMENTARY, Oct. 1994, at p. 21. *See also* Fennell, *The Silencers: A New Wave of Repression is Sweeping Through the Universities,* MACLEAN'S, May 27, 1991, at p. 40 (some male professors argue that forced hiring quotas are fracturing the university along gender lines; one called the process "tribalizing the university") *See also,* Novak, *Back to School,* FORBES, Sept. 2, 1991, at p. 132 ("diversity of viewpoint is extremely valuable in a democracy—but not when its components are kept hermetically sealed from one another in isolated enclaves").

[10]*See* Mortimer B. Zuckerman, *The Professoriate of Fear,* U.S. NEWS AND WORLD REPORT, July 29, 1991, at p. 64 (arguing that special programs for black students are not working). Law schools have also become "politicized." See Andrew J. Kleinfeld, *Politicization: From the Law Schools to the Courts,* ACADEMIC QUESTIONS, Winter 1993/94, pp. 9-19 (arguing that "the process of dispensing justice" is harmed by the politicization of law schools because judges are pressured into making decisions based on what is "politically correct"). *Id.*

[11]Some have seen their beef boutiques firebombed by groups like the "Animal Liberation Front." William Schmidt, *Britons on the Barricades, on Veal Calves' Behalf,* NEW YORK TIMES, January 13, 1995, at p.A4. To be sure, even non-vegetarians might recoil at the thought of caged calves being force-fed a diet of milk and meal so that their meat will be whiter and more tender. More benign, perhaps (but no less important to their protagonists) are campaigns by various vegetable-liberation fronts against using nonunion labor to pick crops like lettuce or grapes.

[12]*See* MD. CODE ANN., STATE GOV'T § 2-1317 (1984) and Jeff Barker, *Research Leads to a Kinder, Gentler State Seal,* BALTIMORE SUN (1/12/01) at B1.

[13]But the industry appears to be on a hairy-backed mammoth's rebound: nationwide fur sales for 1994 well exceeded a billion dollars. Sharon Linstedt, *Fur Is Making A Comeback,* BUFFALO NEWS, December 4, 1994, at p.13.

[14]As they must be in the faculty lounge, factory assembly-line, or school cafeteria. Indeed the locker room may be the male's last *sanctum profanum*——and then

only when women reporters are not present. See *Buddies at Work: When Men and Women Forge Office Relationships*, Gender- neutrality has also invaded restrooms, where unisex facilities are in some quarters preferred over those once labeled "Men" and "Women." BERGEN RECORD, July 31, 1994, at p.LO1.

[15]*See* Jeff Lyon, *Word Police*, CHICAGO TRIBUNE (October 9, 1994) at p. C10.

[16]Carol Innerst, *"Political Correctness" Gets A Presidential Chastising*, WASHINGTON TIMES, May 6, 1991, at p. A1.

[17]This *bon mot* is courtesy of Judge Alexander Sanders, Jr., president of the University of Charleston, who delivered it in an exceptionally well-crafted speech about political correctness before the Fourth Circuit's Judicial Conference in June of 1995. (Transcript in author's files.)

[18]*See* Tim Miles, *"Politically Correct" Return Fire*, PRESS ASSOCIATION NEWSFILE (May 4, 1994), Home News Section.

[19]Alexander Cockburn, *Bush & P.C.*, THE NATION, May 27, 1991 at p. 685(2) (referring to President Bush's commencement address at the University of Michigan on May 4, 1991). See also PAUL BERMAN, DEBATING P.C. THE CONTROVERSY OVER POLITICAL CORRECTNESS ON COLLEGE CAMPUSES 1 (1992).

[20]E.g., JAMES FINN GARNER, POLITICALLY CORRECT BEDTIME STORIES (1994).

[21]SANDRA STOTSKY, *PEDAGOGICAL ADVOCACY*, ACADEMIC QUESTIONS (Spring 2000) at 27.

[22]At least that's the way it was put by Stanley Fish, a literature professor at Duke University and perhaps the prime poobah of the modern PC movement (as quoted in Jefferson Morley, *A P.C. Guide to Political Correctness: Helpful Hints for Those Baffled by the Cliche of the Decade*, WASHINGTON POST, Jan. 15, 1995, at CO1. Fish is author of THERE'S NO SUCH THING AS FREE SPEECH . . . AND IT'S A GOOD THING, TOO (1994). The first major feminist to use the term was Karen DeCrow, who as president of the National Organization of Women in 1975 stated that her group was moving in an "intellectually and politically correct direction." *Id.* See also *Book Note: When Words Matter*, 108 HARVARD LAW REVIEW 1393 (1995).

[23]Janet Tassel, *The 30 Years' War*, HARVARD MAGAZINE (September 1999).

[24]*Id.* (quoting WASHINGTON POST columnist Donna Brit).

[25]Blue-collar workers themselves do not seem to care what they're called. *See* KENNETH LASSON, THE WORKERS: PORTRAITS OF NINE AMERICAN JOBHOLDERS

(1973)—especially the chapter describing the importance of garbagemen. *See also* John Leo, *Falling For Sensitivity*, U.S. NEWS AND WORLD REPORT, Dec. 13, 1993 at 27, and *Academically Incorrect*, LONDON TIMES, January 30, 1995.

[26]See Part II.

[27]Kate Battersby, *Thou Shalt Try to be A Very Nice Sport*, LONDON DAILY TELEGRAPH, March 23, 1994, at p.38.

[28]The Supreme Court does sometimes draw a line, however, between offensive speech and expressive conduct. Indecent exposure, for example, has yet to be held protected on First Amendment grounds. See, e.g., Barnes v. Glen Theatres, 111 S.Ct. 2456 (1991); Fox v. Washington, 236 U.S. 273 (1915); and Arnold H. Loewy, *Obscenity, Pornography, and First Amendment Theory*, 2 WM & MARY BILL OF RTS. J. 471 (1993). *See also* James Q. Whitman, *Enforcing Civility and Respect: Three Societies*, 109 YALE L.J. 1279 (2000).

[29]Dissenting opinion in Abrams v. United States, 250 U.S. 616, 630 (1919). According to this doctrine, abhorrent ideas will fester if suppressed, but die of their own false weight if given air. Such a view of the Framers' original intent is held by those on the right and left alike. See, e.g., Robert Bork, *Neutral Principles and Some First Amendment Problems*, 47 IND. L.J. 1, 26 (suggesting that the Framers thought speech was special and democracy "meaningless without open and vigorous debate"). But cf. Kenneth Lasson, *Group Libel Vs. Free Speech: When Big Brother Should Butt In*, 230 DUQ. L. REV. 77 (1984) (pointing out the failure of the theory in Nazi Germany during the early 1930's).

[30]The not-sufficiently-correct author was distinguished British historian John Vincent. See *Academically Incorrect*, *supra* note 25.

[31]The quote has often been attributed to Henry Kissinger, but I first heard it in the early 1960's from Richard Macksey, a humanities professor at the Johns Hopkins University, who tells me that it was not original with him, either.

[32]HENRY BEARD AND CHRISTOPHER CERF, THE OFFICIAL POLITICALLY CORRECT DICTIONARY AND HANDBOOK (1992). *See also*, e.g., Mary Matalin and James Carville, *All the Blockhead's Men*, NEW YORK TIMES, September 24, 1995, at section 7, p. 42.

[33]Even the politically-correct Oxford English Dictionary finds it difficult to rid itself entirely of traditional standards, refusing to label "manhole" as *offens.* (offensive). *See* Mark Lawson, *The Word Is Out*, MANCHESTER GUARDIAN (July 5, 1995) at p. T2.

[34] *See also* HENRY BEARD AND CHRISTOPHER CERF, THE OFFICIAL POLITICALLY CORRECT DICTIONARY AND HANDBOOK (1992).

[35] Or emasculated (depending upon your degree of political correctness). See, for example, any of the recent editions of DR. SPOCK'S BABY AND CHILD CARE, in which all children appear to have been born female.

[36] Steve Kogan, *No Freedom But In Harness*, ACADEMIC QUESTIONS (Fall 1997) at 38. See also *Nerds' English*, THE ECONOMIST (July 15, 1995).

[37] George Will, *Sensitivity Cops on the Trail of the "D" Word*, WASHINGTON POST (January 11, 1996) at A23.

[38] Fennell, *supra* note 9. *See also* Jenish D'Arcy, *War of Words: Academics Clash Over "Correctness,"* MACLEAN'S, May 27, 1991, at p. 44.

[39] *See* Wray Herbert, *The PC Assault on Science*, U.S. NEWS AND WORLD REPORT, Feb. 20, 1995, at p. 64 ("[t]he bottom line of deconstructive philosophy is that no text—neither *Lord Jim* nor a Cheerios box top—is privileged over any other").

[40] *See* Alexander Cockburn, *Dangerous Diversions*, THE NATION, May 27, 1991, at p. 690 (stating that "multiculturalism" means race essentialism). But see Irving Howe, *The Value of the Canon: What's Wrong with P.C.*, THE NEW REPUBLIC, Feb. 18, 1991, at p. 40 (arguing that the traditional literary and intellectual canon was based on received elitist ideologies and that humanities teaching was marked by corresponding biases, so that "it is now necessary to enlarge the canon so that voices from Africa, Asia, and Latin America can be heard").

[41] *See* Mortimer B. Zuckerman, *The Professoriate of Fear*, U.S. NEWS AND WORLD REPORT, July 29, 1991, at p. 64.

[42] *See* Irving Howe, *The Value of the Canon,* THE NEW REPUBLIC, Feb. 18, 1991, at 40.

[43] *Id.*

[44] *See* Paul R. Gross and Norman Levitt, *Knocking Science for Fun and Profit*, SKEPTICAL INQUIRER, March/April 1995 at p. 38.

[45] *See* Sandra Reeves, *Courting Differences*, U.S. NEWS AND WORLD REPORT, Sept. 30, 1991, at p. 96.

[46] Andrew Blum, *Profs Sue School on Suspension: Claim Victimized by "Political Correctness,"* NAT'L LAW JOURNAL, June 6, 1994, at A6.

47*See* GERTRUDE HIMMELFARB, LOOKING INTO THE ABYSS : UNTIMELY THOUGHTS ON CULTURE AND SOCIETY 1994. *See also* Himmelfarb, *What to do About Education 1: The Universities*, COMMENTARY, Oct. 1994, at p. 21.

48The latter includes black nationalism. *See* Berman, *supra* note 19.

49Derrick Bell, *Who's Afraid of Critical Race Theory*, 1995 U. ILLINOIS L. REV. 893 at 906 (1995).

50"Rival groups, recognizing no common mission, are engaged in a continual power struggle, not only about such matters as appointments, tenure, and the like, but about the very substance of education—what should be taught and how it should be taught." *See* Himmelfarb, *supra* note 47. *See also* Camille Paglia, *The Right Kind of Multiculturalism*, Wall Street Journal, September 30, 1999.

51Camille Paglia, *The Right Kind of Multiculturalism*, WALL STREET JOURNAL, September 30, 1999.

52*See* Kimberly Shearer Palmer, *When College Students Go "Postmodern,"* WASHINGTON POST, April 4, 2000.

53*See* Janet Tassel, *The 30 Years' War*, HARVARD MAGAZINE (September 1999) (quoting Lawrence Stager, professor of the archaeology of Israel).

54*Reductio Ad Absurdum: Annals of Appeasement*, HETERODOXY (April-May 1999) at 3.

55*See* Robert McLendon, *Political Correctness Can Blunt the Point,* LOS ANGELES TIMES, March 10, 1994, at p. 4 (quoting a Capistrano Valley high school senior who said PC "is a good idea, but it has gone too far. People have become a little bit too sensitive . . . . I believe that people should be polite to each other, but with PC, people are being forced to be polite").

56Cockburn, *supra* note 19 ("Universities are scared of lawsuits and demonstrations initiated by minority groups"); Zuckerman, *supra* note 41 ("To show compassion and to avoid confrontation, academic leaders who would never have given whites separate dorms have given them to blacks, along with their own student unions, homecoming dances, yearbooks and the like"); Marie McCullough, *Swarthmore in '94?*, PHILADELPHIA INQUIRER, June 22, 1994, at B01. ("In the Quaker tradition, Swarthmore strives for accommodation to end conflict"). *See also* Eric Konigsberg, *Mess: A Visit to P.C. Hell*, THE NEW REPUBLIC, May 31, 1993, at p. 14 (noting that leftist students have even "faked hate crimes on occasion to call attention to their causes").

[57]Jenish D'Arcy, *A War of Words: Academics Clash over "Correctness,"* MACLEAN'S, May 27, 1991, at p. 44 (stating that some universities have abolished formerly required courses dealing with European society because of the belief that Western culture has historically been responsible for the oppression of women, blacks, and other minorities). *See also* Stephen Goode, *Campus Radicalism Lacks Mass Appeal,* INSIGHT ON THE NEWS, Feb. 1, 1993, at p. 12 (noting the University of Massachusetts' new diversity requirement that "students must take two courses in cultures not their own").

[58]*Id.* D'Arcy reports that a University of Toronto political philosophy professor was denied tenure at Yale because he was too conservative in his beliefs. *See also* Fennell, *supra* note 9 ("professors who object to the new conformity are heckled into submission or refused full-time professorships"); Jerry Carroll, *Political Corrections Takes a Nosedive,* SAN FRANCISCO CHRONICLE, October 26, 1994 at E7.

[59]WALL STREET JOURNAL, Dec. 21, 1990 at A10.

[60]*See* Clifford Orwin, *All Quiet on the Post-Western Front?,* THE PUBLIC INTEREST (March 1996).

[61]Merle Rubin, *Culture Wars: A Feeding Frenzy of Self-identification,* BALTIMORE SUN, November 19, 1995, at p. 1D.

[62]*See* Goode, *supra* note 57 at 12. "[The country has lost] 'any sense of an integrated knowledge and experience'; everyone is separated into groups that don't speak to one another. Ideally, students should be 'taught within a context of the whole history', and certainly not in fragmented segments. There are traditions that all Americans share, regardless of background" (quoting a "civil rights activist turned professor").

[63]*The Dissolution of General Education 1914-1993: A Report by the National Association of Scholars,* 9 ACADEMIC QUESTIONS (Fall 1996). The SAT exam has also been changed in a capitulation to the forces of PC. Sara Mosle, *Score,* SLATE MAGAZINE, June 21, 2002.

[64]Robert Lerner and Althea Nagai, *Dumbing Down: Multiculturalsim and the Demise of the Liberal Arts at Maryland's Public Universities and Colleges* (Calvert Institute for Policy, March 1999). In contrast to the University of Maryland, which has no mandatory courses, Morgan State University had the most of any school examined—seven, which all undergraduates must take.

[65]Johnella Butler and John Walter, *Transforming the Curriculum* (State University of New York Press, 1991).

[66]David Sacks and Peter Thiel, *The Diversity Myth: "Multiculturalism" and the Politics of Intolerance at Stanford* at 53 (1995).

[67]Sacks and Thiel, *The Diversity Myth*, at 43. *See also* Clifford Orwin, *All Quiet on the Post- Western Front?*, THE PUBLIC INTEREST (March 1996).

[68]William Simon, *PC Has A Price*, 9 ACADEMIC QUESTIONS (Spring 1996) at 49; *see also* Kevin Driscoll, *Literature In An Ivory Tower of Babel*, WASHINGTON TIMES, 11/9/97 at B6; and Konigsberg, *supra* note 56.

[69]Cheryl Lu-Lien Tan, *Curricula: Left, Right or On Course?*, BALTIMORE SUN (9/24/00).

[70]Leo, *supra* note 25.

[71]George Will, *The Mask of Masculinity*, NEWSWEEK (7/19/99) at 68. Will comments that "In olden days, before these things were understood with today's clarity, people thought that when they studied subjects such as philosophy, history, politics, sociology, anthropology, art, music and literature, they were engaged in the study of women and men."

[72]Daphne Patai, *The Vaguest Measure of Faculty Merit*, (part of Symposium: *The Effects of Multiculturalism on Scholarship*, 12 ACADEMIC QUESTIONS (Winter 1998-99) at 35.

[73]Paul Gross and Norman Levitt, *The Natural Sciences: Trouble Ahead? Yes*, 7 ACADEMIC QUESTIONS (Spring 1994). *See also* Steven Greenhut, *Colleges Trash Western Culture Political Piffle*, CINCINNATI ENQUIRER, June 7, 1998 at B5.

[74]*See* Janet Tassel, *The 30 Years' War*, HARVARD MAGAZINE September (1999).

[75]Richard Lacayo, *War of Words*, TIME, July 7, 1997 at 92.

[76]Joining Ellis as other voices in the wilderness are Dinesh D'Souza *(Illiberal Education)*; David Lehman *(Signs of the Times)*; Charles Sykes *(Profscam)*; Camille Paglia *(Sexual Personae)*; Christina Hoff Summers *(Who Stole Feminism?)*; and Paul Gross and Norman Levitt *(Higher Superstition)*. *See* John Ellis, Literature Lost: Social Agendas and the Corruption of the Humanities (1997) at 226, and Driscoll, *supra* note 68. *See also* George Dent, Jr., *Political Discrimination in the Curriculum: A Case Study*, 12 ACADEMIC QUESTIONS 24 (Spring, 1999).

[77]Nancy Amdur, *Move Over Shakespeare, Make Room for "All My Children,"* CHICAGO TRIBUNE, January 4, 1998 at C6; (note rebuttal: many majors take Shakespeare even though not required).

[78]Maureen Dowd: *Liberties; A Winter's Tale*, NEW YORK TIMES, December 28, 1995 at A21.

[79]Leo, *supra* note 25.

[80]WALL STREET JOURNAL, November 11, 1998.

[81]Don Horine, *UF Student: It's Incorrect To Be 'Politically Correct' on Campus*, THE PALM BEACH POST, January 24, 1994, at p.1A.

[82]*See* John M. Ellis, *Literary Studies, Then and Now*, 13 ACADEMIC QUESTIONS 2 (Spring 2000) at 78-81.

[83]Janet Tassel, *The 30 Years' War*, HARVARD MAGAZINE (September 1999). *See also* Kathy Eden, *Great Books in the Undergraduate Curriculum*, ACADEMIC QUESTIONS (Spring 2000) at 63.

[84]*Minor Curricular Adjustment: Politically Correct Political Science Course*, THE NEW REPUBLIC, Jan. 20, 1992, at p. 8.

[85]Walter A. McDougall, *An Ideological Agenda for History*, ACADEMIC QUESTIONS at 30.

[86]Leo, *supra* note 25.

[87]Charles Babington, *Montgomery Wishes You a Gloomy Columbus Day*, WASHINGTON POST, Oct. 7, 1992 at p. D01.

[88]PERSPECTIVES [the newsletter of the American Historical Association] (May/June 1997), as quoted in 11 ACADEMIC QUESTIONS (Spring 1998) at 83. For a thorough going and illustrative defense of multiculturalism, *see* Cary Nelson, *Manifesto of a Tenured Radical* (1997). *See also* James Ceaser, *A Multiculturalist Cornerstone Manifesto*, 12 ACADEMIC QUESTIONS 71 (Spring, 1999) for a satirical counterpoint.

[89]Excerpted from Rebecca Carl, *Creating Asia: China in the World at the Beginning of the Twentieth Century.*

[90]*See* David Kaiser, *My War with the AHA*, 13 ACADEMIC QUESTIONS 2 (Spring 2000) at 70.

[91]Telephone conversation with Alan Sokal, April 16, 2001. *See The Sokal Hoax: The Sham That Shook the Academy*, edited by the editors of Lingua Franca, University of Nebraska Press (September 2000).

[92]*See* Sally Satel, *PC, M.D.: How Political Correctness is Corrupting Medicine*, Basic Books (2001), as quoted by Michael Pakenham, *Political Correctness Kills, and Here's Medical Evidence*, BALTIMORE SUN (1/7/01) at 2F.

[93]Paul Gross and Norman Levitt, *The Natural Sciences: Trouble Ahead? Yes*, 7 ACADEMIC QUESTIONS (Spring 1994).

[94]Janet Tassel, *The 30 Years' War*, HARVARD MAGAZINE (September 1999).

[95]*See* Kathryn Jean Lopez, *Glass Ceilings and Foggy Science*, HETERODOXY (February/March 2000).

[96]"I am in favor of studying literature from all over the world, provided it measures up to genuine aesthetic standards and is not praised simply because it is non-Western in origin." Paul Cantor, *A Welcome for Postcolonial Literature*, 12 ACADEMIC QUESTIONS 22 at 27 (Winter 1998-99) at 27. *See also* Roger Kimball, author of *Tenured Radicals*, writing in WEEKLY STANDARD, SEPTEMBER 29, 1997 at 31.

[97]*See* David Mulroy, *Alphabetic Literacy and the Revitalization of the Liberal Arts*, 12 ACADEMIC QUESTIONS 43 (Spring, 1999).

[98]Cecil Hunt, *Guests in Another's House: An Analysis of Racially Disparate Bar Performance*, 23 FL. ST. L. REV. 721 at 729, 792-93 (1996).

[99]James Shapiro, *When Brevity Rules the Syllabus, "Ulysses" Is Lost*, THE CHRONICLE OF HIGHER EDUCATION (February 12, 1999) at A60. *See also* Alan Saxe, *Changing Face of Education Affects Universities, Too*, FORT WORTH STAR-TELEGRAM (March 15, 1998) at 6.

[100]David Kirp, *Those Who Can't*, CURRENT (September, 1997) at 19.

[101]*Id.*

[102]*See* John Wilson, *Myths and Facts: How Real Is Political Correctness?*, 22 WILLIAM MITCHELL LAW REVIEW 517-520 (1996).

[103]Many such codes are promulgated at state-funded schools. See ARATI W. KORWAR, WAR OF WORDS: SPEECH CODES AT PUBLIC COLLEGES AND UNIVERSITIES (1994).

[104]Nat Hentoff, *Sexual Harassment by Francisco Goya*, WASHINGTON POST, Dec. 27, 1991 at p. A21. See also John Leo, *PC Follies: The Year in Review*, U.S. NEWS AND WORLD REPORT, Jan. 27, 1992, at 22. Similar sensitivity occurs in other venues. In 1993 Vermont officials hung bedsheets over a mural in a state office building because of a complaint by female employees that the painting, a depic-

tion of Christopher Columbus landing in the New World which contained bare-breasted native women, constituted sexual harassment. Nadine Strossen, DEFENDING PORNOGRAPHY: FREE SPEECH, SEX, AND THE FIGHT FOR WOMEN'S RIGHTS 21-22 (1995).

[105]The offending passage was this:

Another problem with sample polls is that some people desire their privacy and don't want to be bothered by a pollster. Let's say Dave Stud is entertaining three beautiful ladies in his penthouse when the phone rings. A pollster on the other end wants to know if we should eliminate the capital gains tax. Now Dave is a knowledgeable businessperson who cares a lot about this issue. But since Dave is "tied" up at the moment, he tells the pollster to "bother" someone else. *Language Censors*, WALL ST. J., Jan. 5, 1993 at A14.

[106]The teaching assistant told the student:

"This is ludicrous & inappropriate & OFFENSIVE. This is completely inappropriate for a serious political science paper. It completely violates the standard for non-sexist writing. Professor [name withheld] has encouraged me to interpret this comment as an example of sexual harassment and to take the appropriate formal steps. I have chosen not to do so in this instance. However, any future comments, in a paper, in class or in dealings w/me will be interpreted as sexual harassment and formal steps will be taken. Professor ... is aware of these comments -& and is prepared to intervene. You are forwarned!" *Id.* (emphasis in original)

[107]Craig Hymowitz, *The Locked Box,* HETERODOXY, May 1995 at 10-12.

[108]While litigation was pending, Cornell re-wrote its rules. The New York Court of Appeals ultimately ruled in favor of Cornell, finding that the university had not breached its employment contract with Maas.

[109]Students at Swarthmore College accused the college's mental health center of having an "outmoded and insensitive approach" to matters such as rape and eating disorders. After months of discussion, Swarthmore finally arranged a hearing by outside experts to evaluate student grievances. The center's director, wounded by what he perceived as a lack of support, resigned instead. Students unhappy with the resignation went public with their complaints. They were denounced by Swarthmore's president, whom they accused of a cover-up. Marie McCullough, Swarthmore in '94?, PHILADELPHIA INQUIRER, June 22, 1994, at B01.

[110]Ted C. Fishman, "Kangaroo Campus", PLAYBOY MAGAZINE, Oct. 1994, at p. 41.

[111]Strossen, *supra* note 104 at 28.

[112]Adrienne Drell, "Seminary Professor to Fight Despite Libel Suit Dismissal," CHICAGO SUN- TIMES, Jan. 30, 1995 at p. 19.

[113]Telephone conversation with Graydon Snyder, December 12, 1995.

[114]Marvel & Kessler, *supra* note 6. The complaining students said this wasn't the first time Dr. Silva had made them uncomfortable by using sexual innuendos, such as when he told a woman on her knees rummaging through a card catalog that "It looks like you've had a lot of experience down there"—a statement she took as demeaning. The professor claimed that he was merely lauding her studiousness.

[115]Marvel & Kessler, *supra* note 6. *See also* television interview, Eye to Eye with Connie Chung (CBS, April 7, 1994).

[116]*Id.*

[117]J. Donald Silva v. The University of New Hampshire et al, 888 F. Supp. 293 (1994).

[118]*Id.*

[119]Besides reinstating him, the university paid Dr. Silva approximately $250,000. (Telephone conversation with Silva's counsel, Michael McDonald, Esq., of the Center for Individual Rights in Washington, D.C.)

[120]His victory in court, however, has not stifled continued criticism. New Hampshire Representative Richard L. Cogswell, for example, wrote a blistering letter to a local newspaper, in which he asked: "*SHOULD* a tenured professor . . . at a major New England university, who is being paid by the parents and good taxpayers of the State of New Hampshire, *be using sexually explicit language and metaphors*, to teach young, impressionable, male and female students at UNH? The answer is NO!!!!!" Silva: Lesson Unlearned, Offender Unpunished, NEW HAMPSHIRE FORUM, December 9, 1994, at p.23 (emphasis in the original).

[121]Louis Jacobs, *A Report: Political or Pedagogical Correctness?*, ACADEMIC QUESTIONS (Spring 1993) at 59.

[122]Telephone interview with Michael Kraus, May 26, 1999. *See* Andrew Klienfield, 7 ACADEMIC QUESTIONS (1993-94).

[123]Telephone conversation with Murray Dolfman, July 13, 1999. *See* Nat Hentoff, *Campus Court- Martial*, WASHINGTON POST (December 15, 1988) at A25.

[124]Alyson Todd, "Growing Up Absurd at Wellesley," *The Heterodoxy Handbook: How to Survive the PC Campus* (David Horowitz and Peter Collier, eds.) 165-171 (1994). *See also* Kenneth Lasson, *Political Correctness Askew,* 63 TENN. L. REV. 689 (1996) at 707 n. 124.

[125]Robert Holand, *No Mere Phantasm, PC Has Chilled Free Speech in Academy,* RICHMOND TIMES DISPATCH (10/28/98).

[126]Nadine Strossen, *supra* note 104.

[127]"Not too many men have wised up to worldly women," said comedienne Roseanne Barr. "They want the dumb-bimbo blondes . . ." *Saturday Celebrity,* BOSTON HERALD, July 1, 1995 at p. 9.

[128]"In popular as well as feminist dogma, women who get implants are either brazen hussies or pathetic neurotics under the thumb of men . . ." Nina Martin, *Farewell Perfect Breasts,* HEALTH, September 1995 at p.82.

[129]"The fatal woman of the Romantics, the Lola of the Victorians, is still with us, though often reduced to a common streetwalker." Reagan Upshaw, *John Bellany at Terry Dintenfass,* ART IN AMERICA, May 1995, at p.114. The preferred occupational title for prostitute is now *sex worker.* "Prostitute" is said to be judgmental and difficult to define without including wives, who "also exhange sexual services in return for support." See also *sex care provider, sexual surrogacy,* and *persons presenting themselves as commodity allotments within a business doctrine.* Beard & Cerf, *supra* note 32.

[130]Some notable women themselves have come to admire streetwalkers. "They are goddesses," says renegade feminist Camille Paglia. Roger Clarke, *Pagan Deities in Drag,* THE INDEPENDENT, April 1, 1995 at p.26. Political correctness has also caught up with James Bond, the master chauvinist whose track record with women has outraged feminists for decades. "Gone are the bikini-clad bimbos in the latest Bond adventure Goldeneye," writes film critic Martina Devlin (*Bond's Goldeneye is Still on Girls—But Bimbos Are Out,* PRESS ASSOCIATION NEWSFILE, January 22, 1995.) [Subotnik at 116]

[131]Janet Tassel, *The 30 Years' War,* HARVARD MAGAZINE (September 1999).

[132]John Leo, *The 1999 Sheldon,* U.S. NEWS & WORLD REPORT, January 24, 2000. In February 2002, $2,000 worth of copies of a conservative student magazine were stolen at UC/Berkeley. Cybercast News Service, February 27, 2002.

[133]*See* Subotnik, *What's Wrong with Critical Race Theory?: Reopening the Case for Middle Class Values,* 7 CORNELL J. L. & PUB. POL. 681 (1998).

[134]*Id.*

[135]One member of the faculty responded to the students by telling them to "grow up." The professor's lawyer dismissed the complainant as a prude and his complaint as "fundamentalist Christian McCarthyism." William P. Cheshire, *PCU—Sexist Talk A Matter of Gender*, NEW YORK TIMES NEWS SERVICE, April 2, 1995.

[136]*Career Day for Girls Spurs Debate*, CHICAGO TRIBUNE, April 9, 1995 at p.2A. "After all," one businesswoman commented, "The idea of the day is so much more than a career day. It's specifically designed to reverse the *negative* messages that girls get: messages that they should be pretty and thin, quiet and polite." Apparently, this woman believes that girls should be fat and ugly, loud and rude. *Id.* (emphasis added).

[137]Robert McLendon, *Political Correctness Can Blunt the Point*, LOS ANGELES TIMES, March 10, 1994, at p.4.

[138]Cathleen Schine, *Endpaper: Academic Questions*, THE NEW YORK TIMES, June 12, 1994, at p.82.

[139]*See* Fennel, *supra* note 9.

[140]Leo, *supra* note 104.

[141]Fennell, *supra* note 9.

[142]The fraternity went to court, citing both the First Amendment and a provision of the California Code prohibiting sanctions on the basis of speech. The court ordered the university to reinstate the fraternity, and various administrators to undertake "First Amendment sensitivity training." Nat Hentoff, *Sombrero Scrap*, THE WASHINGTON POST, January 1, 1994 at p.A23. At the University of Florida, a sorority held a fund-raising event to benefit proverty-stricken children. The sorority sisters planned to do stepdancing, but backed down when the president of the National Panhellenic Council ordered the African dance "not to be imitated. Dave Gentry, *A Few Hopeful Signs This Year Amid the Usual Campus PC*, THE WASHINGTON TIMES, July 5, 1995 at p.A17.

[143]Jacobowitz is currently a student at Fordham Law School. *See* Beth Pinsker, *Speech Battles Rattle Ivory Towers, 5 Years After "Water Buffalo" Flap: Eden Jacobowitz Ends Up In Law School*, SOFTLINE INFO, October 16, 1998; *Buffaloed*, TIME MAGAZINE, November 29, 1993, at p.67; and Charles Krauthammer, *Defining Deviancy Up*, THE NEW REPUBLIC, November 22, 1993, at p.20.

[144]*See* Symposium Edition, *Political Correctness in the 1990's and Beyond*, 23 NORTHERN KENTUCKY LAW REVIEW 508 (1996), and Eric Gouvin, *Catty Remarks about Animal Correctness*, 47 JOURNAL OF LEGAL EDUCATION 433 (1997).

[145]Gentry, *supra* note 142. At the University of Cincinnati—whose official administrative handbook states that only white people can be racist—students at a rally supporting the Persian Gulf War shouted racial insults at a group of Arab students. (The university did not know what to label the one black student spotted in the crowd. An Egyptian student suggested calling him a "European-influenced African.") John Leo, *A Political Correctness Roundup*, U.S. NEWS AND WORLD REPORT, June 22, 1992, at p.29. Professor Robert Lande of the University of Baltimore relates a similar story. When he was a student at Harvard, a comment was made that "only whites can be racist." A classmate from Singapore reacted with incredulity: in his country, the saying is that. if you see an Indian and a snake and have but one bullet, you shoot the Indian—because snakes aren't as dangerous.

[146]After a hearing in federal court, the school later agreed to revoke what remained of his suspension. The case is still pending. Leslie Alan Horvitz, *Public Interest Law Center Fights Political Correctness*, THE WASHINGTON TIMES, November 6, 1995, at p.16.

[147]Leo, *supra* note 25.

[148]*Id.*

[149]Wall Street Journal, Dec. 21, 1990 at A10.

[150]Colegrove v. Green, 328 U.S. 549, 556 (1946).

[151]Stanley Fish, *Fraught with Death: Skepticism, Progressivism, and the First Amendment*, 64 COLORADO L. REV. 1061, 1083 (1993); Adam Begley, *Souped Up Scholar*, N.Y. TIMES MAGAZINE, May 3, 1992, at p.38.

[152]See, e.g., Doe v. University of Michigan, 721 F.Supp. 852 (E.D.Mich. 1989). See generally David A. Hoekema, *Campus Rules and Moral Community: In Place of In Loco Parentis* 104-11 (1994).

[153]112 S. Ct. 2538, 2541 (1992).

[154]315 U.S. 568 (1942).

[155]112 S. Ct. at 2545 (holding that the government may not regulate use based on hostility or favoritism towards the underlying message).

[156]Alabama, Alaska, California, Colorado, Connecticut, Delaware, Florida, Georgia, Hawaii, Illinois, Iowa, Kansas, Louisiana, Maine, Massachusetts, Michigan, Minnesota, Nebraska, Nevada, New Hampshire, New Mexico, New York, North Carolina, Oklahoma, Oregon, Pennsylvania, Rhode Island, South Dakota, Tennessee, Texas, Utah, Vermont, Virginia, Washington, West Virginia, Wisconsin, and Wyoming. The District of Columbia and Puerto Rico have similar laws.

[157]In Maryland, for example, even if the harassment is not associated with a separate crime, the perpetrator can be found guilty of a misdemeanor and imprisoned up to three years or fined up to $5,000. Md. Ann. Code, art. 27 § 470A. The constitutionality of the Maryland statute has been questioned in light of the *R.A.V.* decision, because a person's speech may be used to prove a biased motive. Kevin Sullivan, *Area Jurisdictions Call Hate-Crime Laws Solid; Statutes Said to be Narrower Than St. Paul's,* WASHINGTON POST, June 23, 1992 at p. A06. But the law was upheld in Ayers v. Maryland, 335 Md. 602, 645 A.2d 22, 35, 38 (1994), where the state's hate-crime statute was found not to violate the First Amendment—even though it permits the trial court to inquire into the defendant's beliefs and associations, and despite the fact that a defendant's prior racist speech may be used to prove motive.

[158]The University of Baltimore, for example, encourages all faculty to take part in an annual "staff diversity training session." Part of the training includes tips for the faculty on how to handle diversity in the classroom and how to avoid gender specific terms when teaching. Clay Ballantine and Cheryl Blackburn, UNIVERSITY OF BALTIMORE; STAFF DIVERSITY TRAINING, Nov. 15, 1994 (a collection of articles from a variety of sources on file with the author).

[159]Charles Babington, *Diversity and Grade School Politics; Mandating Female, Minority Candidates Stirs Outcry in Montgomery,* WASHINGTON POST, June 3, 1994, at p. D01.

[160]Ben Wildavsky, *First Amendment vs. Anti-Hate Efforts: Rethinking Campus Speech Codes,* SAN FRANCISCO CHRONICLE, March 4, 1995 at A1.

[161]*See* Alan Kors and Harvey Silverglate, THE SHADOW UNIVERSITY: THE BETRAYAL OF LIBERTY ON AMERICA'S CAMPUSES (1998).

[162]Tom Mashberg, *Debates Rage on Campus over Free-Speech Rules,* BOSTON HERALD, October 31, 1999 at 1.

[163]347 U.S. 483 (1954).

[164]Charles R. Lawrence, *If He Hollers Let Him Go: Regulating Hate Speech on Campus,* DUKE LAW JOURNAL 431, 441 (1990).

[165]Nooshin Namazi and James H. Cahill, *University Hate Speech Codes: A Necessary Method in the Process of Eradicating the Universal Wrong of Racism*, 10 TOURO LAW REVIEW 561, 582-85 (1994).

[166]Lauri A. Ebel, *University Anti-Discrimination Codes v. Free Speech*, 23 NEW MEXICO L. REV. 169, 181 (1993).

[167]Lawrence, *supra* note 164 at 446-47.

[168]For a discussion on why Brown and other cases invalidating governmental discrimination does not justify regulation of private racist speech, see Nadine Strossen, *Regulating Racist Speech on Campus: A Modest Proposal?*, 1990 DUKE LAW JOURNAL 484, 541-547 (1990).

[169]See Steven Fleischman, *Dear Professor Lawrence, You Missed the School Bus*, 72 Boston U. L. Rev. 953 (1992). But see Mari Matsuda, *Public Response to Racist Speech: Consider the Victim's Story*, 87 MICH. L. REV. 2320, 2378-79 (1989).

[170]Karst, *Citizenship, Race and Marginality*, 30 WM. & MARY L. REV. 1, 1 (1988).

[171]Vince Herron, *Increasing the Speech: Diversity, Campus Speech Codes, and the Pursuit of Truth*, 67 SO. CAL. L. REV. 407, 430-431. West Virginia University limits free speech to two tiny designated areas on campus. WASHINGTON TIMES, March 26, 2002.

[172]See generally Herron, *supra* note 171 at 418-432 (quoting Rhode, *Campus Speech Codes: Politically Correct, Constitutionally Wrong*, L.A. LAW., Dec. 1991 at 48-49).

[173]*Id.* at 421.

[174]*Id.* at 424-425.

[175]42 U.S.C. § 2000e-2(a)(1) (1995).

[176]Suzanne Sangree, *Title VII Prohibitions Against Hostile Environment Sexual Harassment: No Collision in Sight*, 47 RUTGERS L. REV. 461, 482 (1995).

[177]Jules B. Gerard, *The First Amendment in a Hostile Environment: A Primer on Free Speech and Sexual Harassment*, 68 NOTRE DAME L. REV. 1003, 1006 (1993).

[178]29 C.F.R. 1604.11 (1995) (emphasis added). Similarly, a "racially hostile environment" can be created by harassment that is "physical, verbal, graphic, or written."

[179]John P. Walters, *The Indistinct Difference Between Guidelines and Regulations*, THE WASHINGTON TIMES, March 8, 1995 at p.A19.

[180]Keith R. Fentonmiller, *Verbal Sexual Harassment as Equality Depriving Conduct*, 27 UNIV. OF MICH. JRNL. OF LAW REFORM 565, 574-77 (1994).

[181]Meritor v. Vinson, 477 U.S. 57, 65 (1986). See Gerard, supra note at 1005.

[182]See Steven Wulf, *Federal Guidelines for Censorship*, 8 ACADEMIC QUESTIONS 58 (1995).

[183]*See* Kenneth Lasson, *Group Libel Versus Free Speech: When Big Brother* Should *Butt In*, 23 DUQUESNE L. REV. 77 (1984).

[184]United States v. X-Citement Video, Inc., 982 F.2d 1285, 1296 n.7 (9th Cir. 1992) (Kozinski, J., dissenting in part).

[185]*See* Burlington Indus., Inc. v. Ellerth, 118 S.Ct. 2257 (1998) and Faragher v. City of Boca Raton, 118 S.Ct. 2275 (1998).

[186]*Robinson v. Jacksonville Shipyards* was, in short, wrongly decided. Where work environments are made hostile solely because of verbal expression—however abhorrent it may be—it should be protected. A finding of liability for discrimination based on a Title VII hostile-environment claim, where the offensive conduct was merely expressive and not targeted at an individual or group with the intent to harass, is a clear violation of the Constitution as embodied in the First Amendment.

[187]Walters, *supra* note 179.

[188]*Id.*

[189]Wulf, *supra* note 182.

[190]*See generally* Harry Tepker, Jr. and Joseph Harroz, Jr., *On Balancing Scales, Kaleidoscopes, and the Blurred Limits of Academic Freedom*, 50 OKLAHOMA LAW REVIEW 1 (1997).

[191]*See* Symposium Edition, *Political Correctness in the 1990's and Beyond*, 23 NORTHERN KENTUCKY LAW REVIEW 507 (1996).

[192]*See* John Wilson, *Myths and Facts: How Real Is Political Correctness?*, 22 WILLIAM MITCHELL LAW REVIEW 521-523 (1996); Michael S. Greve, *Do "Hostile Environment" Charges Chill Academic Freedom?*, ABA JOURNAL, Feb, 1994 at 40; and Cynthia G. Bowman, *Street Harassment and the Informal Ghettoization of Women*, 106 HARVARD L.REV. 517 (1993). The case referred to in the footnote is Cohen v. San Bernardino Valley College, 883 F. Supp. 1407 (2995), reversed

in part in 92 F.3rd 968 (1996). *See* Harry Tepker, Jr. and Joseph Harroz, Jr., *On Balancing Scales, Kaleidoscopes, and the Blurred Limits of Academic Freedom,* 50 OKLAHOMA LAW REVIEW 1 at 24- 26 (1997).

[193]*See, e.g.,* Clark D. Cunningham and N.R. Madhava Menon, *Race, Class, Caste ... ? Rethinking Affirmative Action,* and Cass R. Sunstein, *Affirmative Action, Caste, and Cultural Comparisons,* 97 MICH. L. REV. 1296 (1999).

[194]Janet Tassel, *The 30 Years' War,* HARVARD MAGAZINE (September 1999).

[195]Shelby Steele, *We Shall Overcome—But Only Through Merit,* WALL STREET JOURNAL, September 16, 1999.

[196]Edward Blum and Marc Levin, *Remember Lino Graglia,* HOUSTON CHRONICLE, November 10, 1999 at A37.

[197]Lynda Richardson, *The Mentor Conservatives Turn To for Inspiration; A Gadfly and Confessor to a Harvard Lineage,* New York Times, October 16, 1999. Latter-day interpretations of "gender equity" under Title IX have resulted in the cancellation of more than 400 men's athletic programs around the country. *See* Jessica Gavora, *Tilting the Playing Field: Schools, Sports, Sex, and Title IX* (2002). Rules are sometimes bent in order to hire minority faculty members. *College Puts Diversity Ahead of Protocol,* CHRONICLE OF HIGHER EDUCATION, September 28, 2001 at 12.

[198]As the "diversity specialist" explaining the University of Arizona's Diversity Action Plan stated, even nerds and people who dress differently should be included because "We don't want to leave anyone out." *See* Leo, *supra* note 25.

[199]Himmelfarb, *supra* note 9. *See also, Academic Watch,* NATIONAL REVIEW, Nov. 19, 1990, at p. 18 (stating that Baruch College in New York was deferred accreditation "on the grounds that it was not graduating enough blacks and Hispanics [although there] was no complaint about the number of blacks and Hispanics admitted to the college").

[200]Margaret J. Radin, *Reply: Please Be Careful with Cultural Feminism,* 45 STANFORD L. REV. 1567, 1569 (1993).

[201]Duncan Kennedy, *Rebels from Principle: Changing the Corporate Law Firm from Within,* HARV. L. SCH. BULL., Fall 1981, at 40.

[202]David Fraser, *If I Had A Rocket Launcher: Critical Legal Studies as Moral Terrorism,* 51 HASTINGS L.J. 777, 804 (1990). *See also* Fraser, *Truth and Hierarchy: Will the Circle Be Unbroken?,* 33 BUFF. L. REV. 729, 773 n.156.

[203]I made this observation at much greater pretension and length in *Scholarship Amok: Excesses in the Pursuit of Truth and Tenure*, 104 HARVARD L. REV. 926 (1991). For a delightful ranking of *The Top Ten Politically Correct Law Reviews*, see Arthur Austin, 1994 UTAH L. REV. 1319 (1994).

[204]Sanford Pinsker, *Politicized Academia?*, CHRISTIAN SCIENCE MONITOR, August 20, 1998 at 11. Bowling Green's actions were widely criticized by mainstream journalists, civil libertarians, and the National Association of Scholars. *See* George Dent, Jr., *Political Discrimination in the Curriculum: A Case Study*, 12 ACADEMIC QUESTIONS 24 (Spring, 1999).

[205]The speakers included trustees at the largest public university systems in America, a former writer for TIME and the NEW YORK TIMES, and a professor of geology at Brooklyn College. Columbia's course catalogue states that the university aspires to be a "community of discourse." While this self-perception may apply to such courses as "Pirates, Boys, and Capitalism" or "Gender and Deviance," it doesn't seem to embrace points of view that dissent from "the smothering orthodoxy that covers Columbia like an invisible fog." Daniel Flynn, *Columbia Ends Free Speech*, 6 HETERODOXY 9 at 9 (November 1998).

[206]*See* John Wilson, *Myths and Facts: How Real Is Political Correctness?*, 22 WILLIAM MITCHELL LAW REVIEW 517 at 529 (1996). In the spring of 1999 the University of Oklahoma finally abandoned the effort by declaring that it could not find someone suitable to fill the position. WASHINGTON POST, May 8, 1999 at A5.

[207]See Berman, *supra* note 19. *See also* Carroll, *supra* note 58 ("If the campus is where PC began, it has strong roots in the media"); Stephen Goode, *Campus Radicalism Lacks Mass Appeal*, INSIGHT ON THE NEWS, Feb. 1, 1993 at p. 12(8) (stating that "the news media bows at the alter of the political correct").

[208]Jon Weiner, *"Rape by Innuendo" at Swarthmore*, THE NATION, Jan. 20, 1992, at p. 44.

[209]One such letter had been written by the student responsible for putting together the guide in question.

[210]Eventually, TIME ran the letter, but in a context that robbed it of its significance (alongside a letter attacking heavy metal rock music and another defending THE NEW REPUBLIC). *Id.*

[211]Hugo Young, *Commentary: Middle America's Loud Voice of Hate*, THE MANCHESTER GUARDIAN, May 23, 1995, at p.13.

[212]Peter Johnson, *Rush Limbaugh's Right of Way: Politically Incorrect and Loving It*, USA TODAY, Oct. 28, 1992, at p. 01D.

[213]Jamin Raskin, *The Great PC Cover-Up*, 14 CAL. L. REV. 68 (1994). *See also* Morley, *supra* note 22 (observing that politically correct may mean "conforming to liberal or far-left thought on sexual, racial, cultural or environmental issues).

[214]Jenish D'Arcy, *A War of Words: Academics Clash over Correctness*, MACLEAN'S, May 27, 1991, at p. 44; Michael Novak, *Back to School*, FORBES, Sept. 2, 1991, at p. 132.

[215]*See generally* Berman, *supra* note 19.

Conclusion

[1]Alan Kors and Harvey Silverglate, THE SHADOW UNIVERSITY: THE BETRAYAL OF LIBERTY ON AMERICA'S CAMPUSES at 370 (1998).

[2]Stephen Buckley, *Professor Changing the World One Curriculum at a Time*, WASHINGTON POST, Aug. 19, 1993 at p. M01.

[3]*See* John Ellis, *Literature Lost: Social Agendas and the Corruption of the Humanities* (1997) at 226. *See also* George Dent, Jr., *Political Discrimination in the Curriculum: A Case Study*, 12 ACADEMIC QUESTIONS 24 (Spring, 1999).

[4]*Sexual Harrassment and Academic Freedom: A Statement of the National Association of Scholars* (Statement available by fax or mail via National Association of Scholars, 575 Ewing Street, Princeton, New Jersey). *See also* James Q. Whitman, *Enforcing Civility and Respect: Three Societies*, 109 YALE L.J. 1279 (2000). *Emphasis supplied.*

[5]Charles J. Sykes, *Oh, Say, Can We Whine*, CHICAGO TRIBUNE, Sept. 20, 1992 at C16.

[6]See statements promulgated by the National Association of scholars, available at nas@nas.org.

Acknowledgments

The writing of this book was made considerably easier by the contributions of various research assistants, library staff, secretaries, editors, and designers.

I am indebted to my student researchers: Melissa Tillett, whose cheerful diligence helped give the manuscript its currency and coherence; Carolyn Knight Buppert, whose insightful suggestions on feminism sought valiantly to keep me honest and, in many cases, did; and Jill Loper, whose unflagging civility made plumbing the depths of political correctness more bearable. Valuable editorial comments were offered along the way by Peter Yu of the *Harvard Law Review,* Carolyn Brown of the *Journal of Legal Education,* and Lela Mahoney of the *Tennessee Law Review.*

Martha Kahlert, Barbara Jones, and Ella Agambar, all from the University of Baltimore School of Law, provided superb secretarial support. The research and technical assistance lent by the UB law library staff—the best I have worked with anywhere—was excellent.

I am especially grateful to Bruce Bortz of Bancroft Press, whose unique publisher's perspective was accompanied by much encouragement and numerous thoughtful suggestions on the text; to Steve Parke for his creativity on the cover; and to Theresa Williams for hers on the typography and page design.

Finally, I thank my wife and family for putting up with the multifarious spells of moodiness that often accompany the lonely pursuit of writing books—especially this foray into the even lonelier world of academic scholarship.

Additional Praise

"With passion, clarity, 'smoking guns,' and humor, University of Baltimore law professor Kenneth Lasson joins the few academic liberals who have impeached American higher education for academic high crimes and misdemeanors. Lasson provides evidence beyond a reasonable doubt that many college administrators and faculty are guilty of supporting political correctness, radical feminism, and trivial scholarship."
—DR. EVELYN AVERY, BOARD MEMBER, NATIONAL ASSOCIATION OF SCHOLARS
—DR. SHELDON AVERY, AWARDS CMTEE, NATIONAL ASSOCIATION OF SCHOLARS

"Employing an exemplary sense of humor, the multi-faceted Professor Lasson exceeds his usual high intellectual standards with his latest book, *Trembling in the Ivory Tower*. With wide-ranging scope, and good solid common sense, he skewers academe and its many foibles. And he does so using a clear and delightful writing style that, heaven knows, I wish other academicians could imitate."
—H. MEBANE TURNER, PRESIDENT EMERITUS, UNIVERSITY OF BALTIMORE

"Like Martin Anderson's *Impostors in the Temple*, Ken Lasson's *Trembling in the Ivory Tower* shows that our colleges and universities are corrupt, and are becoming ever less congenial to teaching and learning. *Trembling Tower*, however, is unique in showing that faculty members' major daily preoccupation—obtaining tenure and advancement through fraudulent publications—as well as the folkways that fall under the category of political correctness, constitute the very matrix of this corruption. This book is significant also because Lasson is a card-carrying member of the Liberal tribe that is solely responsible for the state of modern American academic life. And there's more. By leavening deadly serious topics with learned humor, as he does in *Trembling*, Lasson has not only provided an enjoyable book to read, but proves that having a law degree is no bar to good sense and good humor."
—ANGELO CODEVILLA, PROFESSOR OF INTERNATIONAL RELATIONS, BOSTON UNIVERSITY

"If Kenneth Lasson's description of the American academy is accurate, and it is, I'll get into trouble if I say anything nice about his book. So be it. *Trembling in the Ivory Tower: Excesses in the Pursuit of Truth and Tenure* is a wonderful work—relentlessly serious in its condemnation of scholarly gobbledygook, radical feminism, and political correctness, but also reaching 10 on the hilarity index. As I read *Trembling*, I was reminded of another Baltimorean, H. L. Mencken, who laughed (and made others laugh) as he chronicled the decline of civilization. Although a white male, Lasson represents the most underrepresented group in today's multicultural universities: those who care about the English language and rational thought."
—ERIK M. JENSEN, DAVID L. BRENNAN PROFESSOR OF LAW, CASE WESTERN UNIVERSITY

"Even without Lasson's measured, witty commentary, his exhaustive and entertaining evidence would have the practitioners of academicism, radical feminism, and PCism laughed out of court. But they're not in court, where facts and truth, analysis and argument, reason and commonsense prevail (at least usually). They're in colleges and universities, where such principles often no longer obtain. Higher education has been politicized, and its politics now are radical. Lasson's modest suggestions—civility, tolerance, and a dose of Western Civ—will help to restore sanity and balance, a sense of humor and moderation, and perhaps even some amiability."
—LAURIN A. WOLLAN, JR., PRESIDENT, FLORIDA ASSOCIATION OF SCHOLARS

"This book deftly deflates both the pompous and petty in American higher education, and honors those who seek to maintain (against increasing odds) the established norms of Western civilization and rational discourse. Lasson teaches us the value of true intellectual diversity on campus, as opposed to the politically correct diversity promoted by radical feminists and deconstructionist faculties to the exclusion of individualistic values, historical perspective, and scientific method. A most welcome challenge to the PC-Thought-Police."
—GERALD ZURIFF, PROFESSOR OF PSYCHOLOGY, WHEATON COLLEGE

"Can such academic travesties as multiculturalism, deconstruction, and political correctness actually be funny on occasion? In *Trembling in the Ivory Tower*, Professor Kenneth Lasson amply proves they can. In his blis-

tering examination of academic fads and foibles, hidden treats include a hilarious disquisition on the law review essay with the greatest number of footnotes ever, and on the Mine Eyes Glazeth Over (MEGO) syndrome. Lasson's wit illuminates his sometimes acerbic truth-telling, painting a full and fascinating picture of what happens when academe abandons its once proud motto: "the truth shall set you free," and replaces it with dreary litanies recited by devotees of multiculturalism and political correctness. Filled with courage and common sense, Lasson's tribute to rational argument sparkles."
—ROBERT LERNER, PH.D., LERNER AND NAGAI QUANTITATIVE CONSULTING, & INDEPENDENT SCHOLAR

"Trembling in the Ivory Tower" is that all too rare book that successfully speaks to both an academic and a lay audience. Lasson skillfully exposes the way in which free speech has been stifled and standards of rigorous scholarly inquiry debased on American colleges in recent years. This book's timely and provocative arguments deserve a hearing from anyone who cares about preserving an unfettered marketplace of ideas on our campuses—and, for that matter, everywhere else in our democratic society as well."
—SAMUEL I. "SANDY" ROSENBERG, MEMBER, MD HOUSE OF DELEGATES, AND ADJUNCT PROFESSOR OF LAW, UNIVERSITY OF BALTIMORE AND UNIVERSITY OF MARYLAND SCHOOLS OF LAW

"In a courageously frank analysis of current trends in many American institutions of higher education, Lasson exposes frightening examples of exaggerated political correctness, deteriorating course standards, and poor levels of writing. He challenges the academic community, while it is still not too late, to counter the damaging effects of radical feminism, the downgrading of European culture, totalitarian attitudes, and the employment of jargon and gibberish. His powerfully argued case deserves careful consideration and widespread discussion."
—STEFAN REIF, PROFESSOR OF MEDIEVAL HEBREW STUDIES, DIRECTOR OF GENIZAH RESEARCH, AND FELLOW OF ST JOHN'S COLLEGE, UNIVERSITY OF CAMBRIDGE, ENGLAND

About the Author

Kenneth Lasson has taught at Cambridge University, University of Haifa, University of Aberdeen, and Loyola College (MD); and worked at Brookings Institution, Goucher College, and University of Maryland School of Law.

His nine previous books have been reviewed in the *New Yorker, New York Review of Books*, and *Washington Post*, among others.

He has appeared as a guest on "The Today Show," "Larry King" (radio), "The Diane Rehm Show" (NPR), "NBC Nightly News," and "Chris Matthews' Hardball (CNBC), among others.

His writings have appeared in *The Atlantic Monthly, Washingtonian Monthly, Washington Post, Miami Herald, Philadelphia Inquirer, Baltimore Sun*, and *Jerusalem Post*.

A fulltime law professor at the University of Baltimore, he lives in Baltimore with his wife, and has three grown children.